Bed & Breakfast – Australia's Best

Jane Schonberger
George Morency

Lanier Publishing
PETALUMA, CALIFORNIA

Please visit our web site: www.TravelGuideS.com
E-mail: Lanier@TravelGuideS.com

A *Lanier* Guide
▲

Other Books from Lanier Publishing

The Complete Guide to Bed & Breakfasts, Inns and Guesthouses
All-Suite Hotel Guide
Elegant Small Hotels—U.S.A.
Elegant Hotels—Pacific Rim
Condo Vacations: The Complete Guide
Family Travel Guide Online
Golf Resorts: The Complete Guide
Golf Resorts International
22 Days in Alaska
Cinnamon Mornings & Raspberry Teas
Bed & Breakfast Cookbook
Sweets & Treats
Moving Mom & Dad

For further information, please contact:
 Lanier Publishing
 Drawer D
 Petaluma, CA 94953

© 2000 by Lanier Publishing Int., Ltd.
All rights reserved. Published 2000

1999 edition. First printing

ISBN 1-58008-196-7

Distributed to the book trade by:
 Ten Speed Press
 P.O. Box 7123
 Berkeley, CA 94707
 website: www.tenspeed.com   tel. 1-800-841-2665

Cover by Laura Lamar
Cover photo "Apple Tree Cottage," Adelaide Hills, South Australia
Photo courtesy of South Australia Tourism Commission
Photograph by Adam Brozzone

Design & Production by Sally Carpenter

Typeset by John Richards

Printed in Canada on recycled paper

Contents

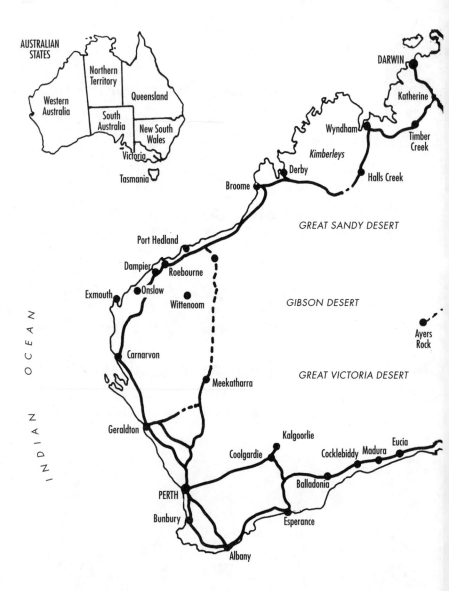

AUSTRALIAN STATES

Western Australia

Northern Territory

Queensland

South Australia

New South Wales

Victoria

Tasmania

DARWIN

Katherine

Timber Creek

Wyndham

Kimberleys

Halls Creek

Derby

Broome

GREAT SANDY DESERT

Port Hedland

Dampier

Roebourne

Onslow

Exmouth

Wittenoom

GIBSON DESERT

Ayers Rock

Carnarvon

GREAT VICTORIA DESERT

Meekatharra

Geraldton

Kalgoorlie

Coolgardie

Cocklebiddy

Madura

Eucla

INDIAN OCEAN

PERTH

Balladonia

Bunbury

Esperance

Albany

ACKNOWLEDGMENTS

Thanks go to the many individuals who helped make the revised edition of this book a reality. First, to Phil Wood, publisher of Ten Speed Press, who supported the original edition of the book; Pamela Lanier and Julio Valdes of Lanier Publishing, whose love of travel spawned a unique and thriving business; Sally Carpenter, who worked through the logistics with us and shepherded the book to completion; the individual State Tourism offices for their help and support; Richard and Kim Rene, our intrepid Melbourne-based international media and marketing gurus, who acted as our "B&B Special Forces" Down-Under; additional research associates, Kylie Glover and Andrew Patterson in Sydney; the many hosts who took us in, shared their lives with us, and showed us the "real" Australia; Lillian Morency and Marcia and Mickey Schonberger, who have finally accepted the fact we will never have corporate careers; and lastly, thanks to our daughters, Alexandra and Madison, who put up with us as we worked furiously to meet our deadlines and never (almost never) complained.

Introduction

Australia is a land of astonishing contrasts: dry and sparsely vegetated in parts, yet teeming with remarkable plant and animal life that has survived over millions of years. It is one of the last refuges in an overcrowded and polluted world. To see a landscape stretching to infinity, to stand under the black, starry Outback sky at night, to walk down an endless white sand beach—these are all Australian experiences. And for those who have a sense of adventure—there is no better place on earth.

When we traveled to Australia ten years ago to research the first edition of this book, the country's tourism industry was still in its infancy. Bed and breakfast style lodgings were beginning to spring up, but we had to search long and hard to find them. They were considered alternative accommodations and the hosts were regarded as pioneers. Over the last decade, Australians have discovered there is a large market for bed and breakfasts and they can now be found in every city and burg. The idea for B&B accommodations originated in England, where families seeking to supplement their incomes, hung signs out their doors and opened their spare bedrooms to passing motorists. Now the B&B business has gained international popularity and it's possible to stay in a bed and breakfast establishment in almost any corner of the globe.

This book features a variety of Australia's best guesthouses, historic homesteads, country inns, and small resorts as well as private homes, farms, and Outback stations. Regardless of what each place is called, they're all based on the similar philosophy of providing personalized service in small, intimate, usually owner-operated establishments. Discerning travelers can be assured that all the properties meet high standards and offer special features not always reflected in a standardized rating system.

The quality of accommodations vary greatly, and in an effort to take some of the guesswork out of choosing, we have selected those B&B's that we feel best meet an international standard while maintaining a "unique" Australian flavor. We believe the best B&B's reflect the spirit and atmosphere of a particular region and have hosts who can provide guests with a personal introduction to the finest the area has to offer. The best B&B's also offer an opportunity to meet other people and foster new friendships, whether with the hosts themselves or with other guests.

The isolation of many properties in Australia often makes it impractical for them to offer only the traditional bed and breakfast. Many establishments, therefore, provide dinner as well as bed and breakfast, or in some cases, fully inclusive packages (all meals, tours of the properties and activities) to their guests. For the sake of convenience, we refer to all these establishments as B&B's.

While researching this book, we reviewed over 2,000 properties and inspected over 300 of them across the country. Not all the properties visited are included in this guide. It is a subjective collection of those that we feel are the best. We know more and more travelers are looking for alternatives to the sterile environments offered by hotel/motel chains; whether a chic guest house in the Blue Mountains, a small private hotel in a trendy Melbourne suburb, a country retreat in the Clare Valley, or a homestead in the Outback, we hope this guide will offer them the freedom to choose.

Distances

The vast distances and remoteness of many areas in Australia are a surprise to many visitors. The island continent is about the size of mainland USA although the population is less than that of California. Sydney to the Great Barrier Reef is a three and a half-hour flight (approximately 1600 kilometers), and Ayers Rock is about 2400 kilometers from Sydney. Outback stations can be a day or two drive from a major city or only accessible by light aircraft.

Generally, public transportation—planes, trains and buses—will take you to all the capital cities, major cities, towns, and places of tourist significance. If you want to get off the beaten track, it's probably best to consider renting a car or looking into various fly/drive packages. There are few places on earth with as much variety as Australia, but it's important to realize the limitations the great distances may impose and not be too ambitious in your itinerary. While each area has a great deal to offer, be realistic about what you can and can't accomplish during the length of your visit.

School & Public Holidays

On public holidays, some attractions, all banks, and some shops are closed. The following is a list of Australia-wide public holidays you should be aware of.

January 1—New Year's Day
January 26—Australia Day
March/April—Good Friday/Easter Monday
April 25—Anzac Day
June (second Monday)—Queen's Birthday
December 25—Christmas Day
December 26—Boxing Day

Each state has other public holidays, such as Bank Holiday and Labor Day, at different times of year, so be sure to check with the State Tourism offices. School holidays also vary from state to state (generally they are during

Christmas, May, and August), so be forewarned because this is the time that families take their vacations. It's often difficult to find rooms during school holidays, and when you do, you'll find yourself in the company of lots of kids. If you do plan on traveling during school holidays, be sure to book well in advance. A list of Australian school holidays can be obtained from the Australian Tourist Commission (www.aussie.net.au).

Climate

Australian seasons are opposite those in the northern hemisphere. August is mid-winter and Christmas falls in the middle of the summer. Because Australia is such a large country, there is good weather somewhere almost year round. Australian winter is mild by northern standards and is considered the off-peak time to travel. Throughout Australia's winter months, the waters of the Great Barrier Reef are at their clearest and the Top End enjoys it's most comfortable temperatures. The southern states, Tasmania in particular, are best visited in the summer when the temperatures are more moderate. The snowfields of New South Wales and Victoria offer good skiing in the winter, and the climate in the Red Centre is desert-like all year round, hot and dry during the day and often cold at night.

Reservations/Deposits

Because many of the properties listed in this book have limited space and are popular, it is almost a necessity to make reservations, especially on the weekends or school holidays and during high season. Even the most popular places have cancellations, and a last minute call sometimes proves fruitful. It's generally easier to find accommodations during the week and it's not necessary to book as far in advance. You'll discover a marked difference between weekend and weekday stays in the guest and country houses and both have their advantages. Weekends are usually a bit more festive, with city dwellers escaping to the country for some R & R and a little partying. It's a great chance to meet some Sydney-siders or Melburnians while they're relaxed, away from their jobs and willing to socialize. Often these meetings result in invitations to dinner back in the city or introductions to other friends along the way. During the week, you're more likely to meet other travelers, or sometimes, have the whole place to yourself. The hosts are more relaxed during the week, and might take the time to personally show you the area's attractions or help organize special outings.

Rates

Rates change fast and it's impossible to keep up. We've listed the high-low range for the 2000–2001 season. Many innkeepers have unadvertised off-season or mid-week rates and discounts for children, so it's a good idea to ask. All rates are quoted in Australian dollars, which was approximately the equivalent of .65 at the time of this printing. A standard annual rate increase is approximately 10%.

Goods and Services Tax

It should also be noted that at press time, the Australian Government has introduced a Goods and Services Tax (GST) of 10% that will be added to the standard tariff beginning July 2000. After July 2000, all tariffs will be quoted inclusive of this tax.

Useful Information

The emergency phone number in Australia is 000 for police, ambulance and fire.

Australia's electric current is 240/250 volts AC, and Australian sockets take a three-pin plug. Check to see if you need an adaptor plug and a transformer—while many of the large hotels supply these, most of the establishments in this book do not.

Tipping is not obligatory in Australia. Generally, tips are only given when the service has been exceptional.

Variety of Accommodations

The range of accommodations in Australia are extreme and vary widely from state to state, but the hospitality remains constant and that's what makes a stay in one of Australia's homes or small inns such a pleasure. Tasmanian bed and breakfasts, for example, are modeled more on the traditional English B&B, which caters to the passing trade, while Victoria and South Australia's B&B's are often destinations in and of themselves. These grand homes, originally built by convict labor, have been transformed into gracious country houses providing gourmet meals and genteel activities. The Northern Territory and Western Australia are still somewhat undeveloped in terms of tourism, however, there are a number of stations, private homes, and guesthouses, which have opened their doors to guests and offer a glimpse into rural Australia. Many of Queensland's B&B's are wooden pioneer-built homesteads, constructed on stilts and well suited for the hot summers. New South Wales has a tradition of guesthouses, as well as a variety of host farms, where travelers get a chance to experience the Australian bush.

Hosts generally have an intimate knowledge of the area they live, and their first hand experience is an invaluable resource when planning daily activities. They can point out special attractions and cater to individual interests; tour books just can't be as personal. Whether the city or the Outback, Australians are known for their hospitality and there is no better way to experience their warmth than by staying in their homes or in small private hotels or guesthouses.

What's Included/What's Not Included

At the minimum, every property in this book provides bed and breakfast. Generally breakfasts fall into one of three categories: Continental Breakfast usually includes fruit, cereals, toast, and tea/coffee. A Full Breakfast consists of a continental breakfast supplemented by a cooked dish. Many establishments offer gourmet, silver-service breakfasts, which may be three-course meals featuring a variety of homemade delicacies including homemade breads and preserves. Full breakfasts are often quite substantial and will hold you until dinner. Breakfast Provisions are all the makings for breakfast provided in a hamper or in the kitchen of a self-contained cottage. These provisions range from continental to full (farm fresh eggs, etc.), and guests can prepare and eat their morning meal at their own convenience.

Most of the properties in this guide feature private accommodations and facilities. Ensuite bathrooms (a uniquely Australian term), mean a bathroom that adjoins the bedroom. Private bathrooms indicate that the facilities are for your exclusive use, and Share Bath means that you may be sharing the bathroom with other guests. Spas are the equivalent of a Jacuzzi, and spa baths are a common amenity.

Handicap Access is not as stringently mandated in Australia as it is in the United States. Even those properties that indicate they have handicap access may only have limited access (e.g. the home may be accessible but there is inadequate access to the home), and it may not meet legal standards. It's best to check with your hosts to understand what level of accessibility they have.

All of the bed and breakfasts in this guide are Hosted, which means you'll be met by the owners who are available throughout your stay to answer questions and help out with any special arrangements. Most hosts are as attentive or discreet as you need them to be, and they'll take their cues from your behavior. Many properties provide afternoon tea, pre-dinner drinks, and nightly port and chocolates. Tea and coffee are usually available throughout the day along with fruit or light snacks. In addition to breakfast, many of the hosts will prepare a memorable dinner with prior notice, or pack a picnic hamper for lunch. If there is anything at all you need, chances are your hosts will try to accommodate you.

As you peruse this guide, you'll find a number of different types of accommodations listed. Some of the more common are:

Homestay B&Bs

There are hundreds of welcome mats out in Australia, and those who stay in the home of an Australian family will find a different view of Aussie life.

"Homestays" can be arranged in big cities, beachside suburbs, and little towns throughout the country. These B&B's aren't fancy inns or guest-houses; they are 'fair dinkum' Aussie homes. Some are historic homesteads, others are modern luxury homes, and still others are city apartments, but all have hosts who have a keen interest in people and sharing their local knowl-edge. Arrangements to stay at these B&B's can be made direct, or through a central reservation office. Whenever possible, special attention is placed on matching the interests of both hosts and guests and arranging an itinerary to suit personal needs.

Farm and Station Stays

Spending a few days on a farm is the ideal way to meet some "real Austra-lians" while getting to know the true Australian pioneer spirit. Escaping from the city and exploring the bush provides an opportunity to get in touch with those who remain part of Australia's unique history and tradition of living off the land. As a guest on a farm or station, you'll have a chance to share in daily activities, join a cattle muster, experience the excitement of shearing season, enjoy "down home" cooking, and try some of Australia's wonderful wines. Bush cooking—a damper and billy tea -over an open fire and under a starry night sky, is often one of the highlights of a farmstay. You can try your hand at some of the farm chores, or if you're a city person and the cows and sheep look better from a distance, you can just sit back under a shady verandah and soak up the beauty of the surrounding countryside.

There are many different types of farms throughout Australia including dairy, sheep, wheat, and cattle properties. Often the large properties are home to tens of thousands of sheep or cattle. Some Outback stations are larger than many small states or countries. While a rental car is the ideal way to explore Australia's rural countryside, most host farmers will meet their guests at nearby coach or train stations, usually at no extra charge.

The two basic types of farm stays are based on the style of accommoda-tions, and each will appeal to a different type of traveler. Farm Holidays generally refer to bunkhouse accommodations in converted shearer's quar-ters. Privacy is limited, but the price is quite moderate making this a good choice for families or large groups. Host Farms, provide accommodations within the family homestead, often with private baths. Meals are usually taken with the hosts, and you are truly treated as part of the family. Most of the farm stays in this book are Host Farms, where the proprietors go out of their way to provide something special (including additional meals if requested).

Self-Contained Suites or Cottages

Self contained or self-catering accommodations are often offered in a sepa-rate cottage or suite on a large, rural property. All you have to do is bring your own food (and sometimes linen) and enjoy the surroundings. The price is generally moderate, and these self-contained cottages are a good choice for families who need the extra space and convenience of self-catering. All of the self-contained accommodations included in this book are hosted—meaning that the owners meet guests—provide breakfast, and are generally available during the day if you need them.

Guesthouses, Country Houses, Country Retreats

While everyone's idea of an ideal retreat differs, in most cases it means an escape from the daily hassles of city life. Fortunately, the Australian country-side offers an abundance of opportunities to get away from it all. Hosts may refer to these getaways as inns, guesthouses, small hotels, country houses, or country retreats. It's not important to label them, only to know that each hostelry offers a cozy ambience, individual décor, intimacy, and attention to detail not found at larger hotels and resorts. Hosts will treat you like a special houseguest and provide homemade, usually gourmet, meals. The choices range from large, gracious Victorian homes to solitary island resorts. However, each has its own distinct character and none are stamped from a corporate plan. You won't find a paper strip across the toilet or a chain lock on your door, but you'll probably find fresh flowers, a carafe of port, or some freshly baked biscuits.

Private Hotels/Boutique Hotels

Not to be confused with a Sheraton or Hilton, private hotels are usually small, intimate hostelries, often located in historic buildings. More often than not, they're in city centers and many were originally licensed hotels or pubs. Some still retain a liquor license. Private hotels are definitely not part of a chain and are either owner operated, or managed with great care and personal attention.

Boutique Hotels offer many of the same amenities as larger hotels, but they are much smaller and personalized. A good choice for business travelers, they offer many of the necessary facilities (e.g. telephones in the rooms) and an international standard of service and accoutrements.

Pubs

While out on the road, you'll frequently come across that famous Australian institution—the country pub. It is usually the stateliest building on the street and seems to beckon travelers to come in for a cold beer or a counter meal. Many of these pubs, or hotels as they are generally called, also provide inexpensive accommodations. This book doesn't include any pubstays, but they can be an interesting option. The rooms aren't usually luxurious (in fact most are pretty spartan), but they are generally clean and comfortable. Don't expect air-conditioning or private bathrooms, but do expect a family atmosphere, local characters, and a distinctly Australian ambience.

Itineraries

In daring to try something different, you will find that not all of the properties listed will be to your liking. Some are posh, offering every possible amenity and a price to match; others are small and intimate with a great deal of character but fewer amenities. The quality varies from region to region, and in some remote areas, the choices are limited. When a perfect choice doesn't exist in a place that really should be visited, we have recommended the best available.

Every attempt has been made to provide the most up to date information, but changes do occur. Owners move, new establishments open, homes switch back over to private residences. Your hosts are often the best resource for finding out about these changes, and they are usually happy to make suggestions about other places to stay along your itinerary. They know better than anyone else the new places that have opened, what changes in ownership have taken place, and whether the level of quality is being maintained. If you follow the suggestions in this book and stay in the recommended places, we guarantee you'll see an Australia that few tourists have a chance to experience, and when you bid your host goodbye, it will be like saying farewell to a newfound mate.

Happy Trails,

Jane Schonberger & George Morency

As you use this guide you may find changes. Prices and information contained in these listings are correct to the best of our knowledge. We cannot, however, guarantee all details and suggest that travelers verify important information when booking. We welcome your comments and suggestions about the establishments listed, new places that have opened their doors, or ones we may have overlooked. Please contact us at ausbb2000@aol.com.

Aussie Glossary

As with all nations, Australia has developed its own unique vernacular. To help in your travels, here are some Australian terms and colloquialisms.

Abo	Aboriginal
Alice (The)	Town of Alice Springs in the heart of Australia
Aussie	Australian
Arvo	Afternoon
Bangers	Sausages
Barbie	(not a doll!) Short for barbeque
Barrack	To support or cheer for a sports team. (Don't use the word root.)
Bathers	Swimsuit
Beaut	Beautiful, good, great
Billabong	Pond in an otherwise dry stream
Billy Tea	Tea boiled over an open fire in an old tin can
Bird	A girl
Bitumen	Paved road
Bloke	A male
Blowies	Blow flies
Blue	Fight
Boot	Trunk of a car
Boghouse	Toilet
Brekkie	Breakfast
Brolly	Umbrella
Brumby	A wild horse
Bugs	Australian crustacean
Bum Bag	Fanny pack
Bush	Countryside, anywhere away from the city
Bushranger	Desperado
Bushwalk	A nature hike
Chook	Chicken
Corroboree	Aboriginal ceremonial dance—a celebration or meeting.
Cozzy	Swimsuit (also Bathers)
Cuppa	Cup of tea or coffee
Cup (The)	Popular Melbourne horseracing event
Damper	Unleavened bread traditionally cooked in a campfire.
Didgeridoo	Long, tube-like aboriginal instrument
Dingo	Native Australian wild dog

Dogsleg	Zig-zag in the road
Drover	Mounted herdsman
Dunny	Outhouse
Ekka	Exhibition; State Fair
Entree	Appetizer (not the main course)
Fair Dinkum	The real thing; genuine
Fossiking	Hunting gems or semi precious stones
Galah	Noisy parrot
G'Day	Hello
Gaol	Jail
Good on ya	Well done; for sure
Grazier	Large scale sheep or cattle farmer
Hectare	2.47 acres
Hooly Dooly	Good, great, groovy
Homestead	Main residence on a sheep or cattle station (ranch or farm)
Hotel	Generally a drinking establishment
Jackaroo	Station hand (female—Jillaroo)
Joey	Baby kangaroo
Journo	Journalist
Jumper	Sweater
Kilometre	.62 miles
Kiwi	New Zealander
Lamington	Square cake covered in chocolate icing and coconut
Larrikan	Young hooligan
Lift	Elevator
Lollies	Candy
Mate	A friend
MCG	Melbourne Cricket Ground
Middy	Mid-sized glass of beer
Milkbar	Corner shop
Merino	Breed of sheep
Mozzies	Mosquitoes
Museli	Breakfast cereal
Mustering	Roundup of sheep or cattle
Never never	Way out in the Outback
No worries	No problem
Outback	Remote part of the bush, Back of Bourke
Oz	Australia
Pinch	Steal
Pommie	An Englishman
Pram	Baby carriage
Pub	Public House, bar

Roo	Kangaroo
Roo bar	Protective bar on the front of a car.
Root	F#*k
Seppo	American (Septic Yank)
Sheila	Girl or woman
Singlet	Tank top
Spot on	Right on
Station	Large ranch
Sandshoes	Sneakers
Scrub	Untamed vegetation of stunted growth
Serviette	Napkin
Shag	Have sex
Slab o beer	Case of beer
Snowfields	Ski mountains
Spa	Jacuzzi
Sticky Beak	Nosy; to pry or meddle
Strine	Australian dialect
Struth	Surprise, amazement; mild horror
Stubbie	Short beer bottle
Swag	Bed roll
Ta	Thank you
Ta Ta	Goodbye
Tea	Evening meal
Telly	Television
Tinnie	A can of beer
Top End	Far north section of Northern Territory—around Darwin.
Torch	Flashlight
Track	Walking trail
Tucker	Food
Uni	University
Ute	A utility or pick-up truck
Vegemite	Popular food spread made of yeast extract.
Veggies	Vegetables
Walkabout	To travel aimlessly; disappear for a while
Wallaby	Member of kangaroo family
Whacked	Intoxicated or very tired
Whinger	Whiner
Yabby	Small freshwater crayfish
Yank	An American

New South Wales

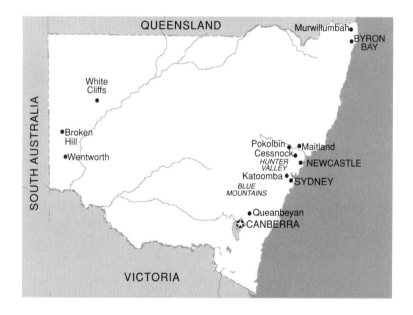

The site of Captain Cook's original landing in Australia, New South Wales is the oldest and most populous state in the country. Situated on the eastern seaboard, with Queensland to the north and Victoria to the south, the state is divided naturally into four areas—the sparsely populated Outback, the lush highlands of the Great Dividing Range, the farm country of the range's western slopes, and the rich subtropical coastal region.

New South Wales is best known for the capital city of Sydney, a free-spirited and vibrant metropolis built around a beautiful harbor. Undoubtedly one of the most beautiful cities in the world, it's easy to see why it was chosen as the site of the XXVII Olympic Games. Water is an integral part of Sydney's legacy and it is everywhere. With a long Pacific coastline and a natural harbor that goes deep into the countryside, it's no wonder that Sydney takes full advantage of its seemingly endless series of small bays and inlets. Ferries bus people back and forth from **Circular Quay** in the City Center, to harbor-side suburbs with houses that crowd to the water's edge. The harbor bustles with activity as boats of every conceivable description ply the smooth, deep waters. With a multitude of bayside beaches and 29 surf beaches, all within a short distance of the City Center, it's clear why late business appointments on a hot Friday afternoon are uncommon.

Sydney has all the attributes of a great cosmopolitan city—a diverse mix of cultures, clean streets, good public transportation, a strong commitment to the arts, lovely parks and museums, fine hotels, and restaurants—and famous landmarks like the Opera House and the Harbour Bridge. The real charm of Sydney lies not in its grand houses or important public buildings, but in its small streets and intimate 19th century neighborhoods—many of which are beautifully preserved. The Rocks, the oldest section of the city, has been transformed from a once unsavory district with taverns and brothels teeming with sailors off the whaling and sealing ships, into one of the prettiest areas of the inner city. This same commitment to careful preservation has been carried out in many of the city's outlying neighborhoods and suburbs—the most notable being **Darlinghurst**, **Woollahara** and **Paddington**.

The New Year in Sydney gets off to a dramatic start each year with a spectacular fireworks display over the harbor and numerous festivals and other events interspersed throughout the year. Each January, the Sydney Festival celebrates the arts; February brings the Gay and Lesbian Mardi Gras, a Sydney icon, featuring a fantastic parade down Oxford Street; and in December, the Sydney to Hobart Yacht Race is a Boxing Day tradition. But visitors to New South Wales also have the opportunity to get out of the city and explore lush rainforests, snow-capped mountains, and semi-arid desert—all of which are easily accessible by road, rail, or air.

Inland, it's only a short drive from Sydney to the **Blue Mountains**, which are part of the **Great Dividing Range**, one of the largest mountain ranges in all of Australia. The name is derived from the color given by vapors from the eucalyptus trees that proliferate on the slopes. A nostalgic world of colonial villages, grand old mansions, and formal gardens, the area is famous for the guesthouse tradition that thrived at the turn of the century. The many country inns, private hotels, and guesthouses have recently experienced a strong resurgence of popularity, and Sydney-siders fill all of the available rooms on weekends.

Just two hours north of Sydney is the Hunter Valley, a large picturesque area of gentle lowlands. The site of the first vineyards in Australia, a number of the wineries are still producing some of Australia's finest wines. Many of the historic homesteads and grand mansions in the Hunter Valley date back to the early days of the colony, and today, the area enjoys a well-deserved reputation for providing excellent accommodations, delicious cuisine, and warm hospitality.

New England—North West, 567km north of Sydney and 467km south of Brisbane, is surrounded by unique Australian landscapes, quiet country towns, regional cities, rich pastoral lands, and mountains that unfold into open plains. The two major centers for the New England region are Australia's Country Music Capital, Tamworth, and the university town of Armidale. The New England region is also dotted with many exciting attractions and activities that showcase the region's beauty and way of life.

To the South West, the **Canberra-Snowy Mountain** region combines Australia's capital city with the country's highest mountains—and best skiing. **Canberra**, the seat of Australia's Federal Parliament, was designed by Walter Burley Griffin, a 35 year-old landscape architect from Chicago and 1911 winner of a worldwide design competition to build a new national capital. A beautiful garden city in its own right, the city boasts many historic places of interest including the National Library and National Gallery, the High Court, the Australian Mint, and the War Memorial.

In vivid contrast with the rest of Australia, which can be characterized as the flattest continent in the world, the Snowy Mountains high country presents unsurpassed beauty. Home of the rugged mountain men who chased wild horses and made famous in several films including *Man From Snowy River*, the area is also known as the Australian Alps—offering magnificent skiing during the winter and spectacular wildflowers, bushwalking, fishing, and water sports in the summer.

The mighty **Murray River** is a spectacular feature of Australian nature. It begins in the Australian Alps, is harnessed by the massive Hume Dam, travels over 2500km to form the border between Victoria and New South Wales, before finally ending its journey in South Australia. Along the Murray, enjoy wonderful riverside scenery, cruise on a paddle steamer, relive the history of river towns, visit the boutique wineries, and experience the incredible wildlife of the river.

The New South Wales coast stretches 1400 kilometers from **Tweeds Head** on the Queensland border, to **Eden** near the Victoria border in the south. The spectacular curves of the Pacific Highway wind along a coast of sheltered bays, coastal lakes, secluded, sandy beaches, through scenic villages and towns with names like Byron Bay, Coff's Harbour, Port Macquarie and Bateman's Bay. The extraordinary beauty, temperate climate, easy access, excellent diving, swimming, surfing, sailing, fishing, and first class tourist facilities, combine to make the coast a year round tourist destination.

The northern stretch of coast in tropical New South Wales includes the **Northern Rivers** region. A natural paradise, its beauty lies in unspoiled beaches, volcanic mountains, lush countryside, and world heritage listed national parks. Cape Byron, Australia's most easterly point, is located here along with **Byron Bay**, a popular tourist destination. The Byron Bay Hinterland offers an alternative lifestyle with great markets, homegrown food, and old-fashioned Australian hospitality. Tweeds Heads, near the New South Wales–Queensland border, is a surfer's paradise. Check out the famous "Barrels" at Angourie Beach.

Heading south towards Sydney, you'll discover Australia's Holiday Coast, which embraces beautiful beaches, dense, lush forests, and a myriad of rivers and waterways. The Great Lakes region offers clean clear expanses of water and over 1,000 kilometers of National Park ideal for sailing, fishing, canoeing, and windsurfing. Port MacQuarie has 13 golden beaches and beautiful mountain and river scenery. The northern part of Australia's Holiday Coast, from Nambucca Valley to Coff's Harbour, is characterized by hinterland rainforests and golden sand beaches.

The Illawarra region of New South Wales stretches from the 'Mountains to the Sea'. From the beauty and history of the Southern Highlands' lush rural countryside, to the rolling waves of the Pacific Ocean, the Illawarra is a rich and colorful concentration of contrasting scenery, lifestyles, and pleasure activities within one hour by road or train from Sydney. Drive through the picturesque mountain rainforest or travel aboard the historic scenic railway "The Cockatoo Run," which meanders up the Illawarra Escarpments through pristine rainforests unveiling views from Kiama to Sydney's Royal National Park.

The South Coast of New South Wales features sensational beaches, dramatic coastline and quaint villages. Stretching from the village of Berry to the Victorian border south of Eden, the road that hugs the South Coast forms a popular route from Sydney to Melbourne.

Inland, the Riverina stretches from the rugged snow capped mountains in the Kosciuszko National Park, through to the gentle slopes of the rich Murrumbidgee Valley, across fertile irrigation areas and out to the vast outback plains and moonscape of the Mungo National Park.

Most visitors to New South Wales, particularly first time visitors to Australia, don't realize that there are miles of rugged Outback in the Far West region of the state. Here, the stark beauty of the Outback extends endlessly to the distant horizon—from red-ochre sand and gray-green salt-bush to pockmarked lunar landscapes. A good base from which to explore this fascinating area is the historic town of **Broken Hill**, where it's possible to tour the opal mines and neighboring ghost towns, go on a camel safari, purchase aboriginal art or explore one of the many nearby National Parks to view the prolific native wildlife.

New South Wales has plenty to offer both the active traveler and adventure travel enthusiast. With four wheel driving, scuba diving and snorkeling, bushwalking, ballooning, horseback riding, white-water rafting, bicycling—the list is limited only by time and sense of adventure!

For more information:

Tourism New South Wales
GPO Box 7050
Sydney, NSW 2001
61 2 9931 1111
www.tourism.nsw.gov.au

Canberra Visitor Centre
Northbourne Ave
Dickson ACT 2602
61 2 6205 0044
www.canberratourism.com.au

As a result of the new tax system changes, including the introduction of the Goods and Services Tax on 1 July 2000, some prices shown in this publication may be subject to change on or after that date. Persons intending to purchase any of the advertised services for use on or after 1 July 2000 should confirm the likely prices with the service provider.

REGIONAL DIRECTORY

➤ denotes review

ACT

➤ **Avalanche Homestead**   1126 Orila Rd / PO Box 544, Queanbeyan, NSW 2620   *Unique, modern homestead near Canberra*

BLUE MOUNTAINS

Arabanoo Bed & Breakfast   23 Taylor Ave., Wentworth Falls, NSW 2782 61 2 4257 2325
Elegant B&B with views to Sydney from the verandah

➤ **Araluen Bed & Breakfast**   59 Wilson St., Lawson, NSW 2783
61 2 4759 1610
Beautifully appointed home in the original Blue Mountains Village

➤ **Avonleigh**   174 Lurline St., Katoomba, NSW 2780   61 2 4782 1534
*A lovely guest house that represents the graciousness and elegance of a
bygone era*

Kashelda   905 Comleroy Rd., Kurrajong, NSW 2758   (02) 4576 1268
Private, peaceful home with rural views

➤ **Kurrara Guesthouse**   17 Coomonderry St., Katoomba, NSW 2780
61 2 4782 6058   *Unique Victorian guesthouse (c. 1897) captures the
nostalgia and charm of a bygone era*

➤ **Lakeside Lodge**   30 Bellevue Rd., Wentworth Falls, NSW 2782
61 2 4757 3777
Secluded lakeside accommodations close to major mountain attractions

Moments   86 Fletcher St., Wentworth Falls, NSW 2782   (02) 4757 4455
Lovely, rambling mountain home with panoramic views

Moniques Bed & Breakfast   31 Falls Rd., Wentworth Falls, NSW 2782
61 2 4757 1646
1930's self-contained 3 bedroom cottage situated in lovely garden

Montrose House   15 Hat Hill Rd., Blackheath, NSW 2785
61 2 4787 7775
Historic country house set in $1^1/_2$ acres of superb gardens

➤ **Parklands Country Gardens & Lodges**   Govetts Leap Rd.,
Blackheath, NSW 2785   61 2 4787 7771
Luxury accommodations in 28 acre heritage garden

Pegums   25 Honour Ave., Lawson, NSW 2783   61 2 4759 1844
A small historic guesthouse specialising in home cooking

➤ **Whispering Pines**   178 Falls Rd., Wentworth Falls, NSW 2782
61 2 4757 1449
Quiet B&B hospitality surrounded by spectacular mountain views

➤ **Woodford of Leura**   48 Woodford St., Leura, NSW 2780   61 2 4784 2240
*Four bedroom guesthouse offers country hospitality in the heart of the
Blue Mountains*

BYRON HINTERLAND

➤ **Dunvegan**   PO Box 894, Byron Bay, NSW 2481   61 2 6687 1731
Boutique retreat in the beautiful Byron Bay hinterland

➤ **Green Mango Hideaway**   Lofts Rd (off Coolamon Scenic Drive),
Coorabell (PO Box 171 Bangalow), NSW 2479   61 2 6684 7171
Peaceful and secluded property with Balinese accents

CENTRAL COAST

Waterside   Central Coast region; Coffs Harbour

GREAT LAKES

Karingal   98 Coomba Rd., Pacific Palms, NSW 2428   61 2 6554 0122
Modern home set on 5 acres of natural bush with views of Wallis Lake

HUNTER VALLEY

Belltrees   NSW 61 2 6546 1156   *Once a family home, now an exclusive rural retreat in Upper Hunter Valley*

Bluebush Estate   Wilderness Rd., Lovedale, NSW 2320   61 2 4930 7177
Tranquil setting on edge of vineyard overlooking Molly Morgan Range

➤ **Capers Guest House**   Wollombi Rd., Wollombi, NSW   61 2 4998 3211
Luxury boutique sandstone guesthouse and cottage with magnificent views

➤ **The Carriages Country House**   Halls Rd., Pokolbin, NSW 2321
61 2 4998 7591   *A luxurious guesthouse on a country lane nestled in the heart of the Hunter Valley*

➤ **Casuarina Restaurant & Country Inn**   Hermitage Rd./PO Box 218, Pokolbin/Cessnock, NSW 2321/2325   61 2 4998 7888
A stunning boutique resort set in the tranquil surrounds of a vineyard, native gardens and orchards

➤ **Catersfield House**   96 Mistletoe Lane, Pokolbin, NSW 2320
61 2 4998 7220
A gracious country home situated amongst historic vineyards

Chez Vous   138 DeBeyers Rd., Pokolbin, NSW 2320   61 2 4998 7300
One bedroom cottage on tranquil two and a half acres in Hunter Valley

➤ **The Convent Pepper Tree**   Halls Rd, Pokolbin, NSW 2320
61 (2) 4998 7764
The Convent Pepper Tree—if it isn't heaven then it's very close

➤ **Montagne View Estate**   555 Hermitage Rd., Pokolbin, NSW 2335
61 2 4998 7822
Elegant country guesthouse set in a vineyard with beautiful mountain views

➤ **The Old George & Dragon Restaurant**   48 Melbourne St., East Maitland, NSW 2323   61 2 4933 7272
Historic inn offering award-winning cuisine and deluxe accommodations

Villa Provence   15 Gillards Rd., Pokolbin, NSW 2320   61 2 4998 7404
Fully self-contained luxury villas

Windsor's Edge   McDonalds Rd., Pokolbin, NSW 2320   61 2 4998 7737
Self-contained cottages on private vineyard in Pokolbin

➤ **The Woods at Pokolbin**   Halls Rd., Pokolbin, NSW 2320
61 2 4998 7368
Exquisite country house for two to eight guests nestled in the Pokolbin Woods

NORTH WEST / NEW ENGLAND

➤ **Lalla Rookh Country House**   Werris Creek Rd., Duri, NSW 2344
(02) 6768 0216
Comfortable modern homestead in New England Region

OUTBACK

➤ **The Imperial**   88 Oxide Street/PO Box 1062, Broken Hill, NSW 2880
61 8 8087 7444
Heritage accomodations capture the gentle spirit of an Australia long past

➤ **PJ's Underground**   Dugout 72, White Cliffs, NSW 2836 61 8 8091 6626
Unique underground accommodations built in historic opal mines

SOUTH COAST

➤ **Ulladulla Guest House**   39 Burrill Street, Ulladulla, NSW 2539
(02) 4455 1796
Award-winning guesthouse overlooking a picturesque harbour

SYDNEY

➤ **Coningsby**   14 Beaconsfield Parade, Lindfield, NSW   (02) 9416 4088
Historic property fifteen minutes from Sydney

➤ **Paddington Terrace**   76 Elizabeth St., Paddington, NSW 2021
(02)9363 0903
Victorian Terrace house in heritage suburb of Sydney

➤ **Palm Beach's "Chateau Sur Mer"**   124 Pacific Rd, Palm Beach, NSW
2108   61 2 9974 4220
*Large Mediterrean style residence with superb ocean views in the
exclusive haven of Palm Beach*

➤ **Pittwater Bed & Breakfast**   15 Farview Rd. / (Mail) PO Box 441,
Newport Beach 2106, Bilgola Plateau, NSW 2107   (02) 9918 6932
Luxury B&B close to the beach

Simpsons   8 Challis Avenue, Sydney, NSW 2011   61 2 9356 2199
Gracious and elegant small hotel near Sydney's King's Cross district

Victoria Court Sydney   122 Victoria Street, Sydney-Potts Point, NSW
2011 61 2 9357 3200
Charming Victorian boutique hotel in the heart of Sydney.

Wahroonga Valley Bed & Breakfast   53 Roland Ave., Wahroonga,
NSW 2076   61 2 9489 5745   *Traditional bed and breakfast set in a lovely
garden on Sydney's North Shore*

TWEED COAST

➤ **Hillcrest Bed and Breakfast**   Upper Crystal Creek Rd., Crystal Creek,
NSW 2484   (02) 6679 1023
Luxury accommodations with panoramic views in Tweed Shire

Wollumbin Palms Retreat   6 Mt. Warning Rd., Murwillumbah, NSW
2484 (02) 6679 5063
Uniquely designed luxury lodges in the Rainforest

Araluen

O verlooking the quiet fairways of the friendly Central Blue Mountains Golf Course, Araluen (Aboriginal for "Place of the Waterlilies") is just 100 metres from the first tee. The well appointed home of Gai and George Sprague offers relaxation and pampering in three comfortable queen-sized bedrooms with modern ensuites. Set in an acre of cottage and native gardens, Araluen boasts a large sunny living room with polished timber floors and open fire place. The whole house—including reading, games and dining rooms—has central heating (and cooling for summer). Spacious and finely furnished, Araluen also features a quiet reading room and huge games room with billiard/pool table and piano.

The wrap-around verandahs are an ideal place to relax and listen to the birdlife; you can even hand-feed the magpies in the award winning gardens. Gai is a trained chef and a "compulsive cook" so there are always baked goodies around the house for you to enjoy with tea or coffee. And breakfast is a special event at Araluen. With an extensive menu complemented by home-made breads and jams, it is served—at whatever time you choose—in the dining room that overlooks the golf course. (By prior arrangement Gai can also provide picnic baskets or dinner at home, although there is an abundance of eatery choices in the area—including two BYOs within walking distance.)

Courtesy mountain bikes are available and there are tennis courts nearby. Guests are also offered complimentary green fees at the golf course, and even if you are a novice, you'll be treated like VIPs. Nearby, an easy bush track winds through secluded glades busy with bird life, and passes Adelina, Junction, Cataract, and Federal Falls. All are within a 4km circuit and are a delight for picnics. And you'll be well placed to explore all the history and charm of the Blue Mountains villages. Your hosts can also help find and enjoy the particular attractions that match your interests—anything from abseiling to art, from grand escarpments to fine foods. Guests say they feel totally relaxed when they walk into Araluen, and quite spoilt while they are there. "A perfect balance of pampering and privacy!"

Name: Araluen Bed & Breakfast

Category: Bed & Breakfast

Location: Blue Mountains region; Lawson (nearest city)

Address: 59 Wilson St., Lawson, NSW 2783

Phone: Tel. 61 2 4759 1610 **Fax** 61 2 4759 2554

E-mail: araluen.bnb@bigpond.com

Web site: www.araluen.com

Innkeepers: Gail & George Sprague

Rates: From A$120-190 per double includes full breakfast; dinner by arrangement

Rated: ****½ AAA

Number of rooms: 3 Queen

Baths: 3 Ensuite

Services & amenities: Games room, mountain bikes, award-winning gardens, near golf course

Restrictions: None

Handicap access: yes

Avalanche Homestead

L ocated just 45 kilometers southeast of Canberra near Queanbeyan, Avalanche Homestead provides a startling contrast to the sights and sounds of Australia's nearby capital city. Here guests can relax in a luxurious country home in comfortable rural seclusion amidst some of the most spectacular high country scenery in Australia.

The homestead was built in 1978 on 2000 acres of bushland bordering an 80,000-acre nature reserve. The focal point of the house, constructed of double brick and local timbers, is an enormous combination living room/dining room with lofty 38-foot high-beamed ceilings and huge walls of glass providing commanding views of the surrounding countryside. The house was originally designed for entertaining and owners Frank and Faye Biddle have taken advantage of the unique architectural layout to provide a comfortable and hospitable atmosphere for their guests.

Only 14 guests can be accommodated at a time—in seven comfortably appointed double/twin rooms with ensuite bathrooms located in a separate guest wing. The rooms look out onto a large swimming pool and yard and have panoramic views of the surrounding Tinderry mountains. Although most meals are served in the homestead, barbecues and picnic lunches are popular in warm weather. Faye uses only the best home-grown produce and meats in preparing her sumptuous meals, and with advance notice, will be happy to cater to any special dietary requirements that guests may have.

During their stay, guests at Avalanche can do as much or as little as they wish. Flexibility is the rule at Avalanche – meal times, menus, style of dress and the way guests choose to spend their day. Because of the wide variety of activities available, the Biddles recommend that visitors plan to spend at least several days. Guests can take part in calving, mustering and other cattle property activities according to season, take a four wheel drive tour of the property, go horseback riding or bushwalking to view a wide variety of native bird and wildlife including kookaburras, cockatoos, parrots, wild ducks, kangaroos, wombats, lizards and hares. The property also has a trout lake and great fishing is available. At dusk, guests relax in the living room with a cool drink and watch the kangaroos grazing in the neighboring valley through the giant picture window.

Name: Avalanche Homestead

Category: B&B/Farmstay

Location: ACT: Canberra (nearest city); 45 km

Address: 1126 Urila Rd/PO Box 544, Queanbeyan   2620

Phone: Tel: 61 2 6236 3245 Fax: 61 2 6236 3302

Innkeepers: Frank & Faye Biddle

E-mail: info@avalanchehomestead.com.au

Web site: website: www.avalanchehomestead.com.au

Bedrooms: 1 King; 3 Queen; 3 Twin

Baths: Ensuite

Rate: From A$195-245 per double includes full breakfast and activities

Services and amenities: Swimming pool, BBQ, horseback riding, fishing

Rating: Four state awards for excellence

Restrictions: Children by arrangement

Handicapped facilities: Limited

Avonleigh

O riginally constructed as a gentleman's residence in 1916 and set on nearly an acre of green lawns edged with pine trees, Avonleigh is one of the original grand homes of the area. Largely untouched by the ravages of time, Avonleigh has been meticulously restored and enlarged to recapture the ambience of another era. The original section of the Federation residence houses the formal lounge and dining areas. A new wing, built in a similar architectural style, contains 12 quiet guestrooms decorated with country cottage prints and furnished with Edwardian beds and period pieces. A charming Teddy Bear can be found in each room to provide company. The décor and furnishings throughout the house, many locally collected, capture a unique graciousness and charm. The two lounges feature lofty ornate ceilings, Victorian chaises scattered about, Australian landscapes, tapestries adorning the walls and open fires crackling in the winter.

Modern comforts have not been forgotten however—each of the rooms have ensuite facilities, the house is centrally heated, and big, fluffy quilts cover the comfortable beds. Dining at Avonleigh is a treat not to be missed, with a frequently changing menu that offers a tempting choice of dishes prepared from the freshest of seasonal produce. Breakfasts are hearty and the perfect beginning to a crisp mountain morning. Visitors to the Blue Mountains will delight in the special world of elegance that Avonleigh provides while taking advantage of its excellent location. Only a short stroll from the spectacular lookouts at Echo Point and the famous Three Sisters rock formation, Avonleigh offers easy access to bushwalks, historical sites, art galleries and an array of local attractions.

Name: Avonleigh

Category: Guesthouse

Location: Blue Mountains region; Katoomba (nearest city)

Address: 174 Lurline St., Katoomba, NSW 2780

Phone: Tel. 61 2 4782 1534 **Fax** 61 2 4782 5688

E-mail: avonleigh@hotmail.com

Web site: www.bluemts.com.au/avonleigh

Innkeepers: John & Joanna Chung

Rates: From A$100 per person includes dinner, bed & breakfast

Number of rooms: 12 Queens

Baths: 12 Ensuite

Services & amenities: Guest lounge; tea/coffee, licensed restaurant; golf, swimming, tennis nearby

Restrictions: No children

Handicap access: no

Capers Guesthouse

A delightful mix of luxury accommodations and stunning views, Capers Guesthouse is a sanctuary of comfort, peace and privacy for a handful of guests. Impeccable levels of service and thoughtful attention to detail make Capers a country retreat of distinction. Originally part of Sydney Hospital, the 550 convict hewn sandstone blocks (each weighing approximately 1 ton) were dismantled and transported to Wollombi in 1995. Owners Anne and John Kelly, former interior decorators from Sydney, took on the job of meticulously cutting them and construction of the guesthouse commenced September 1997. Capers celebrated its grand opening on May 8th 1999, and during the dedication it was declared "a labour of love that should stand the test of time."

The style of the building was designed to reflect the period of its origins; a simple, Colonial country house set high on the hillside. Accommodations are in five luxury bedrooms all with ensuites, some with open fireplaces, spa baths, private garden courtyards, and all with French doors opening onto grand stone flagged verandahs. All guest rooms are both generous in size and appointments with ducted air conditioning and central heating, tea and coffee making facilities, stunning views, hair dryers, toiletries, crisp white linen and lace, soft, fluffy towels and bathrobes. Each guestroom has been individually designed and luxuriously furnished with the casual elegance of Colonial style and echoes of times past.

The lounge and dining rooms open directly onto large verandahs with breathtaking views of the Wollombi Valley. Both rooms hold the magic and mystery of Australia's convict past with sandstone walls and fireplaces adorned with the convicts' markings chiseled in nearly 150 years ago. Capers is definitely a spot where you can spoil yourself. Linger over memorable breakfasts on the large stone terrace verandah while watching the steaming winter mists rise from the millpond. Winter fare consists of piping hot porridge and a delicious cooked country breakfast, and in the summertime, fresh fruit platters and fluffy omelets make a perfect start to your day. Capers also boasts a three-bedroom, luxury four-star country cottage, which is available year round for groups of up to six people.

Name: Capers Guest House

Category: Guesthouse & self-contained cottage

Location: Hunter Valley region; Cessnock (nearest city)

Address: Wollombi Rd., Wollombi, NSW 2325

Phone: Tel. 61 2 4998 3211 **Fax** 61 2 4998 3458

E-mail: capers@hunterlink.net.au

Web site: www.capersguesthouse.com.au

Innkeepers: John & Anne Kelly

Rates: From A$200-240 per double includes full breakfast/A$150 for cottage

Rated: ****

Number of rooms: 1 King, 4 Queen, 2 Double, 1 Twin

Baths: 8 Ensuite

Services & amenities: Air-conditioning, 3 stone fireplaces

Restrictions: No smoking; 2 night minimum for cottage on weekend

Handicap access: Cottage only.

The Carriages

Perfectly positioned along pretty Halls Road in the middle of The Hunter Valley Wine Country, The Carriages offers guests the opportunity to enjoy the tranquility of an elegant country house set amongst beautiful gardens and surrounded by famous vineyards. Nestled in the lee of a creek in the quiet seclusion of thirty-six acres, The Carriages provides the ultimate in luxury and comfort. Six of the eight guest suites in the main building are sumptuously appointed with their own fireplaces and decorated with antique country pine furniture, cushy sofas and queen-size beds with feather doonas in true guesthouse style. The rooms also offer a host of amenities including a television, telephone, tea/coffee making facilities and garden views. The recently opened and popular Gatehouse is a separate cottage featuring two large suites with sitting areas and double spa baths. Built for the discerning traveler with five-star taste, this self-contained cottage is a lavish and romantic retreat. A central guest lounge with open fire, television, and full kitchen facilities, separates the two suites. The Gatehouse, designed as an adults only accommodation, has a private verandah and is surrounded by nicely landscaped gardens. In the morning, a gourmet basket includes all the makings for a scrumptious breakfast.

Unique to The Carriages, are its horse-drawn carriages available to tour the wineries. Capture the romance and history as you observe a whole new view of the vineyards. The guesthouse is situated in the heart of one of Australia's premium wine growing districts making the winery tours an exceptional treat. If wine tasting is not for you, relax by the superbly landscaped swimming pool after an energizing game of tennis. In the winter, doze in a cozy cane chair on the sun-drenched verandah, or simply enjoy the romance of the open fireplace in the privacy of your own room. When the sun goes down, there are a number of superb restaurants including Robert's at Peppertree, just a short stroll away. Savour a fabulous meal and then return to your suite for a restful night's sleep.

Name: The Carriages Country House

Category: Boutique Guesthouse

Location: Hunter Valley region; Cessnock (nearest city)

Address: Halls Rd., Pokolbin, NSW 2321

Phone: Tel. 61 2 4998 7591 **Fax** 61 2 4998 7839

E-mail: bj&lise@thecarriages.com.au

Web site: www.thecarriages.com.au

Innkeepers: Ben & Lisa Dawson

Rates: From A$150–245 per double includes gourmet breakfast basket

Rated: **** AAA

Number of rooms: 8

Baths: Ensuite

Services & amenities: Tennis court, air-conditioning, open fires, swimming pool, landscaped gardens

Restrictions: No pets; children not catered to

Handicap access: no

Casuarina

A member of Small Luxury Hotels of the World, Casuarina Restaurant and Country Inn was established by well-known chef, food writer, and Vigneron, Peter Meier in the 1980's. The Hunter Valley's only five-star property follows the European tradition of providing accommodations to complement the cuisine. Casuarina is set in the tranquil surrounds of a vineyard, native gardens and orchards at the base of the Brokenback Range right in the heart of what some locals call "God's own Country."

The fabulous food is just one reason to come to the remarkable Casuarina. The fantasy factor is another. Each of the nine luxuriously appointed, split-level suites follows an evocative theme. All have a similar floor plan, with an elevated bedroom area, spacious sitting room, and French doors that open to a shady verandah with the grapes of the Chardonnay vineyard almost within arm's reach. The Bordello Room is a favorite with its gigantic four-poster bed draped in voluptuous pink and a strategically placed mirrored ceiling. Antique furnishings such as an 1850's French sideboard and Victorian chaise add to the romance of the room.

Almost as decadent as the French Bordello, Casanova's Loft features a bathroom with a king-size spa and separate shower. A magnificent antique Queensland maple staircase leads up to the bedroom with its draped four-poster bed. The furnishings are late 1800's French, the exposed timber ceilings are finished in a limewash, the walls painted in a soft Mediterranean blue, and the Axminster carpets in a patterned terracotta. A bit more subdued is the Federation Suite highlighting Australian architecture and furnishings. The suite features an original bedroom suite made from Queensland maple circa 1910 and an ornate plaster ceiling that is a replica of the ones used in the early 1920's. An archway bordered in original leadlights, separates the elevated bedroom from the lounge area with its Federation tiled floor. With no two rooms alike, it's possible to return to Casuarina over and over again and have an entirely different experience. In addition to the impressive accommodations and gastronomic pleasures, guests can take part in cooking and wine-tasting classes. If the level of tutelage matches the rest of the quality found here, these classes are well worth the time.

Name: Casuarina Restaurant & Country Inn

Category: Luxury Guesthouse

Location: Hunter Valley region; Cessnock; 15 km (nearest city)

Address: Hermitage Rd./PO Box 218, Pokolbin/Cessnock, NSW 2321/2325

Phone: Tel. 61 2 4998 7888 **Fax** 61 2 4998 7692

E-mail: casuarina@bigpond.com

Web site: www.casuarina-group.com.au

Innkeepers: Peter & Glennis Meier

Rates: From A$230-280 per double includes full country breakfast

Rated: ***** AAA; Amex Best Restaurant (3x)

Number of rooms: 4 King, 5 Double

Baths: 9 Ensuite

Services & amenities: Grass tennis court, swimming pool, Finnish sauna, croquet court, close to Cypress Lakes Golf Club

Restrictions: No children; no pets

Handicap access: yes

Catersfield

S ituated in the heart of the Hunter Valley vineyards with spectacular views of the surrounding mountains, Catersfield is a gracious country home close to all the area's major attractions. A long driveway wends its way up to the front door where you'll be greeted by hosts Rosemary Cater-Smith and Alec Cater. The attractive guesthouse has nine spacious, individually themed rooms with large ensuites and a host of amenities including air-conditioning, television, refrigerator and tea/coffee making facilities. The French Room is a popular choice with its subdued décor and outstanding views to the horizon. The Summerhouse features a calming spa where you can soak and take in the surrounding scenery at the same time. Guests can also relax in the lounge with its floor to ceiling brick fireplace and elegant seating plan. Weather permitting, the front deck provides another pleasant environment for a rest. With its comfortable table and chairs and market-style umbrella, you can soak up the picturesque landscape and watch the sky turn shades of red and orange as the sun sets behind the mountain range. During the hot weather, a swimming pool refreshes after a day scouting the nearby wineries.

A hot breakfast is served daily and other meals are available at Café Monteverdi. Numerous cellar doors are within walking distance providing ample opportunity to sample the fine local wines. The area also offers hot-air ballooning, horse and carriage rides, sky-diving, golf, horseback riding, bicycling and many outstanding restaurants. Rosemary and Alec are familiar with the entire valley and can offer suggestions that will help personalise your visit.

Name: Catersfield House

Category: Guesthouse

Location: Hunter Valley region; Cessnock; 3 km (nearest city)

Address: 96 Mistletoe Lane, Pokolbin, NSW 2320

Phone: Tel. 61 2 4998 7220 **Fax** 61 2 4998 7558

E-mail: casfield@hunter-region.org.au

Web site: www.casfield.hunter-region.org.au

Innkeepers: Rosemary Cater-Smith & Alec Cater

Rates: From A$90-195 includes full breakfast & buffet

Number of rooms: 9 King, Queen, Twin

Baths: 9 Ensuite

Services & amenities: Air-conditioning, swimming pool, BBQ, spa

Restrictions: No smoking; no pets

Handicap access: yes

Coningsby

Enjoy the quiet ambience of this lovely heritage home (circa 1905) where guests relax beside a comforting fire with a favourite book, stroll through the magnificent grounds, or recline on verandahs overhung with greenery. Set in peaceful gardens with its own tennis court, swimming pool and billiards room, Coningsby is a perfect home away from home for visitors to Sydney. The rooms are exquisitely furnished with guests' comfort always in mind. Each air-conditioned bedroom has its own ensuite or private bathroom and an elegant drawing room where afternoon tea is served. For those guests who enjoy a game of tennis, there is an all-weather grass tennis court with tennis balls and rackets provided. Follow up with a swim in the glorious, sun-drenched, 15m pool, or play snooker or billiards on the full size table in the Billiards Room.

Coningsby is set in the leafy North- Shore suburb of Lindfield, only 3 minutes walk to the railway station (with a direct line to the Olympic Stadium), shops, banks, post office and numerous restaurants. Coningsby is a private haven, an ideal base from which to explore the world-renowned wine district of the Hunter Valley, the spectacular Blue Mountains, or closer to home, Sydney's magnificent beaches or the many wonders of Sydney City itself. After a day of sightseeing, the home and garden offer guests a unique chance to forget the everyday rush. Crackling open fires, English afternoon teas, leisurely hot breakfasts, fresh fruit and flowers, tranquil gardens and active sports, all help to make your stay at Coningsby a treasured memory.

Name: Coningsby
Category: Homestay
Location: Sydney region; Sydney; 15 minutes (nearest city)
Address: 14 Beaconsfield Parade, Lindfield NSW 2070
Phone: Tel. (02) 9416 4088 **Fax** (02) 9416 3557
E-mail: coningsby@enternet.com.au
Web site: people.enternet.com.au/~coningsby
Innkeepers: Lord & Lady Roberts
Rates: A$120 - A160 includes full English breakfast
Number of rooms: 1 King, 1 Double, 1 Twin
Baths: 2 Private, 1 Ensuite
Services & amenities: Air-conditioning, heating, tennis court, pool, billiard room
Restrictions: Smoke-free environment
Handicap access: no

The Convent Pepper Tree

T he Convent Pepper Tree was built in 1909 in Coonamble, some 600km west of the Hunter Valley, for the Brigidine Order of Nuns newly arrived from Ireland. In the 1990's, The Convent was divided into four sections and transported to its present site on seven low loaders. Several small country laneways and bridges had to be adjusted to accommodate the bulky convoy. The Convent was rebuilt as faithfully as possible, even to the point of having the new timber made in the same mill in Coonamble where the original timber was cut.. All of the pressed metal interiors are original, although many of the walls have been moved to enlarge the rooms, which are now elegant and luxurious suites.

Many of the Nuns have visited the newly restored Convent and have commented on how happy they are to see their old home restored to its former glory. In fact, the Nuns have shown their appreciation by returning the original foundation stone, stained glass windows and etched wooded doors, which they had kept when they moved into their new modern home in Coonamble.

The Chapel was in Room 1. Rooms 6 and 7 were initially the music rooms, school rooms and kindergarten. The parlours are the office and the dining room. The library is now Room 4, and the boarders' section has become rooms 14, 15, 16 and the verandah. The Nuns-only section is the remainder of the top floor.

The décor of the rooms has a French Baroque flavour, illuminated through the constant use of cherubs, angels, gilt and toiles du jour window furnishings. The white cane furniture alludes to long sultry afternoons spent relaxing in the high ceiled, airy rooms. Mosquito nets add a touch of romance and are reminiscent of hot Coonamble nights without screened windows. The Convent facilities include an indoor heated spa, swimming pool, tennis court, sunny breakfast room, and formal guest lounge where pre-dinner Champagne and Canapés are served before guests dine in one of the marvelous restaurants of the Hunter Valley.

Name: The Convent Pepper Tree

Category: Boutique Guesthouse

Location: Hunter Valley region; Polkobin (nearest city)

Address: Halls Rd, Pokolbin, NSW 2320

Phone: Tel. 61) (2) 4998 7764 **Fax** (61) (2) 4998 7323

E-mail: convent@peppers.com.au

Web site: www.peppers.com.au

Innkeepers: General Manager

Rates: From $A300 per double includes pre-dinner drinks, canapes, country breakfast

Rated: ****1/2

Number of rooms: 9 Deluxe, 8 Superior

Baths: Ensuite

Services & amenities: Spa, pool, tennis court, guest lounge, licensed restaurant

Restrictions: None

Handicap access: no

Dunvegan

F our-star rated Dunvegan proudly preserves the traditions and generous hospitality of the MacLeod Clan of Skye. Hosts Barbara and David
Powell pamper their guests with lavish treatment including indulgent
breakfasts and gourmet dinners enjoyed in elegant surroundings. This delightful country guest house set high in the rolling hills and surrounded by
macadamia and banana plantations, is just 10 minutes from some of the best
surfing and fishing beaches in the area. An exclusive retreat that caters to
adults, Dunvegan offers four private and handsomely appointed bedrooms,
each with a different character and ensuite. All rooms open onto wide verandahs, which offer stunning hinterland views. The only interruption may be
the sound of early morning birdcalls. Fresh flowers, comfortable beds, fine
linens, ceiling fans, and fine furnishings are just a few of the personal touches
that can be found in each of the rooms.

The large, five year old Australian homestead is quite striking with its high
ceilings, spacious rooms, walls of glass and polished timber floors. The
charming hosts will join guests for complimentary pre-dinner drinks, which
can be enjoyed fireside in the huge sitting room or on the beautifully landscaped terrace. Over drinks, relax and soak up the blissful, private surroundings. There's no rush here and schedules are always flexible. Breakfast is
served at a convenient time either in bed, in the sunny conservatory, out on
the terrace or on your private verandah. Spend the day at the nearby beach
exploring the delights of Byron Bay, or take advantage of the tropical rainforests and stunning mountain scenery within easy driving distance. Barbara
and David are only too happy to arrange fishing, bushwalking, golf, or for the
more adventurous, hang-gliding, cycling or rafting.

Name: Dunvegan

Category: Country Guest House

Location: Byron Hinterland region; Byron Bay (nearest city)

Address: PO Box 894, Byron Bay, NSW 2481

Phone: Tel. 61 2 6687 1731 **Fax** 61 2 6687 1731

E-mail: dunvegan@nor.com.au

Web site: www.byron-bay.com/dunvegan/index/html/

Innkeepers: Barbara & David Powell

Rates: From A$140 per double includes breakfast (dinner by arrangement)

Rated: ****AAA

Number of rooms: 2 Queen, 1 King or Twin, 1 Double

Baths: 4 Ensuite

Services & amenities: TV/Video, complimentary pre-dinner drinks, bathrobes, port & chocolates, tea/coffee

Restrictions: Not suitable for children

Handicap access: no

Green Mango Hideaway

With a tropical atmosphere reminiscent of Bali and a reputation for fine food and warm hospitality, this secluded bed & breakfast in the hills behind Byron Bay provides the perfect environment for a relaxing stay. Situated in lush gardens with abundant birdlife, it features a palm-fringed saltwater pool and Thai-style bathhouse with spa. The ambience of the property is complimented by the indoor décor—artifacts and furnishings from various parts of Asia, muslin canopies above the beds and oriental rugs scattered on timber floors. Green Mango accommodates just eight guests in four rooms. There are two guestrooms on the ground floor of the main house, each with queen-size bed, ensuite bathroom and French doors that open onto a private section of the verandah with table, chairs and hammock. Upstairs, there is a spacious and romantic room with king-size bed, sitting area, ensuite and wide balcony overlooking the pool. Also in the house, is a large and comfortable guests' sitting room with open fire, library of books and large selection of music. The dairy bails features a suite of three rooms: bedroom with queen-size bed, bathroom and colourful sitting room with glass and timber doors that open onto a private deck. With its westward view, it's a great place to enjoy the sunset.

A full breakfast, served at a table near the pool, might consist of a fresh fruit platter, cereal, home-baked bread and a cooked dish such as scrambled eggs with smoked salmon. Dinner is available several times a week by arrangement, and there is a wonderful selection of local restaurants to sample.

The area of New South Wales where Green Mango Hideaway is located, is renowned for its beauty—its green rolling hills, stunning beaches and pockets of rainforest. The charming local villages are fun to explore with their antique shops, galleries, cafes and restaurants. Many artisans live in the area and their work, from pottery and ceramics to woodwork and candles, is displayed at the colourful weekend markets. There is a wealth of activities available to the visitor including bushwalking, hang-gliding, kayaking, swimming, surfing, horseback riding, golf, and bird-watching. As Green Mango Hideaway is just a 15 minute picturesque drive from the bustle of Byron Bay and close to all the scenic attractions of the hinterland, it makes the perfect base for exploring this glorious region. A warm welcome from your hosts Susie & Mick is assured.

Name: Green Mango Hideaway

Category: Bed & Breakfast

Location: Byron Hinterland region; Byron Bay (nearest city)

Address: Lofts Rd (off Coolamon Scenic Drive), Coorabell (PO Box 171 Bangalow), NSW 2479

Phone: Tel. 61 2 6684 7171 **Fax** 61 2 6684 7181

E-mail: relax@greenmango.com.au

Web site: www.greenmango.com.au

Innkeepers: Susie & Mick

Rates: From A$125 per double includes full breakfast; dinner by arrangement

Rated: **** AAA

Number of rooms: 3 Queen, 1 King

Baths: 4 Ensuite

Services & amenities: Pool, spa house, tropical gardens

Restrictions: Not suitable for children

Handicap access: no

Hillcrest Bed & Breakfast

Perched atop a hill on five landscaped acres and surrounded by undulating pastures of a 200 acre farm, Hillcrest Bed and Breakfast enjoys
panoramic views from Mt. Warning to the Queensland Border Ranges.
Hosts Clive and Tracy have attended to every detail with their guests comfort
in mind; from the guest wing with private entrance, quality linens, huge fluffy
towels, and separate guest lounge to the home-made breads for breakfast and
the complimentary homemade cake/biscuits served with afternoon tea. Each
guest bedroom opens to a large verandah where a table and chairs await
guests who want to enjoy the stunning views. The inviting guest lounge opens
to a central atrium, which features a decorative fishpond and the gentle
sound of running water. Enjoy complimentary port and chocolates in the
lounge after dinner, or on a balmy night, unwind by the solar heated pool and
take in the splendour of the Northern NSW night sky. A few short steps from
the pool and stone waterfall, is a gazebo and BBQ area—the perfect place to
take afternoon tea or sip on a cool drink while looking out across two huge
Lilly-filled dams to the Queensland Border Ranges. Clive and Tracy pride
themselves on the quality of their food, and guests are treated to home-made
bread and conserves each morning. Dinner is available on request, and
Tracy is happy to prepare a light lunch or picnic. For those who want to
venture out to dine, Murwillumbah offers a choice of international restaurants, and the nearby seaside town of Kingscliff is famous for its "restaurant
strip" along the promenade. The Tweed Shire is home to four World Heritage

listed National Parks with some of the most spectacular rainforest in the world. There is much to see and do in the area and travelers should allow at least several days to fully enjoy it. A few of the many attractions include a guided Rainforest Safari (discount to Hillcrest guests), a river cruise and the best horse trail ride in Australia. Murwillumbah Gold Club is a short drive from the front gate and pristine beaches, art galleries, shops, restaurants, a race track and transportation services. As Hillcrest caters for a maximum of two couples, to ensure total peace and individual attention, reservations are recommended. Ask about Honeymoon Specials and small groups.

Name: Hillcrest Bed and Breakfast

Category: Country House

Location: Tweed Coast region; Murwillumbah (nearest city)

Address: Upper Crystal Creek Rd., Crystal Creek, NSW 2484

Phone: Tel. (02) 6679 1023

E-mail: hillcrest@norex.com.au

Web site: www.cheekynet.com.au/hillcrest

Innkeepers: Clive and Tracy Parker

Rates: A$95 - A105 per double including country style breakfast and home made cake/biscuits with afternoon tea.

Number of rooms: 2 Queen, 1 Double

Baths: 1 Ensuite, 1 Private

Services & amenities: Solar heated salt-water swimming pool, gazebo with gas BBQ, central atrium with decorative fishpond, guest lounge with colour TV/video. Large verandahs. Horseriding nearby.

Restrictions: Maximum 2 couples at one time. No children.

Handicap access: no

The Imperial Heritage Accommodation

The Imperial Heritage Accommodation offers a glimpse into the gentle spirit of an Australia long past. Located 500 km north east of Adelaide, The Imperial is near the center of Broken Hill in the vast Outback region near the South Australia-New South Wales border. A scenic drive will take you through one of the oldest landscapes in the world, a land that legend says was shaped by the ancient serpents and giants who inhabited the Dreamtime. A modern city, Broken Hill offers a range of activities from underground mine tours to the extraordinary scenery of modern sculptures surrounded by wildlife in the wilderness. The unofficial "capital" of the region, Broken Hill is also home to the School of the Air, the Royal Flying Doctor Service and many internationally recognized artists. Nearby Silverton, just 30kms from Broken Hill, is regarded as the film capital of the Living Outback. Easily accessible, the tiny town is renowned for its classic images of red earth, scarlet sunsets and camels in the main street.

For intrepid visitors to the region, The Imperial Heritage Accommodation has five large, well appointed bedrooms, all with ensuite facilities. Quality furnishings, individual heating and cooling, televisions, mini refrigerators and writing desk, make each room as comfortable as possible. During free time, a relaxing lounge, billiard room, garden, barbeque and solar heated pool are among the many special amenities that guests enjoy. Hosts Steve and Robbie Marcus have created a distinctive Outback experience by establishing the only four and a half star bed and breakfast style accommodations in this historic town. They provide a myriad of personal touches and definitely know how to make their travelers feel welcome. A stay at The Imperial shows guests the way to live and a way to feel at home in the very heart of Australia.

Name: The Imperial

Category: Guesthouse

Location: Outback region; Broken Hill (nearest city)

Address: 88 Oxide Street/PO Box 1062, Broken Hill, NSW 2880

Phone: Tel. 61 8 8087 7444 **Fax** 61 8 8087 7234

E-mail: imperial@pcpro.net.au

Web site: www.sabnb.org.au

Innkeepers: Steve & Robbie Marcus

Rates: From $A 128-135 per double includes full breakfast

Rated: **** 1/2 AAA

Number of rooms: 5 Queen

Baths: 5 Ensuite

Services & amenities: Heated swimming pool, billiard room, guest lounge, garden

Restrictions: No smoking, no children, no pets

Handicap access: no

Kurrara Guesthouse

F rom as early as the turn of the century, people have sought the clean air and immaculate beauty of the Blue Mountains as an escape from city life. Historically a retreat from the summer heat of Sydney, the Blue Mountains have become the ultimate 'winter' escape as well. The chill of the crisp mountain air, the hope of a sprinkling of snow, and the nostalgia of grand old guesthouses, continues to draw people to the beautiful Blue Mountains, especially Katoomba, the "Queen City of the Hills."

Established in 1897, the Kurrara Guesthouse (Aboriginal for "High Campsite") is sharing in the renewed popularity of guesthouses in the Blue Mountains. Renovated and beautifully restored, it boasts seven guestrooms, each with ensuite facilities. The home, complete with two sitting rooms and a large breakfast room, is also centrally heated and has four lovely open fireplaces. It's perfect for a romantic getaway or a nostalgic glimpse into the past. Owners Peter Said (a Registered Nurse) and Alan Sexton are well versed in looking after people, and they know the meaning of simple, old-fashioned hospitality. In true Kurrara style, they make certain that guests instantly become part of the family. As an example of their attention to personal needs, nature loving guests can arrange for specially designed picnic backpacks—complete with gourmet food, maps, a compass, first aid equipment and foot rub. When you return, they'll point you toward the heated spa so you can rest your weary bones.

Each of the seven beautifully appointed guestrooms feature private facilities and richly elegant decor. Your experience will be memorable, whether you choose from the master suite with four poster bed, open fire, clawfoot bath and private verandah, or one of the other charismatic rooms that showcase a colourful view of the historic town of Katoomba and beyond. Each morning, a three-course breakfast includes cereals, preserves, seasonal muffins, local fruits and a variety of daily cooked specials. Traditional afternoon teas are served in the sitting room or garden, and in the evening, enjoy a drink by the fire in the parlour. In ways large and small, Kurrara reflects the essence of old world charm; the aroma of home baked breads, cakes and cookies, hand stirred jams, memorable tunes played on the old grammophone, cozy open log fires, antiques, quilts and much much more.

Name: Historic Kurrara Guesthouse

Category: Guesthouse

Location: Blue Mountains region; Katoomba; 1 km (nearest city)

Address: 17 Coomonderry St., Katoomba, NSW 2780

Phone: Tel. 61 2 4782 6058 **Fax** 61 2 4782 7300

E-mail: asexton@ozemail.com.au

Web site: www.bluemts.com.au/kurrara

Innkeepers: Peter Said & Alan Sexton

Rates: From A$120 midweek per double includes full breakfast/afternoon tea

Rated: **** AAA

Number of rooms: 2 King or Twin, 5 Queen

Baths: 7 Ensuite

Services & amenities: Two guest lounges, coffee/tea, heated spa

Restrictions: No smoking

Handicap access: yes

Lakeside Lodge

A t the edge of Wentworth Falls Lake is Lakeside Lodge, the only water-front bed and breakfast in the beautiful Blue Mountains. The large sandstone family home is secluded and quiet, yet close to all the major mountain attractions. It's just a short stroll to Wentworth Falls Village, the train station, a golf course and spectacular bushwalks. Even the historic towns of Leura and Katoomba are only a few minutes drive away.

The romantic and uniquely situated Lakeside Lodge offers two luxurious suites, both with large double beds and superb views to the lake. The Lakeside Suite features a twin shower and two recliners to relax and read in after that long bushwalk, while the Spa Suite features big comfortable lounge chairs and a relaxing double spa. Right outside the door, you'll find your favourite leisure activities including fishing, boating and the wonderful lake walk with its abundance of wildlife.

After a restful night's sleep, wake to a hearty cooked breakfast that can be enjoyed on the patio or in the cozy sunroom. Both spots take advantage of the lovely lakeside location and peaceful surroundings. Former guests have referred to Lakeside Lodge as a "private paradise" and it's easy to under-stand why. Host Michaela Russell tries to make certain that every visit to Lakeside Lodge is "a stay to stay with you forever." Warm and inviting in winter with its log fire and central heating, this extraordinary property is equally heavenly during the summer months. And if the serenity of the environment isn't relaxing enough, therapeutic massages can be arranged. Also ask about mid-week and Yuletide deals.

Name: Lakeside Lodge

Category: Bed & Breakfast

Location: Blue Mountains region; Wentworth Falls (nearest city)

Address: 30 Bellevue Rd., Wentworth Falls, NSW 2782

Phone: Tel. 61 2 4757 3777 **Fax** 61 2 4757 3444

E-mail: lakeside@mountains.net.au

Web site: www.lakesidelodge.com.au

Innkeepers: Michaela Russell

Rates: From A$130 midweek per double includes full breakfast

Rated: Blue Mountains Tourism; Silver Member

Number of rooms: 2 Queen, 1 Single available

Baths: 2 Ensuite

Services & amenities: Boating, fishing, mountain walks, in-house therapeutic massage

Restrictions: Not suitable for children

Handicap access: no

Lalla Rookh Country House

A bed & breakfast for discerning travelers, lovers of art, pottery and old books. Set in 400 acres of farming and grazing land with wonderful views to the mountains, Lalla Rookh Country House is a great place to relax on the easy inland route from Sydney to Brisbane. Explore this beautiful home with its interesting old furniture, extensive library, pottery collection and 'treasures' collected in Australia and overseas. The living area at Lalla Rookh is spacious with leather chairs, Tibetan rugs and a profusion of books and magazines. The sitting room is intimate and ideal for reading or writing. Evening is a time for fine food and good conversation. Drinks are enjoyed on the vine covered terrace or in front of the fire, and dinner is served in the gracious dining room with its antique furniture, silver and crystal. Australian wines accompany the meal, and dining is a relaxed leisurely affair.

Hosts Bob & Sue Moore have been sharing their home, their lifestyle and their district with guests since 1986, providing quality accommodations and traditional country hospitality in a warm and friendly atmosphere. The sprawling single story home was designed both to suit the climate and create a feeling of space. Constructed of natural materials that blend in with the environment, there is extensive use of wood and slate. High ceilings and a full wall of windows provide plenty of natural light and views of the Great Dividing Range in the distance. The property provides interesting walks and an opportunity to see a range of native birds, or guests may explore the area, which has a gold mining history and abounds with old towns and villages, craft workshops and galleries. Your time at Lalla Rookh Country House will be refreshing and memorable—a guaranteed highlight of your trip.

Name: Lalla Rookh Country House

Category: Homestay

Location: North West/New England region; Tamworth; 20 KM (nearest city)

Address: Werris Creek Rd., Duri, NSW 2344

Phone: Tel. (02) 6768 0216 **Fax** (02) 6768 0330

E-mail: lallarookh@bigpond.com

Innkeepers: Bob & Sue Moore

Rates: A$96.00 (double) A$72.00 (single) includes full cooked breakfast w/ fresh fruit & juice

Rated: ***½ AAA ;1999 Winner B&B of the Year

Number of rooms: 2 Queen, 1 Twin, 1 Double

Baths: 2 Ensuite, 1 Share

Services & amenities: Heating, cooling, electric blankets, large fluffy towels, wood fire, leafy terrace, tea/coffee making, TV

Restrictions: No children. Smoking outside only

Handicap access: yes

THE ACCOMMODATION INDUSTRY
AWARDS FOR EXCELLENCE OF NSW

1999 STATE WINNER

BED & BREAKFAST OF THE YEAR

Montagne View

Montagne View Estate stands on a hill, offering views across forest, farmland and vineyards to the Brokenback Range. Montagne is the French word for mountain, and this impressive property certainly lives up to its name with spectacular vistas you'll remember for a lifetime. Accommodations at Montagne View Estate are in the Gables Guesthouse, which offers all the facilities of a five-star resort while remaining small, private and secluded. Each of the eight air-conditioned studio suites have their own open fire place to warm any occasion and three suites include a full-size corner spa. The list of amenities is extensive and every comfort has been included: split system air-conditioning, television and video with complimentary film library, full stereo with CD, the latest magazines to read, plus a wonderful selection of fresh plunger coffee, Twinings teas and home-made cookies

You'll sleep soundly in these luxurious surroundings and wake up to a magnificent country breakfast with lashings of bacon, free-range eggs, home-made croissants or maybe a smoked salmon and fresh herb omelet. Then spend the day as you wish—perhaps with a game of tennis, practicing your golf swing on the private driving range, cooling down with a swim or relaxing in the spa. At the end of the day take a quiet stroll to Brents, a romantic eatery featuring exquisite modern Australian cuisine and the only restaurant in the Hunter Valley to offer 20 local and Australian wines by the glass. Dine by candlelight in an elegant, relaxed environment that serves the perfect recipe for a romantic dinner for two. Winter means wonderful food, warm puddings and great coffee by the open fire. Summer conjures up images of a glass of wine on the verandah, fresh seafood, a seasonal fruit pudding and a sunset over Brokenback Range. Brents at Montagne View is open for lunch every weekend and for dinner from Wednesday to Sunday, and if you're lucky enough to be an overnight guest, you need only amble over to your deluxe suite and retire for the night.

Name: Montagne View Estate

Category: Guesthouse

Location: Hunter Valley region; Cessnock (nearest city)

Address: 555 Hermitage Rd., Pokolbin, NSW 2335

Phone: Tel. 61 2 4998 7822 **Fax** 61 2 6574 7276

E-mail: thegables@montagneview.com.au

Web site: www.montagneview.com.au

Innkeepers: Brent & Jillian Bultitude

Rates: From A$160-650 per double includes full breakfast; 2 & 3 day all inclusive packages available

Rated: ****1/2 AAA/Best Hosted Accommodation Award

Number of rooms: 8 Queen

Baths: 8 Ensuite

Services & amenities: Swimming pool, tennis court, driving range, video library, games room

Restrictions: Not suitable for children

Handicap access: yes

Old George & Dragon

S ince 1937, The Old George and Dragon has been an important piece of East Maitland's history. Built of beautiful sandstone block, The Old George and Dragon was one of the colony's first hotels. Today, the historic inn continues the tradition of offering its own unique brand of refreshment , fine foods and luxury accommodations. Ian and Jenny Morphy purchased the property in 1982 and after restoring the graceful building and running a successful restaurant for a decade, they decided to add guestrooms as well. Influenced by European inns that provide accommodations for dinner patrons, The Old George and Dragon offers four generous queen-size bedrooms, each with ensuite facilities. The guest wing is furnished with fine antique furnishings, a selection of nineteenth century paintings and individualized décor; the front room features a four poster canopied bed while a large courtyard suite that sleeps three can be accessed through the lovely Mediterranean-style courtyard with its terracotta tile and traditional fountain.

Guests may choose to dine in one of three dining rooms, each with its own distinctive ambience. The central dining room features an open fire, pressed metal ceiling, white tablecloths and soft candlelight. Soaring ceilings, custom drapes, and deep shades of green and burgundy combine to create a formal, yet intimate atmosphere. Guests can also dine al fresco in the leafy courtyard. Ian has a well-deserved reputation as a talented chef, and his stylish modern Australian/French cuisine has won numerous accolades. Ian changes the menu daily to take advantage of fresh ingredients, and both he and Jenny believe that creating a meal is a process to be savoured rather than rushed. Favourite dishes include Roast Duck with oranges, Grand Marnier and red cabbage, Braised oxtail with parsnip mash and deep-fried leek, and truffle centered risotto with fennel peas and Harvey Bay scallops. If it sounds amazing, it is and the loyal clientele and numerous regional and national awards are testament to the fact. The Old George and Dragon offers overnight packages that include a three course dinner and light breakfast. After indulging in exquisite world-class cuisine and luxurious accommodations, discover East Maitland's renowned antique shops, the historic river port of Morpeth or the nearby Hunter Valley vineyards.

Name: The Old George & Dragon Restaurant

Category: Restaurant/Superior Rooms

Location: Hunter Valley region; Maitland (nearest city)

Address: 48 Melbourne St., East Maitland, NSW 2323

Phone: Tel. 61 2 4933 7272 **Fax** 61 2 4934 1481

E-mail: oldgeorge@netcentral.com.au

Web site: www.maitlandtourism.gov.au

Innkeepers: Ian & Jenny Morphy

Rates: From A$280 per double includes dinner, bed and light breakfast

Number of rooms: 4 Queen

Baths: 4 Ensuite

Services & amenities: Award-winning restaurant and wine list

Restrictions: No smoking in guest rooms

Handicap access: no

Paddington Terrace

This century old terrace house is located in the heart of Paddington, a heritage suburb where visitors can sense the early history of Sydney. Like Georgetown or The French Quarter, Paddington is a charming inner city neighborhood filled with art galleries, boutiques, restaurants, pubs and bookstores. Rows of Victorian Terraces, with their distinctive lace balconies, line the picturesque streets of the world's only complete Victorian suburb.

History and heritage are a great passion at Paddington Terrace, and hosts Diane and Ron Johnson have written a self-guided walking tour of the historic area that is great fun to follow. It's only a short stroll to Oxford Street with its art house cinemas and Saturday open-air markets. Also nearby are Queen Street's celebrated antique shops and the Sydney Cricket Ground and Football stadium.

After a day of exploration, Paddington Terrace offers relaxing and comfortable accommodations in two gracious rooms that open onto a private balcony. Step outside and watch the activity as you soak up the glorious energy of the city. Each morning, breakfast is served in a sunny conservatory overlooking a courtyard and lush reserve filled with greenery. A stopover in Paddington is a truly unique experience, and visitors to Sydney should definitely take the time to discover this exceptional neighborhood and this extraordinary bed and breakfast.

Name: Paddington Terrace

Category: Homestay B&B

Location: Sydney region; Sydney; 3 KM to CBD (nearest city)

Address: 76 Elizabeth St., Paddington, NSW 2021

Phone: Tel. (02)9363 0903 **Fax** (02) 9327 1476

E-mail: paddterr@ozemail.com.au

Web site: www.ozemail.com.au/~paddterr/

Innkeepers: Diane & Ron Johnson

Rates: A$115-$A135 includes continental breakfast

Rated: NSW B&B Council, Australian B&B Association

Number of rooms: 1 Double with balcony, 1 Twin with balcony

Baths: 2 Ensuite

Services & amenities: Guest Lounge, TV in each room, Tea/coffee

Restrictions: No Smoking inside

Handicap access: no

Palm Beach's Chateau Sur Mer

C hateau Sur Mer is a large French Mediterranean style house, high on a hill with beautiful views of the ocean and beyond. The two-story residence, widely recognized for its high standard of accommodations, provides an opportunity to relax in the secluded heaven of Palm Beach, less than an hour from Sydney's central business district. Reminiscent of the South of France, Chateau Sur Mer provides a warm, friendly atmosphere in quiet, relaxing surroundings just a short walk from the beach.

A quick tour of the home's ground floor showcases the cavernous lobby, high-ceilinged lounge, and dining room with its fully stocked fridge. A delicious al fresco breakfast is served on the sublime sea-view balconies and garden patio, often accompanied by various parrots, local kookaburras and currawongs. If preferred, breakfast can also be served in the large dining room.

The most popular guestroom is the romantic Riviera Honeymoon Suite, formerly the master bedroom, an enormous space with superb ocean views, a large sitting area, and a private balcony where you can enjoy an intimate breakfast. The modern St Tropez Suite has beautiful Pittwater views, and all rooms have a queen bed, TV, video, modern ensuite bathroom, reverse cycle air-conditioning, hairdryer, clock radio, a fridge and tea/coffee making facilities.

Palm Beach's long peninsula has the ocean on one side and the aquatic playground of Pittwater on the other. With its excellent surf, sailing, walks and restaurants, Palm Beach has long been the perfect holiday location for the rich and famous of Sydney and the site of many television programs and films. Hosts Colin and Theresa, an English couple who have lived in Australia for 20 years, believe they now live in paradise and they are delighted to share that experience with you. Just a short walk away from Chateau Sur Mer are the beautiful peninsula beaches, prestigious restaurants, golf course, ferry, sea planes, dive centre, the "Bible Garden" (offering the best views of the peninsula), Barrenjoey Lighthouse and the surrounding native reserves abounding in colourful birdlife and natural flora and fauna.

Name: Palm Beach's "Chateau Sur Mer"

Category: Bed & Breakfast

Location: Sydney region; Sydney; 45 km (nearest city)

Address: 124 Pacific Rd, Palm Beach, NSW 2108

Phone: Tel. 61 2 9974 4220 **Fax** 61 2 9974 1147

E-mail: stay@palmbeachchateau.com.au

Web site: www.palmbeachchateau.com.au

Innkeepers: Colin & Theresa McCloud

Rates: From A$130-230 per double includes special continental breakfast

Rated: B&B Council NSW/ Australian B&B Council

Number of rooms: 3 Queen

Baths: 2 Ensuite, 1 Private

Services & amenities: Air-conditioning, TV, Videos

Restrictions: No smoking; no children; 2 night minimum on weekends

Handicap access: no

Parklands

T he splendour of Parklands begins the moment you pass through the sweeping gates. The driveway, lined with century- old pines and cypresses, takes you past glorious flower beds and sweeping green lawns to a trio of luxury garden cottages. Built in traditional Blue Mountains' Weatherboard style, each of the three luxury cottages contains two elegant Garden Suites and two deluxe Loft Rooms, and all twelve units have expansive views of the splendid grounds. The Garden Suites feature large kingsized bedrooms, an airy sitting room with a sofa you can sink into, a romantic wood-fire, shelves full of books and terrace doors that open onto the stunning heritage garden. Equally luxurious and classically furnished, are the upstairs Loft Rooms with their open plan design, raked ceilings and balconies overlooking beds of rhododendrons. All the ensuite bathrooms have extra deep baths (some with aero jacuzzi-spas), underfloor heating and warm fluffy bath towels. The deluxe accommodations are set in 28 acres of gardens, rolling green fields, tree lined avenues and a lake. It is truly one of the outstanding properties in the Blue Mountains where beauty, luxury and privacy combine to guarantee an extraordinary stay.

The property has a rich natural heritage with the garden started over one hundred years ago. Still flowing today is the natural spring, which the Illustrated Sydney News claimed in 1890 to be the "finest drinking water for miles around." This now feeds into a lake, which is a perfect sylvan setting of young willows, wild waterfowl and the whispering of pine needles in a gentle breeze.

One of the joys of spending a night at Parklands is not having to dress for breakfast. Gourmet hampers are delivered to your room complete with starched serviettes and table clothes along with the morning paper. It is not unusual to find smoked salmon and rolled crepes as part of this delicious feast. If you feel like getting dressed, Parklands is in the heart of bush-walking country and near the charming village of Blackheath, which means some of the Blue Mountains finest restaurants. Only a short stroll away are the village's delightful sidewalk cafes and antique shops. This country retreat delivers on every level and is not to be missed.

Name: Parklands Country Gardens & Lodges

Category: Country Retreat

Location: Blue Mountains region; Blackheath (nearest city)

Address: Govetts Leap Rd., Blackheath, NSW 2785

Phone: Tel. 61 2 4787 7771 **Fax** 61 2 4787 7211

E-mail: office@parklands-cgl.com.au

Web site: www.parklands-cgl.com.au

Innkeepers: Colin & Elizabeth Jacobson

Rates: From A$185 per couple includes breakfast; weekend packages available

Rated: ****1/2 AAA

Number of rooms: 12 King, Twin

Baths: 12 Ensuite

Services & amenities: Close to activities; Suites have woodfires, fridge, CD players, central heating, tea/coffee, picnic rugs

Restrictions: No children 1 to 14

Handicap access: yes

Pittwater Bed & Breakfast

No longer a secret, Sydney's famous Northern Peninsula between Pittwater and the Pacific Ocean offers fabulous beaches, national parks and award-winning restaurants. Close to Avalon and Newport village, visitors to the area will find Pittwater Bed & Breakfast, a comfortable family home situated on high plateau with stunning views of the surrounding bush, coastline and city lights. Extensively renovated and furnished to a luxury standard, guest accommodations are one queen-size room with ensuite and a two room suite with double beds and large spa bathroom. Soft and subdued, the guest rooms provide a relaxing refuge after a busy day. A wall of windows in the living room highlights the superb location and guests become transfixed by the view.

James and Colette are charming hosts, who will make every effort to ensure a memorable stay, and their motto is "arrive as guests, depart as friends." Colette is an enthusiastic cook, and her breakfasts are a triumph of fresh home cooking featuring fruit preserves and her famous muffins. Gourmet dinners and lunch can also be arranged, and all meals are prepared using the best and freshest Australian produce. An array of special services are available by arrangement including a personally escorted day tour with picnic lunch, and romantic honeymoon packages that include a candlelit restaurant dinner and complimentary wine. After a day exploring Sydney or the surrounding area, return to Pittwater and relax by the solar heated pool as you enjoy this lovely four and a half star home away from home.

Name: Pittwater Bed & Breakfast

Category: Bed & Breakfast

Location: Sydney/Northern Beaches region; Newport Beach; 1KM (nearest city)

Address: 15 Farview Rd.(Mail)PO Box 441, Newport Beach 2106, Bilgola Plateau, NSW 2107

Phone: Tel. (02) 9918 6932 **Fax** (02) 9918 6485

E-mail: pittwater@intercoast.com.au

Web site: www.atn.com.au/nsw/syd/accom/pittwat.htm

Innkeepers: James & Colette Campbell

Rates: A$150

Rated: ****½ AAA

Number of rooms: 1 Queen, 1 Double

Baths: 2 Ensuite

Services & amenities: Fax & internet connection; local chauffeur service, morning or afternoon tea, heated pool

Restrictions: No smoking indoors

Handicap access: no

PJ's Underground

PJ's Underground is a unique bed & breakfast located underground in the pioneering township of White Cliffs, 255 km northeast of Broken Hill. White Cliffs was the first commercial opal field in Australia, and hot summer temperatures forced opal miners to retreat to the cool, constant 22 degree temperature of their mines after a hard day's work. Today, PJ's Underground offers comfortable accommodations for up to 17 visitors in five guest rooms nestled under the 64 million year old roof of attractively renovated old mines in historic Turley's Hill. The distinctive B&B is proud to be a finalist in the 1997 and 1999 Tourism Awards for Excellence.

Hosts Peter and Joanne Pedler enjoy visitors sharing their unique home and lifestyle, and often invite guests to join them for dinner and an evening's relaxation in their comfortable guest lounge. Many guests find themselves curled up with a good book from PJ's extensive library in an outdoor oasis (a stark contrast to the surrounding countryside where the kangaroos and emus move through the saltbush and bare gibber plains stretching to the horizon). A relaxing afternoon can be spent fossicking for a piece of elusive opal on the old mining field. White Cliffs' miners welcome a friendly tourist face and are often more than willing to stop for a chat. For those seeking cut opal, PJ's Underground sells a range of polished stones and set jewelry, as well as local arts and crafts. After a long day on the tourist trail visiting the Solar Power

Station, opal showrooms and art galleries, come back and soak in the spa also located underground in a century old, open-cut mine. PJ's Underground welcomes visitors to enjoy the peace and tranquility of the bush, experience the wonder of living beneath the earth's surface, and feel a little of the pioneering spirit of the Living Outback.

Name: PJ's Underground
Category: Bed & Breakfast
Location: Outback region; White Cliffs (nearest city)
Address: Dugout 72, White Cliffs, NSW 2836
Phone: Tel. 61 8 8091 6626 **Fax** 61 8 8091 6626
E-mail: pjsunderground@bigpond.com
Web site: www.babs.com.au/nsw/pj.htm
Innkeepers: Joanne & Peter Pedler
Rates: From $A65-180 includes breakfast; dinner also available
Rated: ***½ AAA; 1997/1999 NSW Awards for Excellence
Number of rooms: 5 Doubles (some with extra single bed)
Baths: 3 Share
Services & amenities: Spa, BBQ, Guest lounges, library, on-site mine tour
Restrictions: No smoking
Handicap access: no

Ulladulla Guest House

T he award-winning Ulladulla Guest House, originally built for a local doctor in the 1940s, was converted to a guesthouse in the 1960s, and totally refurbished and upgraded during 1995–1998. Set in the heart of the fishing village of Ulladulla and overlooking a picturesque harbour, this elegant guesthouse exudes charm. With an emphasis on fine art and crafts, hosts Andrew and Elizabeth have filled each room with unique African artworks and antique furniture. An eclectic library provides an extensive collection of books and magazines, and a guest lounge offers a peaceful spot to soak up the atmosphere and read. Luxury guest rooms all feature queen-size beds, custom designed furniture and original artwork. Some feature private spas and marble bathrooms.

In addition to the sumptuous accommodations, visitors to Ulladulla will appreciate its ideal location. The house is a perfect base for exploring the entire South Coast region with its historic pioneer villages, art galleries and antique shops. There is also the wilderness of nearby National parks, as well as scenic beachside golf courses and an assortment of water sports including fishing and diving. After a busy day, the tropical gardens surrounding the guesthouse offer an oasis of tranquility. Enjoy a sauna after a workout in the gym or arrange for a massage to help you completely relax. The pampering doesn't stop there. Breakfasts are a three course extravaganza consisting of fresh fruits, cereals, home-made muesli and a choice of traditional and gourmet hot dishes to help start the day off right. With attention paid to every detail, it's easy to understand why Ulladulla Guest House has received numerous Tourism Awards for Excellence since it opened in 1997.

Name: Ulladulla Guest House

Category: Guest House

Location: South Coast region; Ulladulla (nearest city)

Address: 39 Burrill Street, Ulladulla, NSW 2539

Phone: Tel. (02) 4455 1796 **Fax** (02) 4454 4660

E-mail: elizans@shoalhaven.net.au

Web site: www.oztourism.com.au/~gdaymate/uladullagh.htm

Innkeepers: Elizabeth & Andrew Nowosad

Rates: A$100-190 includes full breakfast

Rated: ****1/2 AAA

Number of rooms: 10 Queen

Baths: 10 Ensuite

Services & amenities: Heated pool, spa, sauna, gym

Restrictions: No Smoking indoors

Handicap access: yes

Victoria Court

V ictoria Court, a small historic boutique hotel, is centrally located on
    quiet, leafy Victoria Street in elegant Potts Point, the heart of Sydney's
    gastronomic district. It is an ideal base from which to explore and do
business in Sydney, as it is within minutes of the Opera House, the Central
Business District, the Harbour, Chinatown and the famous Beaches.

Victoria Street is an address much favoured in the history of Sydney. In
earlier times, it was the preferred residential choice of some of the city's most
influential and wealthy merchant families who lived there because it was so
close to the magnificent harbour. Right at its heart stands Victoria Court,
whose buildings date from 1881 and retain the gracious ambience of that age,
while incorporating all the refinements of a modern, first class establishment.

Guests are offered friendly and personalised service in an informal atmosphere and amidst Victorian charm. Not unexpectedly, no two rooms are
alike and cater to various budgets. Most rooms have marble fireplaces, some
have four poster beds, and others feature balconies, which offer views over
Victoria Street, classified by the National Trust as a street of historical significance. All rooms have ensuite bathrooms, hairdryers, air-conditioning, co-

lour television, radio-clock, coffee/tea making facilities and direct dial telephones. The focal point of Victoria Court is the verdant courtyard conservatory, where to the melodious accompaniment of a bubbling fountain, breakfast is served.

In the immediate vicinity of the Victoria Court, are some of Sydney's most renowned restaurants as well as countless cafes with menus priced to suit all pockets. Within a short radius, a wide variety of cuisines are offered including Australian, Italian, French, Thai, Chinese, Japanese, and Indian, to name but a few. Public transportation, car rental offices, travel agencies and major banks are within close range. An airport bus service operates to and from the hotel, while for those with their own transportation, security parking is available.

Name: Victoria Court Sydney

Category: Boutique Hotel

Location: Sydney region; Sydney (nearest city)

Address: 122 Victoria Street, Sydney-Potts Point, NSW 2011

Phone: Tel. 61 2 9357 3200 **Fax** 61 2 9357 7606

E-mail: info@VictoriaCourt.com.au

Web site: www.VictoriaCourt.com.au

Innkeepers: Michele & Bill Lawrence

Rates: From $A99 per double includes buffet breakfast

Rated: **** AAA

Number of rooms: 20

Baths: 20 Ensuite

Services & amenities: All rooms have air-conditioning, TV, telephone; guest lounge with fireplace; airport bus; close to Opera House and harbour

Restrictions: None

Handicap access: yes

Villa Provence

T he enchanting Villa Provence offers a little bit of Gallic magic in the heart of the Hunter Valley. Overlooking 23 acres of vineyards and rolling hills, the classic Provençal-style villas could just as easily be located in the South of France. Looking every bit as if it has been part of the Hunter Heritage since the first vines were planted in the early 1800's, Villa Provence consists of nine fully self-contained Southern European style luxury villas. Each villa has a queen-sized bedroom with seating area, spacious lounge with sofa bed, and French doors that open onto a patio or verandah with expansive views of the Brokenback Ranges. A kitchenette allows you to prepare and eat meals at your leisure, whether it's a quick breakfast before you head out for the day, or a relaxed dinner where you sample regional wines and local delicacies. The popular Champagne Suite is the most luxurious and a favourite with Honeymooners.

Wine is only one facet of the Hunter Valley's appeal; the rest is inspired by superb cuisine, jazz festivals, bike rides, hot-air balloons, bushwalks, country markets, operas and vintage fairs, art and antique galleries. At Villa Provence, you can choose to be as active or relaxed as you like. The property offers a myriad of diversions including nearby bushwalks, a game of boules, a private barbecue area, a refreshing swim in the pool, or a leisurely walk to the cellar door for wine tastings and sales. For a special treat, hosts Tracy and William can arrange bicycles or a horse and carriage for your sojourn around the vineyards. There are more than 70 regional wineries, and the Hunter Valley wine country boasts a staggering array of varietals and styles. Secluded, yet central to many award winning wineries, and restaurants, Villa Provence offers a special touch of France in Australia's best-known wine region. For privacy and comfort, the accommodations are unrivaled, and for those looking for a bit of culture and sophistication, Villa Provence delivers.

Name: Villa Provence

Category: Guesthouse/Self-contained villas

Location: Hunter Valley region; Cessnock (nearest city)

Address: 15 Gillards Rd., Pokolbin, NSW 2320

Phone: Tel. 61 2 4998 7404 **Fax** 61 2 4998 7405

E-mail: villapvc@hunterlink.net.au

Innkeepers: Tracey & William Campbell

Rates: From A$180 per double includes room only

Number of rooms: 9 Queen

Baths: 9 Ensuite

Services & amenities: Swimming pool; all villas have air-conditioning, TV, lounge & kitchenette

Restrictions: No smoking; no pets; 2 night minimum on weekends

Handicap access: no

Whispering Pines by the Falls

A grand heritage mountain estate, Whispering Pines is perched on a 1,000 ft. knife-edge escarpment at the head of the majestic Wentworth Falls, overlooking the beautiful Blue Mountains. Nestled in four acres of rambling gardens surrounded by towering cedars and pines, this century-old guesthouse adjoins the famous Blue Mountains National Park. Guests are just seconds from spectacular lookouts and the start of some of the most magnificent walking trails in the mountains. In this remarkable setting, Whispering Pines offers a blend of luxury, privacy, and quiet hospitality.

The spacious suites, antique furnishings, brass beds and period fittings perfectly complement the charm and romance of the grand Australian country house. A long staircase leads to the Verandah Suites, which have dramatic views over the Jamison Valley to Mt. Solitary and beyond; Garden Suites look out over the delightful woodland gardens. The lower level of the house includes one guestroom and an elegant sitting room with log fire and over-stuffed armchairs. A tasty breakfast is served daily in the dining room; weekends are a more leisurely affair with a full cooked meal, while mid-week is a bit less formal with a light breakfast served.

Hosts Bill and Maria McCabe pay extraordinary attention to detail and guests are sure to have an unforgettable experience. The peaceful, romantic residence is surpassed only by the stunning scenery that surrounds it. In addition to taking advantage of the superb location and all the natural attractions, guests can arrange for a candlelit dinner at one of the many nearby restaurants.

Name: Whispering Pines by the Falls

Category: Bed & Breakfast

Location: Blue Mountains region; Wentworth Falls; 2 km (nearest city)

Address: 178 Falls Rd., Wentworth Falls, NSW 2782

Phone: Tel. 61 2 4757 1449 **Fax** 61 2 4757 1219

E-mail: wpines@bigpond.com

Web site: www.bluemts.com.au/wpines

Innkeepers: Bill & Maria McCabe

Rates: From A$150-250 includes breakfast

Rated: **** AAA

Number of rooms: 4 Queen, 1 Double

Baths: 4 ensuite, 1 private

Services & amenities: 4 acres of rambling woodland gardens, fireplaces, central heating

Restrictions: No smoking; no children

Handicap access: yes

Windsor's Edge

Windsors Edge Cottages are situated on a privately owned working vineyard in Pokolbin with views of the Brokenback Range and surrounding vineyards. The luxuriously appointed two bedroom cottages are fully self-contained with spa, queen-sized beds, log fire, air-conditioning, BBQ facilities and all the comforts of home. The Country chic bedrooms lead out to a private verandah where you can enjoy a cup of coffee or a glass of wine. If you're feeling energetic, you can play a game of tennis on the synthetic grass, all-weather court. Windsor's Edge is ideally located only minutes from wineries, restaurants and all the other Hunter Valley attractions, and it's easy to spend a few days exploring the scenic region.

The comfortable living area in the cottage allows you to completely relax and unwind. In the kitchen, you'll find a full size refrigerator, microwave and all the cooking utensils needed to prepare an appetizing dinner. Whether a simple affair or a gourmet feast, the dining table is often the site of lively conversation and good food. A colour television, video player, and stereo CD player are just some of the additional amenities to help make your stay more enjoyable. If you don't feel like preparing your own meal, Amanda's On The Edge stylishly incorporates fine dining on the edge of the vineyard. A mélange of favourites, including authentic curries, delectable Asian dishes and traditional Australian fare can be found at this licensed (or BYO) restaurant where presentation is as important as the food. A stay at Windsor's Edge Cottage includes a cheese platter, complimentary port, and light breakfast consisting of juice, toast, cereal, coffee and tea, in addition to a host of other pleasant surprises.

Name: Windsor's Edge

Category: Self-contained cottages

Location: Hunter Valley region; Pokolbin (nearest city)

Address: McDonalds Rd., Pokolbin, NSW 2320

Phone: Tel. 61 2 4998 7737 **Fax** 61 2 4998 7737

Web site: www.winecountry.com.au

Innkeepers: Jessie & Tim Windsor

Rates: From A$100 midweek/170 weekend per double includes light breakfast

Number of rooms: 3 two-bedroom cottages

Baths: Private

Services & amenities: Refrigerator, TV, video, stereo, CD, microwave, log fire, BBQ, tennis court, restaurant, wine-tasting

Restrictions: No pets

Handicap access: no

Woodford of Leura

Located in one of Leura's quietest country lanes, Woodford is a comfortable stroll from the unique heritage village and some of the best lookouts and gardens in the area. Set amidst almost an acre of tranquil Sorensen gardens, this grand old home is a true retreat screened discreetly by towering pines, which successfully exclude unwanted intrusions. The delightful guesthouse offers both suites and double rooms, each with an ensuite or private bathroom and full central heating. All rooms are complete with colour TV, electric blankets and tea/coffee making facilities. The popular Garden Suite has a separate sitting area with comfortable sofa and view of the lovely garden. The Cedar Suite features a king-sized bed and pair of inviting armchairs, while the double rooms have antique iron or brass beds. The gracious residence also features a cozy guest lounge with log fire, a private dining area and an attractive breakfast room. The Spa Room features a large, heated, 4-person spa—an ideal way to recuperate after a full day's activity in the Blue Mountains.

Promising country hospitality in an intimate atmosphere, hosts John and Lesley Kendall (along with Max the Cat), strive to ensure that your stay at Woodford exceeds all expectations. Upon arrival, guests are welcomed with a cup of tea or coffee served by the log fire in winter or in the garden on a warm day. The gracious tradition of "High Tea", with fine china and silver service, can also be arranged in the formal dining room. John has worked in the hospitality industry for over 30 years, and his experience in hotel/restaurant management has been honed into the role he enjoys as "mine host."

Lesley's varied catering experience is reflected in her ability to meet guests' culinary requirements. Served at your individual table, breakfast is an absolute treat at Woodford. Beginning with freshly squeezed orange juice, the sideboard buffet groans with delights such as Bircher Muesli (a sought after recipe by guests), dried fruit compote, yogurt, and fresh fruit. The feast continues with a choice of such made to order entrees as veal chipolata sausages, lean bacon, eggs (fried or scrambled), grilled tomato, smoked salmon with herbed- scrambled eggs, or corn fritters and bacon. All this accompanied by a bottomless pot of tea/coffee and the morning paper.

Name: Woodford of Leura

Category: Bed & Breakfast

Location: Blue Mountains region; Leura (nearest city)

Address: 48 Woodford St., Leura, NSW 2780

Phone: Tel. 61 2 4784 2240 **Fax** 61 2 4784 2240

E-mail: woodford@leura.com

Web site: www.leura.com

Innkeepers: John & Lesley Kendall

Rates: From $A130-160 per double includes full breakfast; mid-week discounts available

Rated: **** AAA

Number of rooms: 1 King or Twin, 1 Queen, 1 Double

Baths: 2 Ensuite, 2 Private

Services & amenities: Guest lounge with fire, spa room, breakfast room, private dining room, spacious grounds

Restrictions: No children on weekends; mid-week by arrangement

Handicap access: no

The Woods at Pokolbin

T he Woods is an exquisite country house nestled in the Pokolbin Woods. Accommodating up to eight guests in four bedrooms, The Woods offers style, seclusion and tranquility in the midst of wine country. For those serious about food and wine, this is the perfect getaway. A leisurely stroll reveals numerous renowned restaurants and wineries that allow guests to indulge in the best that the Hunter Valley has to offer. Or simply relax in comfort and style, making use of an open kitchen, cooking facilities, BBQ and dreamy courtyard. A generous platter of magnificent local cheese awaits your arrival, and in the morning, provisions for a full breakfast (bacon, eggs, cereal, milk, etc.) can be found in the refrigerator to prepare at your leisure.

Owners Anne Marie and Ewen Cameron have thoughtfully created an elegant, country-style environment. Walls of burnt orange, pillars of azure, and natural looking tile give the house a Mediterranean feel. A huge open fire burns during the winter months and air-conditioning keeps it cool in summer. There are two double bedrooms in the self-contained main house, each with a large ensuite and one with a spa bath. Two guest wings each contain a double bedroom and ensuite. The U-shaped structure surrounds a grassy courtyard with a large fountain, and several sets of French doors open onto the cool, brick floored verandah that borders the private plaza. Enjoy a pre-dinner drink or nightcap on the verandah before slipping into the romantic bedroom with its wrought iron bed, fluffy pillows and mosquito netting.

The focal point of the main house is a large kitchen and dining area complete with dishwasher, microwave, cooking utensils and crockery. A long wooden table seats up to eight, and gourmet meals can be prepared as a group endeavor. If self-catering is not your style, there are several restaurants nearby including Roberts at Pepper Tree, which serves hearty Australian fare with European influences. On the weekends, the house is let out to one group at a time; during the week, the tariff is per double, per night. Because there are multiple bedrooms and the house is totally self-contained, this is a great spot for families or couples traveling together.

Name: The Woods at Pokolbin

Category: Self-contained cottages

Location: Hunter Valley region; Cessnock (nearest city)

Address: Halls Rd., Pokolbin, NSW 2320

Phone: Tel. 61 2 4998 7368 **Fax** 61 2 4998 7368

E-mail: woodsatpokolbin@bigpond.com

Web site: www.thewoods.com.au

Innkeepers: Anne Marie & Ewen Cameron

Rates: From A$150 per double per night weekends; A$100 midweek includes breakfast

Number of rooms: 4 Queen

Baths: 4 Ensuite

Services & amenities: Courtyard, BBQ, near restaurants and wineries

Handicap access: no

Queensland

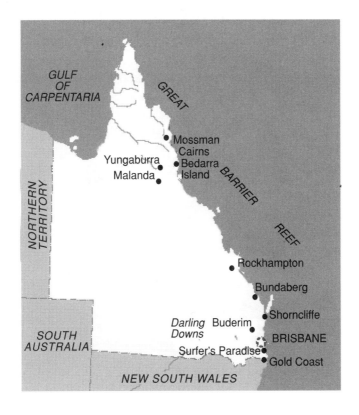

Queensland, Australia's second largest state (covering more than a quarter of the continent), is considered the Holiday or Sunshine State. The geography, climate, flora and fauna are as diverse as the people, and Queensland offers visitors everything from awesome rainforest-clad coastline and the famous Great Barrier Reef, to the sweeping red plains of the rugged Outback and remote pioneer stations.

Although the Reef is perhaps Queensland's most outstanding attraction, there are countless other reasons to visit the Sunshine State. Brisbane, the state's historic and cultural capital, and site of the 1988 World Expo, is a gateway to many of these attractions. A delightful combination of old and new—historic cathedrals and government buildings stand in the shadows of modern glass highrises and concrete towers—the city captures a casual sophistication. Straddling the banks of the meandering Brisbane River, a colourful waterway for ferries, paddle-wheelers and pleasure boats, evergreen Brisbane enjoys a sub-tropical climate and year-round sunshine. Brisbane's top event each year is the Royal Brisbane Show ('the Ekka'), held each August, where crowds pour into the showgrounds to see the best of country life and enjoy an array of activities and entertainment.

Most of the tourism in Queensland is concentrated along the coast. Long deserted beaches with crashing surf, luxury island resorts and the colorful Great Barrier Reef seem to attract the majority of travelers. Marinas up and down the coast service the increasing number of private yachts, cruisers and charter boats that explore the thousands of reefs and islands dotting the Coral Sea.

The Gold Coast, an hour south of Brisbane, is a care-free pleasure playground that rivals the glitz and glamour of Miami Beach, the French Riveria or Spain's Costa Brava. This glittering metropolis, considered a paradise by many sun and fun lovers, offers broad beaches, luxury highrise hotels and outrageous nightlife. Yet not far away are unspoiled tracts of rainforest and wilderness. Just north of Brisbane, is a golden chain of peaceful beaches referred to as the Sunshine Coast. In contrast to the Gold Coast, the Sunshine Coast features many peaceful beaches and small, quaint towns that evoke a more residential feeling. It also has ancient rainforests, tropical fruit plantations and great fishing. Although tourist facilities are proliferating in the area, small guesthouses and bed and breakfasts also provide comfortable accommodations for visitors. The Sunshine Coast Hinterland is considered the "creative heart" of the region with numerous folk festivals and markets.

The most famous of Queensland's attractions, the Great Barrier Reef is among the most beautiful travel destinations imaginable. Stretching 1200 miles down the eastern seaboard, the Reef is the world's largest living structure, a vast network of colorful undersea shoals, reefs and coral quays. There are many ways to experience the Reef, from a private resort on a secluded island where luxury and nature go hand in hand, to a glass bottomed boat that anchors on the outer reef and provides seemingly endless opportunities to snorkel and scuba dive.

The Whitsunday Islands, with their golden sands, sheltered bays and fringing reefs, are located at the southern tip of the Great Barrier Reef; the surrounding waters are considered some of the world's best sailing waters. The jumping off point for many Whitsunday cruises is Airlie Beach, where travelers can find a variety of comfortable B&B's offering friendly, family-style accommodations.

Cairns, Queensland's most northerly city, is an international gateway and the fastest growing tourist development in the country—offering a full range of accommodations and services. It is a tropical city with exotic palms, brightly colored birds and flowers, and an esplanade that runs along the water's edge. From Cairns, it's easy to make arrangements to view the Reef, either from the air or floating on or below the water's surface. Just inland from Cairns, are the Atherton Tablelands, a scenic coastal plateau fringed with volanic crater lakes that offer unforgettable bicycling, hot air ballooning, sea kayaking, white water rafting or spelunking. Great bushwalks and superb scenery can also be found in Kuranda, a picturesque artist village located in the heart of the rainforest, and in Mossman, which sits astride a spectacular gorge.

The Tropical North boasts some of the most spectacular scenery in the world. A third of Queensland lies north of the Tropic of Capricorn, and the Tropical North is a unique part of the world where the rainforest meets the reef. Sugar cane fields and plantations dot the landscape and railway cars can be seen transporting the cane to the processors. Sparsely populated Cape York Peninsula and the savannahs of the Gulf of Carpenteria, are harsh and wild areas promising adventure to hardy travelers.

High temperatures and wet seasons make it more difficult to plan a holiday to the Far North, but the exotic flora and fauna and spectacular scenery make it well worth the time. Travelers to Queensland's Tropical North can stay in comfortable lodges set in a tropical wilderness often accessible only by four-wheel drive or light aircraft. Idle days are passed exploring the sights and sounds of the rainforest and Outback, swimming near uninhabited islands, diving in crystal clear blue waters and fishing off coral reefs.

For something completely different, visitors to Queensland can try a farm or station holiday, which typifies the diversity of the terrain. Whether staying on a vast Outback property or a smaller farm nearer the city, guests can head into the bush and help herd cattle by helicopter, or tour these often historic properties by four wheel drive. Several hours west of

Brisbane is the city of Toowoomba on the Darling Downs, a fertile region filled with cattle, sheep or richly patterned fields of crops. The city is a regional hub for the vast farming interests of the area, and is surrounded by a number of inviting host farms that welcome guests who want a taste of good old-fashioned country hospitality and a chance to experience life on a working farm.

From the vast, disappearing wilderness of Cape York Peninsula to the awesome Great Barrier Reef, Queensland is a land of vast contrasts. And the best way to experience the diversity is to get close to nature. Whether it's relaxing on a private tropical isle, or exploring the bush from a historic homestead; whether it's spending an afternoon fighting Barramundi, or losing time strolling along the miles of deserted beaches, Queensland offers adventure, variety and best of all, year round sunshine.

For more information, check out:
www.DestinationQueensland.com

REGIONAL DIRECTORY

➤ denotes review

ATHERTON TABLELANDS

➤ **Bracken Ridge**   Lot 65 Vance Close/MS 1318, Yungaburra, QLD 4872 61 7 4095 3421
Award winning timber pole home on rural acreage with lake views and access.

➤ **Honeyflow Homestead**   Heidke Road/PO Box 146, Malanda, QLD 4885   61 7 4096 8173
Peaceful Queensland style establishment that exceeds expectations

BRISBANE

➤ **Naracoopa**   99 Yundah St., Shorncliffe, QLD 4017   61 7 3269 2334
Beautiful 1890s home in Moreton Bay suburb with quick access to city, airport and beaches.

Seamount Bed & Breakfast   86 Allpass Parade, Shorncliffe, QLD 4017
61 7 3269 8301
Historic Queenslander built in 1884 overlooking Moreton Bay and Boondall Wetlands

CAIRNS/TROPICAL NORTH

➤ **Collingwood House**   13 Spurwood Close, Mission Beach, QLD 4852 61 7 4068 9037
Tranquil, private rainforest/garden retreat

CORAL COAST

➤ **Dunelm House Bed and Breakfast**   540 Bargara Rd., Bargara, QLD
4670   61 7 4159 0909
Friendly, English-style B&B surrounded by sugar cane fields

DARLING DOWNS

➤ **Old Boyneside**   MS 514/Bunya Highway, Kingaroy, QLD 4610
(07) 4164 4262
Working cattle and grain property near Bunya Mountains

GOLD COAST

➤ **Mermaid Beachside Bed & Breakfast**   115 Seagull Ave./PO Box 252,
Mermaid Beach, QLD 4218   61 7 5572 9530
Luxury seaside accommodations in Australia's premier tourist resort.

GOLD COAST HINTERLAND

Woodleigh Homestead   13 Munro Court, Mt. Tambourine, QLD 4272
61 7 5545 3121
*Mountain retreat overlooking World Heritage–listed Lamington National
Park*

OUTBACK QUEENSLAND

➤ **Planet Downs**   Dawson Highway/PO Box 415, via Rolleston/Virginia,
QLD 4702/4014   61 7 3265 5022
Working cattle station with international standard accommodations

SOUTH EAST

➤ **Ballandean Lodge**   Rees Rd./PO Box 43, Ballandean, QLD 4382
61 7 4684 1320
*Restored turn of the century Queenslander home nestled in the Granite
Highlands*

Vacy Hall   135 Russell St., Toowoomba, QLD 4350   61 7 4639 2055
Heritage listed mansion in the heart of the Garden City of Toowoomba

SUNSHINE COAST

➤ **Buderim White House**   54 Quorn Close, Buderim, QLD 4556
61 7 5445 1961   *Grand manor house at the entrace to the tranquil
Buderim Rainforest Park*

➤ **Chateau Cedarton**   2 Cedarton Dr., Cedarton, QLD 4514
61 7 5496 1789
*Unique Mediterranean style luxury accommodations with superb gardens
and views*

➤ **Eyrie Escape**   Brandenburg Rd, Mooloolan, QLD 4553   61 7 5494 8242
Elegant accommodations and extraordinary views near Sunshine Coast

➤ **The Falls Bed & Breakfast**   20 Kondalilla Falls Rd., Montville, QLD
4560   61 7 5445 7000
Old Queenslander (circa 1910) furnished with antiques.

➤ **The Falls Rainforest Cottage**   20 Kondalilla Falls Rd., Montville, QLD
4560   61 7 5445 7000
An idyllic, romantic retreat for couples

➤ **Maleny Lodge Guesthouse**   58 Maple St., Maleny, QLD 4552
61 7 5494 2370
Charming Queensland Colonial guesthouse north of Brisbane

➤ **Ninderry Manor Luxury Retreat**   12 Karnu Drive, Ninderry via
Yandina, QLD 4561   (07) 5472 7255
*Luxury guest house on the ridge of the majestic Mt. Ninderry looking over
the Maroochy Valley*

Noosa Country House   93 Duke Rd., Noosa Valley, QLD 4562
61 7 5471 0121
*Queenslander style home on 12 acres. Gourmet breakfast served at a
private table on the verandah*

TOOWOOBA/GOLDEN WEST

Jacaranda Grove   92 Tourist Rd., Toowoomba, QLD 4350
(07) 4635 8394
*Luxurious, air-conditioned Federation style retreat with beautiful range
views, antiques and garden*

TROPICAL NORTH QUEENSLAND

➤ **Bedarra Island**   PO Box 268, Mission Beach, QLD 4852
61-7-4068-8233
Exclusive retreat on Great Barrier Reef island with all amenities

➤ **Bloomfield Wilderness Lodge**   PO Box 966, Cairns, QLD 4870
61 7 4035 9166
All inclusive luxury packages in luxury wilderness resort

Daintree Wilderness Lodge   83 Cape Tribulation Rd., Alexandra Bay,
QLD   61 7 4098 9105
*Small intimate lodge offering tranquility among the World Heritage
Rainforest*

Escott Lodge   Escott Station, Burketon, QLD 4830   61 7 4748 5577
*Outback Station in Gulf of Carpenaria with varied styles of
accommodations*

➤ **Lizard Island**   PMB 40, Cairns, QLD 4871   61-7-4060-3999
*Exclusive Great Barrier Reef island in North Queensland with private
villas.*

Orpheus Island
*Exclusive Mediterranean-style bungalows on secluded Great Barrier Reef
island*

➤ **Silky Oaks Lodge**   PO Box 396, Mossman, QLD 4873   61-7-4098-1666
Private chalets and licensed restaurant overlooking Mossman River Gorge

Ballandean Lodge

Midway between Brisbane and Sydney off the New England Highway, atop the Great Dividing Range, you'll find the Granite Highlands and some of the prettiest scenery in all of Australia. This beautiful region is home to the National Parks of Girraween, Bald Rock, Boonoo Boonoo and, for four-wheel drive enthusiasts, Sundown. And nestled between stone-fruit orchards and vast vineyards, sits a beautifully restored turn of the century Queenslander called Ballandean Lodge. This comfortable bed and breakfast, home to Dorothy and Dietmar Gogolka, (along with their dog and two cats), offers peace and tranquility along with gracious hospitality. Accommodations are in tastefully decorated and comfortably furnished queen, double or twin rooms, all with ensuite bathrooms. There is a special view from each part of the verandah, where you can relax, listen to the native birds, and enjoy the sunset. The guests' wing includes a lounge and dining room with a log fire for those pleasantly chilly Granite Highland winter evenings. A traditional full breakfast is served daily in the dining room and evening meals and/or lunch are available by arrangement. Fresh flowers, home made biscuits, jams and pickles, garden and orchard produce in season, are just some of the special treats your hosts provide. Winery tours, picnic hampers, and specialized activities can all be organized.

Each season in this special area is unique. In summer, when local stone-fruit is available right off the trees, the warm pleasant days make way for cool crisp evenings. Autumn brings the grape harvest and an explosion of reds, yellows and oranges as the landscape prepares for winter. And winters are famous for misty mornings, crystal clear days, vivid sunsets and cozy nights beside the fire sipping local wine. Australian native wildflowers bloom in spring, not just in the nearby National Parks, but all along the roadways.

No matter what time of year, a visit to South East Queensland and Ballandean Lodge is a memorable experience. Ask about weekend and midweek packages.

Name: Ballandean Lodge

Category: Bed & Breakfast/Homestay

Location: South East region; Stanthorpe; 20 km (nearest city)

Address: Rees Rd./PO Box 43, Ballandean, QLD 4382

Phone: Tel. 61 7 4684 1320 **Fax** 61 7 4684 1340

E-mail: ballodge@halenet.com.au

Web site: www.halenet.com.au/~ballodge

Innkeepers: Dietmar & Dorothy Gogolka

Rates: From A$105-120 per double includes full breakfast

Number of rooms: 1 Queen, 1 Double, 1 Twin

Baths: 3 Ensuite

Services & amenities: Guest lounge, TV, parking, ceiling fans, laundry facilities

Restrictions: No smoking inside

Handicap access: no

Bedarra Island

J ust off the Queensland coast, midway between Townsville and Cairns, lies Bedarra Island, Australia's ultimate retreat. This romantic rainforest hideaway, offers an exclusive escape for a privileged few to experience the true intimacy of a private island retreat. Bedarra is one of a handful of small island resorts in the world where everything from the luxuriously-appointed villas, to the sumptuous gourmet meals, to the 24-hour open bar, are all included. Each day the island's team of creative chefs, using the choicest and freshest ingredients, prepare innovative haute cuisine that caters to the most discerning of palates. And whenever the mood beckons, the bar awaits with a superb selection of the finest red and white wines available, vintage French champagnes, beers from around the world, spirits, liqueurs, juices and soft drinks.

Each of the 15 private, air-conditioned villas, nestled into the rainforest, has spectacular beach and bay views. A maximum of 30 guests enjoy the island at any time. A million dollar refurbishment, completed in July 1998, completely replaced all the furnishings and fittings in each villa. Designed to harmonize with the natural surroundings, each spacious villa has a balcony and features polished timber floors, a king-sized bed, luxurious bathroom and a separate living area complete with television, fully-stocked refrigerator, video cassette player and a writing desk.

A haven of natural wonders fringed by the warm waters of the Coral Sea, Bedarra Island is an unspoiled wilderness area of rainforest and palm fringed beaches. When tennis, bushwalking, snorkeling, fishing, paddle-skiing and sailing are not enough, you can always explore the nearby Great Barrier Reef. For more adventure, game fishing boats await. For the less active, massages on the beach or in the privacy of your own villa are an ideal option. Luxury yacht charters are also available for sailing expeditions around the picturesque waters, visiting such neighboring islands as Dunk and Timana. For relaxing in glorious seclusion, Bedarra Island is the perfect retreat; explore the pristine rainforest and bask in the sun on the secluded beaches in total privacy or have the chef pack a delicious gourmet picnic, complete with chilled champagne, and hop into a motorized dinghy to find a deserted beach of your own. The exotic location, total privacy and first-class facilities of Bedarra, have found favor with the rich and famous including members of Great Britain's Royal Family, movie stars, rock legends and sports celebrities. From North America, call toll-free for reservations: 1-800-225-9849.

Name: Bedarra Island

Category: Island Resort

Location: Tropical North Queensland region; Cairns; 160 km (nearest city)

Address: PO Box 268, Mission Beach, QLD 4852

Phone: Tel. 61-7-4068-8233 **Fax** 61-7-4068-8215

E-mail: POResorts@aol.com

Web site: www.poresorts.com.au

Innkeepers: General Manager

Rates: From A$800 per person, per night, including all meals, open bar, and return launch transfer from Dunk Island

Number of rooms: 15 Private Villas

Baths: Private

Services & amenities: 24 hour open bar, air-conditioned villas, fully stocked refrigerators, television, sailing, fishing, diving and much more

Restrictions: No children under 16

Handicap access: no

Bracken Ridge

Bracken Ridge is an idyllic bed & breakfast in Tropical North Queensland where guests can enjoy a fabulous holiday and deluxe five star accommodation. With several different styles of lodging to choose from, there is something for everyone. The spacious Queenslander pole home, on rural acreage overlooking spectacular Lake Tinaroo, offers luxury homestay accommodations. The upstairs king-sized bedroom, which features collectible furnishings and a private bathroom with spa bath, overlooks a bushland park setting. Guests can also relax and enjoy the spacious lounge, or sit on the wide verandah and take in the panoramic mountain views. The lower level of the house provides a self-contained luxury unit that was designed and built with guest privacy and comfort in mind. Tastefully furnished with collectables and heirloom Silky Oak furniture, the space is cozy and romantic. Queen-sized bedrooms, kitchenettes, bathrooms and private decks all open onto natural, landscaped native gardens, which are a haven for many different birds and butterflies. For those looking for total privacy, there is also a separate, self-contained cottage on four acres with access to Lake Tineroo. The cottage, with a six person spa pool, provides an ideal romantic retreat for a couple or it can accommodate a family of six.

Bracken Ridge is close to tourist attractions such as Lake Barrine, Lake Eacham, picturesque waterfalls, rainforest walks and the majestic Curtain Fig Tree. Historic Yungaburra Heritage Village, with its fine restaurants, antique and art & craft shops, is only ten minutes away, and Cairns and the Great

Barrier Reef can be reached in an hour. Tinaroo has facilities for fishing, swimming, water skiing and many other water sports. The area abounds in wildlife and is a birdwatcher's paradise. Charter boats are available for barramundi and redclaw fishing, and spotting for bird and wildlife. After an active day, come back, relax in the spa, and enjoy a pre-dinner drink with hosts Myra and John as you watch the spectacular sunset over the lake. Enjoy fine cuisine, fresh local produce, tender Tableland beef, local seafood and fresh redclaw crayfish (in season), and relish the ultimate lifestyle and perfect climate. Dinners are available by arrangement.

Name: Bracken Ridge

Category: Homestay/self-contained suite/cottage

Location: Atherton Tablelands region; Cairns; 60 km (nearest city)

Address: Lot 65 Vance Close/MS 1318, Yungaburra, QLD 4872

Phone: Tel. 61 7 4095 3421 **Fax** 61 7 4095 3461

E-mail: bracken@internetnorth.com.au

Web site: www.bnbnq.com.au/brackenridge

Innkeepers: John & Myra Eggers

Rates: From A$120-145 per double includes full breakfast

Rated: ***** RACQ/1998 /99 Tropical N. Qld Tourism Award

Number of rooms: 1 King in Homestead, 2 Self-contained Suites

Baths: Private (2 with spa)

Services & amenities: Spa, private lake access, charter boat available, BBQ

Restrictions: Not suitable for small children

Handicap access: no

Buderim White House

C apture the mood and essence of romance as you indulge in this grand
manor house on Queensland's Sunshine Coast. Set at the entrance to
the tranquil Buderim Rainforest Park, Buderim White House is presented in magnificent 1890 Victorian Queensland style. Built in 1999, the
stately residence blends traditional architectural detail with superior construction and modern amenities. Warmly furnished in classic timbers, and
complemented with a blend of harmonious antiques and rich elegant décor,
Buderim White House is a delight to the senses. Each luxury suite is exclusively designed for couples with a king-sized hand-carved four-poster canopied bed, Old World open fireplace, comfortable sitting area, and large double hydrotherapy spa. Deluxe rooms with ensuite facilities are also spacious
and no less sumptuous. You'll find thoughtful appointments in all the guestrooms including fresh flowers and chocolates, luxurious white linens and
fluffy bathrobes, and a collection of classical music from Beethoven to Vival-
di. Impressive stained glass windows throughout the house lend an air of
stylish elegance, and lavish fabrics and wall-coverings help create an opulent
environment. A silver service gourmet breakfast is served on your own
private deck, featuring the freshest of ingredients and satisfying, cooked
entrées.

Originally from New Zealand, host Diana Johnston lived in California for
thirty years before marrying her first love who lived in Australia. Both Diana
and Keith have a great deal to offer guests from the United States and abroad.
They pride themselves on excellent service and attention to detail. Given all
early signs, they're well on their way to having one of the premiere properties in the region.

For nature lovers, the Buderim Rainforest Park offers great walking tracks
and just minutes from Buderim White House, are numerous quality restau-

rants (including Harry's On Buderim, one of the top 100 restaurants in Australia), quality shops, championship golf courses and beautiful world-class beaches. Less than an hour from Brisbane, Buderim is perfectly situated to take advantage of the best that South East Queensland has to offer. Ask about special mid-week rates.

Name: Buderim White House

Category: Bed & Breakfast

Location: Sunshine Coast region; Maroochydore; 7 km (nearest city)

Address: 54 Quorn Close, Buderim, QLD 4556

Phone: Tel. 61 7 5445 1961 **Fax** 61 7 5445 1994

E-mail: budwhitehouse@ozemail.com.au

Web site: www.ozemail.com.au/~budwhitehouse

Innkeepers: Keith & Diana Johnston

Rates: From A$120 per double includes gourmet breakfast

Number of rooms: 4 King

Baths: 4 Ensuite

Services & amenities: Open fires, ducted air-conditioning, spa, in-room refrigerators, meeting facilities for 10-12

Restrictions: No smoking; no pets

Handicap access: no

Chateau Cedarton

A little piece of Tuscany in South-East Queensland. Chateau Cedarton is a unique Mediterranean-style bed & breakfast, situated in the beautiful Sunshine Coast Hinterland. Bathed in the Mediterranean colours of vintage buff and varying sea blues, Chateau Cedarton is perched on a foothill, commanding 360-degree views of the Blackall and Conondale Ranges. But this is only part of the magic. Chateau Cedarton holds hidden secrets and surprises that are only revealed to guests.

Four hectares of gardens feature statues of Roman Gods and Centurions standing majestically amidst the old world charm of secluded garden retreats and paths. From the manicured rose gardens, to the native landscaped gardens there are treasures to behold. You may even choose to pause in the gardens for an outdoor game of chess. In the forecourt is a magnificent fountain and aviaries with their Indian Ringnecks, Peach Faces, Lovebirds, and Lorikeets. Victorian style mahogany furniture throughout the guesthouse enhances its luxury and charm.

The guest complex consists of two wings. Guests are greeted at the reception area with its sweeping views of the spectacular Glass House Mountains. Accommodations are in four rooms (with ensuite) on the first level and two rooms (with share bath) on the lower level. All rooms include queen-sized beds, colour televisions, writing desks, refrigerators, radios, mini-bars, and tea/coffee making facilities. Each room is named after a famous individual from the Egyptian and Roman Empires including Cleopatra, Caesar, Mark

Antony and Nefertiti. Attention to detail in the furnishing and decoration of the rooms continues the Mediterranean theme, but subtle differences capture the splendour and character of each namesake and era.

Guests are served a delicious full breakfast each morning and other meals can be enjoyed throughout the day. Alfresco Devonshire teas and light lunches are served on the terraces, beneath protective sails or on the upper deck with its magnificent 360-degree view. With a menu to tempt the tastebuds and the secret recipe to the best scones around, dining at Chateau Cedarton is always superb. Unique by design, with all the flavour and luxury of Europe, this exquisite property is secluded and serene, yet close to all the Sunshine Coast attractions.

Name: Chateau Cedarton

Category: Luxury Bed & Breakfast

Location: Sunshine Coast Hinterland region; Woodford; 16 km (nearest city)

Address: 2 Cedarton Dr., Cedarton, QLD 4514

Phone: Tel. 61 7 5496 1789 **Fax** 61 7 5496 1789

E-mail: chcedarton@eisa.net.au

Web site: www.babs.com.au/cedarton

Innkeepers: Cindy & Robert Lardinois

Rates: From A$140-160 per double includes full hot/cold breakfast

Number of rooms: 6 Queen

Baths: 4 Ensuite, 1 Share

Services & amenities: Bar and restaurant, swimming pool, sauna, spa, library, parking, gift shop

Restrictions: Not suitable for children

Handicap access: no

Collingwood House

F ive-star Collingwood House is an elegant, spacious new residence nestled amidst acres of tranquil rainforest and tropical gardens. It's here that the rainforest meets the reef, and glorious stretches of unspoiled coastline separates the tropical vegetation from the Great Barrier Reef. It's just a five-minute stroll to a picturesque beach with splendid views of nearby Dunk Island. Visitors to the area can enjoy a peaceful and relaxing stay away from the tourist hype, and Collingwood provides an unpretentious environment where the best of nature can be enjoyed in luxurious accommodations.

The three luxuriously appointed, air-conditioned guest rooms have ensuite facilities and private access to covered verandahs. Each of the very discreet bedrooms accommodates two guests who can come and go without having to enter the main area of the house, unless so desired. Large expanses of glass allow for uninterrupted viewing of native wildlife, which may appear anytime.

Breakfast is a delicious, lingering affair by the pool—fresh fruit, lashings of bacon, eggs, sausages, tomatoes, mushrooms, toast and croissants, stacks of hot cakes with maple syrup and endless pots of freshly brewed tea and coffee. This is the time when guests are most likely to see the fantastic cassowary, wallabies, goanna and bird life, which regularly visit the garden and forest. Tasty complimentary snacks are available throughout the day, and guests can lounge by the sparkling pool or relax in the lounge or games room. Collingswood does not cater to children, so adults are assured of a quiet peaceful setting in this idyllic corner of Queensland.

The area has much to offer. In addition to the Great Barrier Reef, there are a number of accessible islands, white water rafting (category 4), sky-diving, sea kayaking and great bushwalks. There is easy access to numerous reef trips, tours and walks, and transportation from Mission Beach to Cairns is easily arranged.

Name: Collingwood House

Category: Bed & Breakfast

Location: Cairns/Tropical North region; Mission Beach; 2 km (nearest city)

Address: 13 Spurwood Close, Mission Beach, QLD 4852

Phone: Tel. 61 7 4068 9037 **Fax** 61 7 4068 9037

E-mail: collingwood@internetnorth.com.au

Web site: www.bnbnq.com.au/collingwood/

Innkeepers: Paul & Jennifer White

Rates: From A$89-99 per double includes breakfast

Rated: ***** RACQ

Number of rooms: 2 Queen, 1 King or Twin

Baths: 3 Ensuite

Services & amenities: Pool, lounge, billiards room, TV, formal dining & bar, BBQ

Restrictions: No smoking inside; no children

Handicap access: no

Dunelm House

D unelm House Bed and Breakfast is located near Bargara Beach "where the land meets the coral." The area's best kept secret, this beautiful beach provides direct access to a coral wonderland. Snorkelers and scuba divers step right off the sand into an underwater paradise.

To take advantage of this extraordinary area, Dunelm House offers friendly accommodations in an English-style B&B. The Queenslander-style house, surrounded by sugar cane fields, is only a short drive to Bargara Beach. Three queen-sized rooms (one with an extra single bed) have ensuite facilities and all the comforts of home. A traditional full English breakfast—bacon and eggs, cereals, fruit, freshly baked bread, and homemade preserves—is served in the dining room, on the verandah, or in the garden by the pool. After breakfast, hosts Rod and Maureen Hall will help organize local activities; they'll also prepare a picnic lunch or evening meal by request.

There are a myriad of nearby attractions to keep guests busy; Lady Elliott Island and Lady Musgrave Island (where the Great Barrier Reef begins) are only a short distance away, and whale watching is popular during the months of August to October. Mon Repos Conservation Park, with the largest concentration of nesting marine turtles on the eastern Australian mainland, is only five minutes away. It's well worth a visit during the months of November to March to see the nesting turtles and the baby hatchings after dark.

And, if the natural wonders aren't enough, other local tourist attractions in Bundaberg include the Bundaberg Rum Distillery, Schmeiders Cooperage, Mystery Craters, the Botanic Gardens with Hinkler House, Fairymead Sugar Museum, original sugar cane steam train rides, Pennylane Gardens, and Avocado Grove. Guests from all over the world have taken advantage of Dunelm House and their comments range from "wonderful aura all around" to "you're the most friendly B&B family we've ever met." Bundaberg is perfect any time of year, with its mild winters and summers cooled by sea breezes, and Dunelm is the perfect place to stay.

Name: Dunelm House Bed and Breakfast

Category: Bed & Breakfast

Location: Coral Coast region; Bundaberg; 9 km (nearest city)

Address: 540 Bargara Rd., Bargara, QLD 4670

Phone: Tel. 61 7 4159 0909 **Fax** 61 7 4159 0916

E-mail: dunelm@telstra.easymail.com.au

Web site: www.babs.com.au/dunelm

Innkeepers: Maureen & Rod Hall

Rates: From A$65 per double includes full breakfast

Rated: **** RACQ

Number of rooms: 3 Queen, 1 with extra single

Baths: 3 Ensuite

Services & amenities: heated pool & spa, TV room, tea/coffee, BBQ

Restrictions: No smoking

Handicap access: no

Eyrie Escape

I f you're looking for a little piece of heaven, Eyrie Escape is as close as you'll get without sprouting wings. Perched on a knoll in Bald Knob, this natural retreat boasts spectacular views across the Blackall Ranges to Montville, and along the Sunshine Coast from Mt. Coolum to the Glasshouse Mountains. Hosts June and Peter Rogers created this elegant escape after traveling the world to discover the ultimate Mecca of relaxation. For peace of mind, a bit of pampering, and views that will literally take your breath away, Eyrie Escape is an extraordinary find.

Each of the three individually designed bedrooms is tastefully appointed with antiques and regional artifacts. Some of the many amenities include remote controlled, reverse cycle air-conditioning, a fridge, television, tea/coffee making facilities, an intercom, as well as an ensuite with shower or bath. A private verandah allows guests to dine outside or relax and enjoy the stunning coastal views.

Privacy and personal preference are touchstones of your indulgent escape. Curl up with a book, listen to music, enjoy a movie on DVD, or soak in the outside spa beneath the stars, a glass of sparkling champagne in your hand. For the more energetic, there is swimming, walking in the rainforest, paddock and orchards of the 32-acre property, or a game of tennis on a court that is perched high above a vast valley. In the winter, relax next to a roaring fire in the sitting or dining room, enjoy a game of billiards, snooker or chess, or just savor the sublime views. Any time of year, this is a retreat for nature lovers who appreciate a combination of luxury and tranquility.

Part of the Eyrie Escape experience is breakfast. Guests have the option of an intimate morning meal on their own verandah, in bed, beside the swimming pool, or in the dining room. Guests rave about June's cheese soufflé, berry compote, and free-range eggs with smoked salmon. On the weekends, a fabulous four course silver service dinner is served in the formal dining room or outside on the patio with the Sunshine Coast lights twinkling below. A stopover at Eyrie Escape is well worth it, and for those without a car, June and Peter will arrange pickups from the local airports and train stations.

Name: Eyrie Escape

Category: Bed & Breakfast

Location: Sunshine Coast Hinterland region; Maleny (nearest city)

Address: Brandenburg Rd, Mooloolan, QLD 4553

Phone: Tel. 61 7 5494 8242 **Fax** 61 7 5439 9666

E-mail: jollyrogers@eyrie-escape.com.au

Web site: www.eyrie-escape.com.au

Innkeepers: Peter & June Rogers

Rates: A$195 per couple includes breakfast & supper; weekend packages available

Number of rooms: 3 Queen

Baths: 3 Ensuite

Services & amenities: Guest lounge, heated pool, spa, tennis court, billiards, TV

Restrictions: No smoking; no children; no pets

Handicap access: no

The Falls

B ask in the romantic era of bygone days; lavender and lace, wonderful views, fresh roses, and old-fashioned hospitality are just some of the characteristics of this elegant guesthouse. The Falls Bed & Breakfast is a graceful old Queenslander adjacent to the Kondalilla Falls National Park in Queensland's Sunshine Coast Hinterland. The sitting room has the warmth of a large fire for cool evenings, and comfortable antique furniture along with a handsome grand piano. The four guest rooms provide total privacy, thoughtfully appointed bathrooms (each featuring large, relaxing showers with good water pressure), and French doors that open onto wide verandahs. Air conditioning and ceiling fans help ensure comfort during warm weather. The elegantly furnished guestrooms show extraordinary attention to detail with fresh flowers, individual décor and intimate sitting areas.

The Falls Bed & Breakfast is a place to unwind in the cool mountain air; a place to rediscover the simple pleasures of life. Enjoy books and magazines, play cards or chess at the inlaid games table, or simply relax in the evening with a drink and coffee in good company. Tea, coffee and homemade biscuits are available throughout the day. Hosts John and Laura Watson can make dinner reservations at one of the many fine local restaurants as well as help arrange a unique outing. For the adventuresome, Harley Motor Bike tours or Off-Beat Rainforest Tours both feature pick-up at The Falls.

A beautiful dining room seats eight, and a delicious full cooked breakfast is served daily. When the weather is warm, an outside deck is the perfect place to relax with its views of the lush landscape. After a delightful breakfast, be romanced by the magic of Montville, the mountain village high above Queensland's Sunshine Coast; an hour north of Brisbane and half an hour from the beach, Montville offers the best of both worlds. There is much to discover while wandering the streets; from the breathtaking natural attractions to the creations of local potters, clock makers, wood turners and fashion designers. The unique ambiance of the village allows for relaxed and friendly shopping, and a surprising range of crafts, visual arts and gifts. Ask about special mid-week dinner, bed and breakfast packages.

Name: The Falls Bed & Breakfast

Category: Bed & Breakfast

Location: Sunshine Coast Hinterland region; Montville; 2 km (nearest city)

Address: 20 Kondalilla Falls Rd., Montville, QLD 4560

Phone: Tel. 61 7 5445 7000 **Fax** 61 7 5445 7001

E-mail: watson1@ozemail.com.au

Web site: www.thefallscottages.com.au

Innkeepers: John & Laura Watson

Rates: From A$140-165 per double includes full breakfast

Rated: **** RACQ/1999 Sunshine Coast & Queensland Tourism Awards

Number of rooms: 2 Queen, 2 Double

Baths: 4 Ensuite

Services & amenities: Guest lounge, tea/coffee

Handicap access: yes

The Falls Rainforest Cottages

Relax and enjoy the peace and romance that is The Falls Rainforest Cottages. This five star retreat has won numerous accolades including 1998 and 1999 Awards for Excellence from both state and regional tourism associations (Sunshine Coast Tourism and Queensland Tourism Awards). Exclusive and private, The Falls offers six Queenslander-style cottages set in a bush reserve; each with far-reaching views of the rolling hills surrounding the property. Soak in the double spa, look through the trees, or gaze at the romantic glow of the wood fire on chilly nights. The cottages are fully air-conditioned and feature double showers and separate double spas, wood fires, televisions, videos, CD stereos and kitchenettes. In addition to all the deluxe amenities, there are little "extras" at every turn—chocolates, homemade biscuits, fluffy robes, bath foam, and fresh flowers, all waiting for you. The Honeymoon Cottages—Tamarind and Lacebark—are among the most popular. Walk to the cottages over a sea of ferns and discover what romantic fantasies are made of.

Guests thoroughly enjoy the tranquility and harmony of this secluded location just 1.5 kilometers from the unique mountain village of Montville and close to the Kondalilla Falls National Park. The Falls Rainforest Cottages is a place to unwind and enjoy the simple pleasures of life. Misty romantic days, and nights hidden away from the rest of the world, are yours in these cozy cottages that provide the perfect country escape. A breakfast basket contains all the provisions necessary for a light morning meal, and special mid-week packages are available that include a gourmet breakfast and romantic dinner at a nearby restaurant. There are also numerous half and full day outings that can be arranged, including scenic drives through the Glasshouse Mountains and Mary Cairncross National Park, rainforest tours, canoeing, whale-watching or horseback riding.

Name: The Falls Rainforest Cottages

Category: Self-contained cottages

Location: Sunshine Coast Hinterland region; Montville; 2 km (nearest city)

Address: 20 Kondalilla Falls Rd., Montville, QLD 4560

Phone: Tel. 61 7 5445 7000 **Fax** 61 7 5445 7001

E-mail: watson1@ozemail.com.au

Web site: www.thefallscottages.com.au

Innkeepers: John & Laura Watson

Rates: From A$180-280 includes continental breakfast

Rated: ***** RACQ/1998 & 1999 Sunshine Coast Tourism Award

Number of rooms: 1 Queen

Baths: Private with spa

Services & amenities: Spa, TV, Video, CD, fireplace

Restrictions: No smoking; no children

Handicap access: yes

Honeyflow Homestead

Honeyflow Homestead was built in 1918 and converted to a guest-house in 1986. Nestled in the Crater Lakes and Waterfalls district of the Atherton Tablelands (Cairns hinterland), between Yungaburra and Malanda, it is the ideal base for a short or long stay. Amid one hectare of gardens with native and fruit trees attracting many different species of birds, the setting is delightfully tranquil. Guests are able to stroll a short distance to the banks of a river where platypus can almost always be sighted.

The guest suites are spacious and well appointed, with ensuite facilities, private sitting rooms with TV, and private access from the wide verandah. Among the many treats that await you, is the home-baked sweet bread in your personal fridge. Relax in the privacy of your own suite or in the communal areas which include a lounge area with open fire, a games/reading room, and dining room with pot-belly stove. In the winter months, the areas are well used, and in the summer months the altitude provides natural cooling from the coast. Dining in at Honeyflow is a lovely experience, with pre-dinner drinks, a delicious three-course country-style dinner, followed by tea/coffee and chocolates. Guests are encouraged to bring a bottle of wine or preferred beverages. In the morning, an extravagant breakfast including home-baked breads, is served in the Garden Room. This room has full-length opening glass panels creating an indoors extension to the garden.

Hosts Greg and Pam have lived and worked in many different places around Australia in varied occupations, and they are outgoing and naturally friendly. Honeyflow Homestead is ideal for those who want to escape and unwind (peace and tranquility are good for the soul), or for guests who want to explore the Tablelands at their leisure, yet still enjoy the comforts of home. For direct bookings of more than three nights, there is a 10% discount and an exclusive "something extra" to use around the Tablelands. This is a popular guesthouse, so book in advance to avoid disappointment and discover what the many regular guests come back for time and again.

Name: Honeyflow Homestead

Category: Guesthouse

Location: Atherton Tablelands region; Cairns; 73 kim (nearest city)

Address: Heidke Road/PO Box 146, Malanda, QLD 4885

Phone: Tel. 61 7 4096 8173 **Fax** 61 7 4096 8173

E-mail: honeyflow@north.net.au

Web site: www.honeyflow.north.net.au

Innkeepers: Greg & Pam Taylor

Rates: From A$125 per double includes full breakfast

Rated: ****½ RACQ/Gold Aussie Host

Number of rooms: 4 Suites

Baths: 4 Ensuite

Services & amenities: Private suites, sitting room, TV, fridge, tea/coffee

Restrictions: No smoking inside

Handicap access: yes

Lizard Island

L ocated 240km north of Cairns and only an hour flight away, Lizard Island is the ideal holiday for those in search of an adventurous reef experience, as well as travelers seeking a true escape from the mainstream world. Its location right on the Great Barrier Reef, provides world class scuba diving, black marlin fishing, pristine white beaches, sophisticated fine dining and seclusion, making the Lizard Island experience treasured and rare. As Australia's northernmost island resort, the secluded 40-room property is located on a 2,500 acre National Park with 24 sandy beaches and coves. With the number of guests limited to 80, it's easy to feel as if you've escaped to your own private paradise. The natural beauty and attractions of Lizard Island are without comparison, and with the July 2000 completion of a $13 million refurbishment, the resort is indeed among the world's finest luxury island destinations. The property was virtually rebuilt from the ground up.

All air-conditioned rooms, suites and villas are furnished in a fresh Australian design, featuring fabrics and colors that harmonize with the natural surroundings. The spacious accommodations are designed to capture sensational water views as well as maximize privacy. The decision of how to spend the day on Lizard is a difficult one. Diving, snorkeling, windsurfing, waterskiing, game fishing, tennis, hiking, sailing and boating are among the activities offered. Being right on the Great Barrier Reef, Lizard Island is world renowned for offering extraordinary underwater adventures. Whether it is a relaxing snorkel among coral gardens right off the beach, or a thrilling night dive, Lizard is unequalled for variety and excitement.

For those preferring to stay above the water, Lizard is every fisherman's dream. Since the waters surrounding Lizard Island were recognized as a major black marlin fishing ground in 1975, there have been seven world records won. But if rest rather than adventure is on the agenda, swimming at secluded beaches, glass-bottom boat trips, picnics, bushwalking or lounging by the pool or bar, are more relaxed options. Fine dining is provided at Osprey's Restaurant, which boasts international standard cuisine. In a menu that changes daily, the focus is on local seafood and other delicacies from the bountiful North Queensland region. The romantically inclined can also choose the ambiance of night dining on Anchor Bay Beach, beneath a private marquee lit by the intimate flicker of flares. A Lizard Island experience is truly one of a kind. Rates include accommodations, all meals and most activities. From North America, call P&O Resorts toll-free for reservations: 1–800-225-9849.

Name: Lizard Island

Category: Island Resort

Location: Tropical North Queensland region; 27 km off coast (nearest city)

Address: PMB 40, Cairns, QLD 4871

Phone: Tel. 61-7-4060-3999 **Fax** 61-7-4060-3991

E-mail: POResorts@aol.com

Web site: www.poresorts.com.au

Innkeepers: General Manager

Rates: From A$680 per person includes all meals

Number of rooms: 40 Rooms with choice of 3 grades of accommodations

Baths: Ensuite

Services & amenities: Tennis, fishing, windsurfing, water-skiing, sailing, glass bottom boats, snorkeling, award-winning restaurant, bar, gymnasium, library, boutique

Restrictions: No children under 10

Handicap access: no

Maleny Lodge Guesthouse

H istoric Maleny Lodge is an elegant Queenslander with bullnose verandahs, high ceilings, and French doors—complete with Australian
antiques and traditional silky oak furnishings. Built in 1894 as a
private residence for the local publican, Maleny Lodge has been completely
restored to its original splendor. Located on the main street of the small
township of Maleny, a leisurely hour's drive north of Brisbane, the guesthouse is only a short stroll to shops, galleries, and restaurants. The area
boasts superb views, a close-knit community of artists and craftspeople, and
proximity to the beautiful Sunshine Coast beaches.

Maleny Lodge offers seven individually decorated guest rooms, all with
ensuites, canopy beds, fluffy towels, robes, fresh flowers, ceiling fans, doonas,
electric blankets and heating. Two of the rooms have televisions and lovely
views over the garden. The dining room, featuring a magnificent mahogany
table that seats 14 comfortably, is a popular gathering spot as is the lounge
room, with large open fire, TV and games room, spacious verandahs and
outside summer house dripping with wisteria and jasmine.

The day begins with a lavish breakfast served on the balcony, weather
permitting. You can expect fresh tropical fruits, local yoghurt, cereals, toast,
muffins, croissants, choice of pancakes, French toast with bacon and banana,
home-cured bacon and eggs with smoked salmon or a special of the day.
Maleny Lodge has an acre of tropical gardens featuring a large salt-water
pool, and the original well that supplied Maleny township water in the early
1900's. The charming B&B is situated close to the Blackall Ranges, and the
surrounding countryside is well-loved for its nature walks, tall forests and

scenic vistas. From the local shops and galleries, to the outstanding natural attractions, there is plenty to do in the area. And at day's end, Maleny Lodge provides a graceful setting and traditional Queensland country hospitality.

Name: Maleny Lodge Guesthouse

Category: Guesthouse

Location: Sunshine Coast Hinterland region; Maleny (nearest city)

Address: 58 Maple St., Maleny, QLD 4552

Phone: Tel. 61 7 5494 2370 **Fax** 61 7 5494 3407

E-mail: malenylodge@mpx.com.au

Web site: web-net.com.au/lodge/

Innkeepers: Lorraine & Peter Duffy

Rates: From A$130-170 per double includes full breakfast

Rated: **** RACQ

Number of rooms: 7 Doubles

Baths: Ensuite

Services & amenities: 10 metre salt water pool, fans, heating, open fires, TV and games room

Restrictions: No smoking, no children under 14

Handicap access: no

Mermaid Beachside

R elax & indulge in this contemporary four and a half star bed & breakfast. Conveniently located in a quiet secure residential area near "The Gold Coast," and Australia's number one tourist destination, Mermaid Beachside provides the best of both worlds. It's just a short stroll from your luxurious room to a patrolled swimming area on the golden sands of Surfers Paradise Beach. The largest shopping centre in the region, Pacific Fair, is only five minutes away. Across the road from Pacific Fair is Jupiter's Casino, which provides for a magnificent night out. Of course, the Surfers Paradise nightlife with its fine dining and unsurpassable clubs is also only minutes away.

Five luxury, air-conditioned, internationally-themed rooms with ensuite bathrooms, are available for guests. The Mediterranean Room features a king or twin beds and a cool, aquatic décor. The English Room is the honeymoon suite with its king-sized bed and tasteful furnishings. The American Room has a bright, Western feel, and The Oriental Room is serene with soothing colors and Japanese prints on the walls. Lastly, there's The Australian Room with its contemporary Aboriginal quilt and red accents.

At Mermaid Beachside, enjoy genuine hospitality from hosts who have traveled the world. Chris & Ros are both avid golfers, and Chris is a professional Golf Club Fitter. They can help organise a golfing holiday at one of the world class golf courses only ten minutes away, or advise on the many local attractions including Seaworld, Dreamworld, Warner Bros. Movie World, Currumbin Wildlife Sanctuary, Wet & Wild Water Park, and the renowned National Parks in the Gold Coast hinterland, all within easy driving. Experience a varied range of breakfast delights on the patio overlooking the pool (heated in winter) before heading out to enjoy the beautiful beach and the plethora of nearby activities.

Name: Mermaid Beachside Bed & Breakfast

Category: Bed & Breakfast

Location: Gold Coast region; Surfers Paradise; 5 km (nearest city)

Address: 115 Seagull Ave./PO Box 252, Mermaid Beach, QLD 4218

Phone: Tel. 61 7 5572 9530 **Fax** 61 7 5572 9530

E-mail: ros@elink.com.au

Web site: www.mermaidbeachside.aunz.com

Innkeepers: Roz Green & Chris Priscott

Rates: From A$110 per double includes breakfast

Rated: **** ½ RACQ

Number of rooms: 5 King, Queen

Baths: 4 Ensuite

Services & amenities: Heated pool, air-conditioning, parking, TV, internet access

Handicap access: no

Naracoopa

N aracoopa Bed & Breakfast provides gracious hospitality in a unique heritage Queenslander style home. Guests enjoy glorious sunsets along the cliffs and beach of beautiful Shorncliffe, a charming suburb of Brisbane that is currently enjoying a resurgence of its turn of the century popularity as a bustling seaside resort town. Although many of the buildings have disappeared, the grand homes of the area are being restored to their former glory and Naracoopa is one of them. The name means House of Plenty and during it's heyday, Naracoopa was the site of many a weekend party. Today, guests can take pleasure in the elegantly restored residence with it's tastefully appointed bedrooms, each individually decorated with antique furnishings, original artwork, fine linens, and private ensuites. Warm, waffle weave, terry robes make it easy to enjoy the luxurious outdoor spa on the deck overlooking the city lights. In the winter, relax by a warming fire.

Hosts David and Grace Cross are Americans who have lived in Australia for 25 years, and they successfully combine the best of both worlds. They are only the third family to occupy the home since 1896, and it is their greatest pleasure to share it with others. A sumptuous breakfast is served on the wide verandah each morning and after feasting on homemade breads and tropical fruits, there is a plethora of local attractions to occupy your time. Naracoopa is a short stroll to Moreton Bay and beautiful Shorncliffe pier. Award-winning restaurants, cafes, golf course, and yacht club are all a short walk away and there is easy access to the Sunshine Coast. Naracoopa Bed & Breakfast has been featured numerous times in the local media and after a stay, it's easy to see why it has garnered so much attention.

Name: Naracoopa

Category: Bed & Breakfast

Location: Brisbane region; Shorncliffe (nearest city)

Address: 99 Yundah St., Shorncliffe, QLD 4017

Phone: Tel. 61 7 3269 2334 **Fax** 61 7 3869 1216

E-mail: naracoopa@uq.net.au

Web site: www.interspace.net.au/inns/naracoopa.html

Innkeepers: David & Grace Cross

Rates: From A$90 per double includes breakfast

Rated: **** RACQ

Number of rooms: 2 Queen

Baths: 2 Ensuite

Services & amenities: Private verandah, TV, Video, Lounge, Bar Fridge, Tea/Coffee, Spa

Restrictions: Children by arrangement

Handicap access: no

Ninderry Manor

O nly a one and a half hour drive north of Brisbane, set high on a ridge just a few minutes from the Sunshine Coast's famous beaches, and surrounded by its majestic hinterland, the luxurious Ninderry Manor is situated to take every advantage of the spectacular views. From the Maroochy Valley to the Glass House Mountains, guests enjoy a special vantage point. When mealtime beckons, enjoy a leisurely breakfast or linger over an intimate candlelit dinner in the spacious guest dining room or under nature's canopy. Breakfasts are served whenever guests are ready and two or three course dinners are available upon request.

Each beautifully appointed guest room has everything needed for an indulgent and superlatively comfortable stay. Queen-size beds, decorator furnishings, fluffy bathrobes, a large ensuite, and private patios overlooking the stunning vista, are features of every room. Relax in the guest lounge, work on your tan by the saltwater pool or simply put your feet up in a shady corner of the vine-covered courtyard. To ensure guests enjoy the very best hospitality that Australia has to offer, hosts Kerry and Peter cater to the personal needs of just six guests. Previous guests rave about the idyllic rural location, delicious food, gracious hospitality and attention to detail.

There is much to do in the area. If you're into exploring, you can discover the historic village of Yandina, the Ginger Factory, the fabulous Sunshine beaches, the famous Saturday Eumundi and Yandina Markets, national parks, rivers, lakes and waterfalls of the Blackall Range. For the active, there is golf, fishing, diving, surfing, tennis, bush walks, bird watching, day tours to Fraser Island, Coloured Sands and whale watching; and for the connoisseur, there are numerous elegant restaurants and art galleries. For a truly unique experience, ask about Ninderry Manor packages designed especially for honeymoons, anniversaries and birthdays.

Name: Ninderry Manor Luxury Retreat

Category: Bed & Breakfast

Location: Sunshine Coast region; Yandina; 5km (nearest city)

Address: 12 Karnu Drive, Ninderry via Yandina, QLD 4561

Phone: Tel. (07) 5472 7255 **Fax** (07) 5446 7089

E-mail: ninderrymanor@ozemail.com.au

Web site: www.ozemail.com.au/~ninderrymanor

Innkeepers: Kerry McLean & Peter Anyon

Rates: A$120 -135 (double) A$70–85 (single) includes gourmet breakfast

Rated: ****½ RACQ

Number of rooms: 2 Queen, 1 Twin (converts to King)

Baths: 3 Ensuite

Services & amenities: Salt water pool

Restrictions: No children; smoking outside only

Handicap access: no

Old Boyneside

O ld Boyneside, operated by the same family for the last 75 years, graciously opens its doors to guests who want to experience the real Australia. This 6,000 acre working cattle and grain property, located in one of the richest agricultural areas of the country, is adjacent to the spectacular Bunya Mountains National Park, home of the massive, ancient Bunya Pine. Hosts Moira and Peter Curtain welcome families from around the world who come for a homespun holiday. A number of guests have turned their visit to Old Boyneside into an annual event. Whether it's to relax and savour the peace and quiet, or join in on the daily farm activities like feeding the animals or collecting eggs, this farmstay offers a memorable getaway. There's even an opportunity to milk the house cow! Other activities on the farm include wagon rides, bushwalking and bird watching. Check out the King Parrots, Magpies, Cockatoos and Blue Wrens who have been spotted around the homestead, along the creek, and throughout the property. Horseback riding is another highlight of an Old Boyneside visit with numerous trails and a horse to suit every age and ability level. Youngsters will delight in this authentic bush experience.

At Old Boyneside, the setting sun doesn't mean the end of fun. The farm's location far from the city, means wide-open skies and the opportunity to see the Southern Cross. Spotlighting excursions can also be arranged providing an ideal opportunity to check out the wildlife at night including the resident possum and owl. Accommodation at this inviting farm are in a spacious guest wing of the homestead. Two handsome guestrooms with comfortable beds share a bathroom and sunroom. There is also a separate, self-contained three bedroom house, which is ideal for families. Hearty repasts are prepared in the family kitchen and guests join their hosts for meals and friendly conversation. A truly unique experience that everyone, particularly families, will remember for a lifetime. Be sure to ask about multi-day packages, including pick-up from Kingaroy and a guided tour of Bunya Mountains, which are available on request.

Name: Old Boyneside

Category: Farmstay

Location: Darling Downs region; Kingaroy (nearest city)

Address: MS 514/Bunya Highway, Kingaroy, QLD 4610

Phone: Tel. (07) 4164 4262 **Fax** (07) 4164 4121

E-mail: farmstay@ozfarmstay.com

Web site: www.ozfarmstay.com

Innkeepers: Peter & Moira Curtain

Rates: A$145 per person includes all meals

Rated: ***1/2 RACQ

Number of rooms: 5

Baths: 2

Services & amenities: Horseback riding

Handicap access: no

Planet Downs

P lanet Downs is true Australiana—with a touch of class. Situated in a valley between the rugged Shotover and Expedition Ranges 650 kilometers northwest of Brisbane, this quarter of a million acre working cattle station combines adventure and luxury with a warm, family-style atmosphere. An eight hour drive from Brisbane or a two hour flight, the vast property is a destination in and of itself.

Unlike many other Outback stations open to guests, Planet Downs was designed and specifically built with guests in mind. Central to the resort is the Gunyah, or main building. Built from Tasmanian red cedar, the large homestead-style building accommodates up to 20 guests in 10 luxurious king-sized suites. Just beyond is the Billabong, a recreation area featuring a filtered swimming pool and all-weather tennis court. All this is set into a landscape of natural rock pools, towering cliffs, and steep gorges perfect for hiking, climbing, swimming, fishing, and photography.

There's plenty to do at Planet Downs, and activity is very much a part of the daily schedule. There are trail rides and camping expeditions into the wild northern area of the property—to secluded tracts of rain forest, cascading mountain waterfalls, and hidden caves filled with 3,000 year old Aboriginal paintings. With over 10,000 head of cattle scattered throughout the countryside, it's possible to join a muster, on horseback or in a four-wheel drive. The Bloxsom family really enjoys showing visitors what life on an Australian cattle property is like, right down to preparing the swag and boiling the billy tea. And after a dusty day or two exploring the bush, guests return to the resort for a hot shower, happy hour, and a chance to watch the sunset from the wide verandahs.

In addition to all the modern conveniences provided in the rooms, the property has a licensed restaurant, which serves delicious home-style cooking (specializing in beef dishes) and a good selection of Australian wines and beers. Both an Outback paradise and a family-run working cattle station, Planet Downs provides a personal glimpse into life in the Australian bush. And, as a member of Small Luxury Hotels of the World, you can be guaranteed first-class accommodations.

Name: Planet Downs

Category: Farmstay

Location: Outback Queensland region; Rockhampton (nearest city)

Address: Dawson Highway/PO Box 415, via Rolleston/Virginia, QLD 4702/4014

Phone: Tel. 61 7 3265 5022 **Fax** 61 7 3265 3978

E-mail: planetd@bloxsom.aust.com

Web site: www.bloxsom.aust.com/planetdowns

Innkeepers: Bloxsom Family

Rates: From A$550-800 per person per night all inclusive

Rated: Small Luxury Hotels

Number of rooms: 10 King, Twin

Baths: 10 Ensuite

Services & amenities: Air-conditioning, potbellied stove, minibars in room; licensed restaurant, swimming pool, all weather tennis court

Restrictions: Minimum stay 3 nights

Handicap access: no

Silky Oaks Lodge

Minutes away from the busy coastal resort town of Port Douglas, lies one of Australia's most exclusive resorts, Silky Oaks Lodge. Situated above the beautiful Mossman River and surrounded by the pristine Daintree Rainforest, Silky Oaks is an idyllic retreat. A rare combination of relaxation, soft adventure and access to tourist attractions entices travelers to Silky Oaks. Indeed, the Lodge's stylish features and facilities, superior standards of service and its unique location, close to the World Heritage-listed Daintree National Park, have placed Silky Oaks in the Queensland Tourism Awards' Hall of Fame.

Each day is filled with new experiences ... discovering the rainforest, exploring via mountain bikes, bird watching, visiting the Great Barrier Reef, heading off on a 4WD Safari, enjoying a game of golf or tennis, or indulging in a shopping spree. More leisurely options include relaxing poolside or on the grassy banks of the Mossman River. You do as little or as much as your personal energy levels dictate.

With just 60 private chalets close to tree top level and overlooking the river, Silky Oaks is small for an international resort, which adds to its charm. Each air-conditioned chalet has been carefully positioned amongst the trees and native flora to maximize privacy. Some include spa baths, and all are spacious, flowing out onto wide verandahs that take full advantage of the surrounding canopy of trees.

At The Tree House Restaurant, talented chefs prepare superb Australian cuisine, using the finest ingredients styled to suit the climate and please discriminating palates. An excellent selection of Australian wines complement the menu. Dining at Silky Oaks is a memorable experience, but not only for its innovative cuisine and attentive service. It is here that you can gain a true understanding of the rainforest experience. No walls or even a pane of glass separate you from the tall trees, or restrict your view of the river below. Brilliantly colored butterflies and small birds pass by your table and add their own charm to the scenery. Beyond the dining room are the bar and lounge, both great spots for relaxing. Past the beautifully timbered walkway is the Jungle Perch overlooking the Mossman River . . . another magical place to enjoy a coffee or an aperitif. Within the grounds is a Wallaby nursery where orphaned young are nurtured. These pretty creatures are very tame and welcome visitors to their temporary shelter. At Silky Oaks Lodge, the essence of the rainforest has been captured for travelers seeking the perfect blend of pampered surroundings, easy access to The Great Barrier Reef, and all the attractions in the region. From North America, call P&O Resorts toll-free for reservations: 1-800-225-9849.

Name: Silky Oaks Lodge

Category: Wilderness Resort

Location: Tropical North Queensland region; Cairns; 83 km (nearest city)

Address: PO Box 396, Mossman, QLD 4873

Phone: Tel. 61-7-4098-1666 **Fax** 61-7-4098-1983

E-mail: POResorts@aol.com

Web site: www.poresorts.com.au

Innkeepers: General Manager

Rates: A$426 per room, per night, including tropical breakfast (taxes included)

Rated: Queensland Tourism Awards' Hall of Fame

Number of rooms: 60 Private Chalets

Baths: Ensuite, Private

Services & amenities: Licensed restaurant and bar, wallaby nursery, tennis, canoeing, swimming, mountain bicycles

Restrictions: No children under 6

Handicap access: no

Victoria

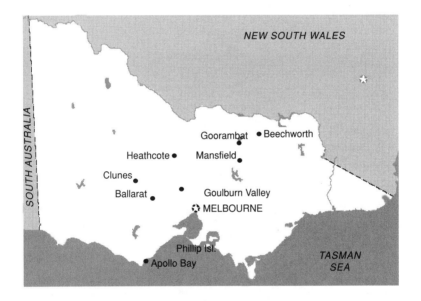

You'll Feel Out Of Place in Victoria

Imagine riding on horseback under the starlit sky of the southern hemisphere. Or imagine waking up in "Snowy River" country to watch the sunrise. Or watch the dew settle on the lush vineyards as you sample a fruity Chardonnay.

Feel like you never felt before. Your senses will come alive with the sights, sounds and aromas that meet you at every turn. And you'll be welcomed into the homes of the friendliest people you have ever met. You'll feel like part of the family in a strange and wondrous land.

Stop imagining and make it real. For more information write to: Tourism Victoria, 2049 Century Park E. #1920, Los Angeles, CA 90067.

A cornucopia of diversity, Victoria brims with attractions and spectacular scenic beauty. What distinguishes the state apart from the rest of Australia, however, is the accessibility of its various enticements. Visitors can travel a short distance from Melbourne, the capital city, and find themselves skiing the mountains of the legendary Snowy River Country, swimming in secluded coves with warm sandy beaches, floating down the Murray River on an old-time paddle steamer, or driving through the splendid Wine Country, Gold Country or Lake Country. Even the unsurpassed beauty of the Outback, with its incredible variety of flora and fauna, is relatively close by.

Melbourne is a charming blend of contemporary sophistication and old world ambiance. A modern metropolis of approximately three million people, Melbourne also boasts an abundance of Victorian architecture. Also known for its urban landscaping, the city is home to the outstanding Royal Botanic Gardens, one of the world's most outstanding examples of landscape gardening. It is almost always lush with greenery and ablaze with bloom. A myriad of annual events keep Melbourne jumping. One of the most notable events is The Spring Racing Carnival, a festival of racing and social events that includes the famous Melbourne Cup (the equivalent of the Kentucky Derby), and Cup Day (the first Tuesday in November). The Australian Open, the first of four Grand Slam Tennis tournaments, is played in Melbourne the last two weeks of January, and in March, the city explodes with energy as it is turned into a race-car circuit for the Qantas Australian Grand Prix.

The completion of the Victorian Arts Centre in 1985 crowned Melbourne as Australia's capital of the arts, and the city reigns as both the culture and fashion mecca of Australia. Next door is the National Gallery, which boasts Australia's largest collection of local and European art. The Centre's Performing Arts venues schedule numerous live performances of world-class opera and ballet. Leading the country's growing fashion industry, the city's trendy boutiques, fashionable department stores, and neighborhood arcades provide everything from haute couture to the hottest trends.

Melbourne's remarkable multi-cultural society has spawned a rich diversity of restaurants. Melbournians take their dining seriously, and Melbourne rivals the world's major cities for variety and quality. Whether dining out in one of the smaller ethnic BYO restaurants that sacrifice décor for quality and authenticity, or in an elegant, first-class dining room that features the eclecticism and creative presentation of modern Australian cooking, the experience will be unforgettable.

Many of the city's restaurants feature wines produced in the region. They have recaptured the fine reputation they enjoyed in Australia before being virtually destroyed by the same vine louse that wreaked havoc with the French and German wine industries almost a hundred years ago. Today, there are more than a dozen wine producing areas in Victoria. Key areas are the Yarra Valley just east of Melbourne (where Healesville Sanctuary can be found and featuring the largest collection of Australian wildlife in the world), Rutherglen in the northeast, the long Murray Valley near the New South Wales/Victoria border, the Goulburn Valley just north of Melbourne, and the area around the towns of Great Western and Geelong on the northwestern shore of Port Phillip Bay. Victoria's climatic range allows production of an entire spectrum of wines—from light chardonnays and sparkling wines, to luscious pinot noirs and hearty cabernet sauvignons—acclaimed and given prizes around the world.

Like its wines, Victoria's countryside is richly varied. Not far from Melbourne are the Dandenong Ranges, noted for excellent bushwalks, stately homes, beautiful gardens, and fine restaurants. A day trip to see the cool, lush forest and prolific birdlife that characterizes the area, can be made on a restored vintage steam train known as "Puffing Billy," a genuine relic of Victoria's early rail days.

Just south of Melbourne is the Mornington Peninsula, the long spit of land that curves down the east side of Port Philip Bay. This popular Melbourne resort area features excellent beaches with great variety—calm water on the bay side and crashing surf on the rugged ocean beaches that face Bass Strait. On nearby Phillip Island, accessible by road or ferry, visitors can experience one of nature's most enthralling spectacles—the parade of Little Penguins wading ashore at dusk. Apart from the natural attractions, Phillip Island hosts the Qantas Australia Motorcycle Grand Prix each October, which causes the island to swell with spectators.

At the southernmost tip of the Mornington Peninsula, is historic Portsea. From nearby Sorrento, a ferry runs across Port Phillip Bay to the fishing port of Queenscliff on the Bellarine Peninsula. This small seaside town has escaped the uncontrolled expansion that has ravaged so many of the larger towns on the Mornington Peninsula, and it remains a picturesque jewel of Victorian architecture with several grand hotels and quaint cottages that are popular weekend getaways for city dwellers.

The Great Ocean Road that begins 30 kilometers from Queenscliff hugs the southern coastline for over 250 kilometers along some of the most spectacular coastal scenery in all of Australia. Among the many memorable attractions along this route are popular beach resorts, breathtaking lookouts, lush rainforests, convict-built lighthouses, beautiful Apollo Bay, and the majestic rock formations of the Twelve Apostles soaring out of the pounding surf.

It was the discovery of gold in the mid 1800's that stimulated Victoria's rapid development as the financial and commercial capital of the country. To the north of Melbourne is the state's historic Goldfields Region, one of the most popular of the state's tourist areas. The enormous wealth created by the gold rush allowed the residents of Ballarat, Bendigo, Maldon (and many others) to build fantastic homes and buildings, creating impressive streetscapes and gardens that must be seen to be believed. Here it's possible to relive the gold rush days at Sovereign Hill, Australia's foremost outdoor museum where history is literally recreated. You can also visit an underground mine, pan for gold, and after a busy day visit Australia's "Spa Centre" in Daylesford, take a long soak in the mineral baths. Central Victoria also hosts a myriad of special events with a Rose Festival, Folk Festival, Winter Festival, and Celtic Festival all taking place at various times of the year.

Named after mountains of the same name in Scotland, the Grampians are a three or four hour drive to the west of Melbourne. The area is noted for fine bushwalks, superb mountain lookouts, sheer cliffs with excellent rock-climbing opportunities, waterfalls, abundant wildlife, and rock caves, many of which are decorated with ancient Aboriginal paintings.

For water sports, the Gippsland Lakes region with over 400 kilometers of inland saltwater lakes and waterways to explore, offers vacationers the ultimate in swimming, fishing, surfing, and boating. A rainbow of adventures can be found at the Lakes including coastal waterway tours, spectacular landscapes, rare plant and wildlife, beaches, art galleries along with fine food and wine. Just north of this region are the mountains of Australia's Great Dividing Range, the highest in Victoria, and the site of the state's booming ski industry.

Because Victoria is so compact, and (for Australia) so densely populated, getting around the state is easy. Victorian roads are numerous, well maintained, and clearly marked. The whole state is studded with guesthouses, farms, and country inns, plus, good public transportation is readily available. Hosts will often pick up guests at the nearest airport, bus or train station, bring them home and make them feel like one of the family. More than places, sights, and sounds, Victoria is people, and Victoria's hosts always offer a warm welcome.

For more information write or telephone:

Tourism Victoria
2049 Century Park East
Suite 1920
Los Angeles, CA 90067
(310) 229 4892 tel
(310) 552 1215 fax
e-mail: tourvic.losangeles@dsd.vic.gov.au

In Melbourne visit:

Victoria Visitor Information Centre
Melbourne Town Hall
Corner of Little Collins & Swanston Streets
Melbourne VIC 3000
61 3 9658 9949

Or visit their website:
www.tourism.vic.gov.au

REGIONAL DIRECTORY
➤ denotes review

BELLARINE PENINSULA
Mietta Queenscliff   16 Gellibrand St., Queenscliff, VIC 3225   61 3 5258 1066
Restored turn of the century Victorian jewel overlooking Swan Bay

CENTRAL/GOLDFIELDS
➤ **AnsoniA**   32 Lydiard St South, Ballarat, VIC 3350   61 3 5332 4678
Boutique hotel and restaurant on beautiful street in the heart of historic Ballarat

➤ **Bodlyn B&B**   9 Errard St. North, Ballarat, VIC 3350   61 3 5332 1318
Elegant brick home with antique furnishings, heating & open fires, and guest sitting room.

➤ **Emeu Inn Restaurant and Bed & Breakfast**   187 High Street, Heathcote, VIC 3523   61 3 5433 2668
Restaurant and B&B offering luxury accommodations and international cuisine in historic surroundings

➤ **Keebles of Clunes**   114 Bailey St., Clunes, VIC 3370   61 3 5345 3220
Restored 1863 Georgian-style hotel in Central Victoria

CENTRAL
➤ **Holcombe Country Retreat**   Holcombe Rd/RMB 3683, Glenlyon, VIC 3461   61 3 5348 7514
Exclusive, self-contained retreat providing fine country living of the highest standard

Moulton   129 Main Road,, Hepburn Springs, VIC 3461
Pond Cottage   Glengrove Farm—Chases Lane, Pipers Creek, VIC 3444   61 3 5422 1447
Self-contained two-story English cottage overlooking a scenic pond

➤ **Tuki Retreat**   Stoney Rises, Smeaton, VIC 3364   61 3 5345 6233
Unique property incorporating sheep farming and trout fishing

GIPPSLAND
➤ **Déjà Vu**   Clara Street (PO Box 750), Lakes Entrance, VIC 3909   61 3 5155 4330
Delightfully different private waterfront suites

Powerscourt   RMB 6095, Maffra, VIC 3860   61 3 5147 1897
Grand country home near Gippsland Lakes

➤ **Sundowner Lodge Guesthouse & Restaurant**   128 Inlet View Rd/PO Box 789, Venus Bay, VIC 3956   61 3 5663 7099
Ultimate romantic coastal hideaway in luxurious boutique B&B

GRAMPIANS
Marwood Villas   Roses Gap Rd., Halls Gap, VIC 3381   61 3 5356 4336
Luxury self-contained villas near The Grampians National Park

GREAT OCEAN ROAD
➤ **Claerwen**   Tuxion Rd., Apollo Bay, VIC 3233   61 3 5237 7064
Elegant modern homestead off scenic Great Ocean Road

MELBOURNE
➤ **The Avoca**   98 Victoria Ave., Albert Park, VIC 3206   61 3 9696 9090
Elegant Victorian terrace house close to beach and Albert Park

Robinson's By The Sea   335 Beaconsfield Parade, St. Kilda West, VIC
3182   61 3 9534 2683
Victorian terrace house overlooking St. Kilda Beach

➤ **Rotherwood**   13 Rotherwood St., Richmond, VIC 3121   61 3 9428 6758
Elegant Victorian style apartments close to the heart of Melbourne

➤ **The Tilba**   Toorak Rd. West & Domain St., South Yarra, VIC 3141
61 3 9867 8844
Gracious small Victorian hotel

MORNINGTON PENINSULA
➤ **Barkly House**   44 Barkly St., Mornington, VIC 3931   61 3 5977 0957
*Stately 1920's home set in tranquil gardens near Mornington shops and
restaurants*

➤ **Cipriani's Flinders Country Inn**   165 Wood St., Flinders, VIC 3929
61 3 5989 0933
*Fine dining and romantic accommodations in a quiet fishing village on
rugged and beautiful coastline*

➤ **Glynt Manor**   16 Bay Rd., Mt. Martha, VIC 3934   61 3 5974 1216
Gracious country manor house that provides luxury accommodations

➤ **Peppers Delgany**   Point Nepean Rd, Portsea, VIC 3944   61 3 5984 4000
Sandstone castle overlooking Port Phillip Bay

➤ **Pines Ridge Country Retreat**   255 Main Creek Rd., Main Ridge, VIC
3928   61 3 5989 6170
Lovely country retreat centrally located on the Mornington Peninsula

➤ **Red Hill Retreat**   RMB 6262, William Rd., Red Hill, VIC 3937
61 3 5989 2035
Boutique accommodations in private, peaceful setting.

➤ **Warrawee Homestead**   87 Warrawee Rd., Balnarring, VIC 3926
61 3 5983 1729
*Enchanting retreat recalling Australia's romantic early colonial days
offering beautiful accommodations and imaginative cuisine*

MURRAY RIVER

Murray House   55 Francis St., Echuca, VIC 3564   61 3 5482 4944
Traditional B&B in historic port town

River Gallery Inn   578 High St., Echuca, VIC 3564   61 3 5480 6902
Historic guesthouse in port area of Echuca

NORTH EAST

➤ **Beechworth House Bed & Breakfast**   5 Dingle Rd., Beechworth, VIC
3747   61 3 5728 2817
*Set in historic gold-mining town, Beechworth House is a convenient
stopover between Sydney, Canberra & Melbourne.*

➤ **Carlyle House Rutherglen**   147 High St, Rutherglen, VIC 3685   61 2
6032 8444
Luxurious, 4¹/₂ star B&B in the centre of historic Rutherglen

➤ **Howqua Dale Gourmet Retreat**   Howqua River Rd./ P.O. 379,
Mansfield, VIC 3724   61 3 5777 3503
*Luxurious country house hotel specializing in all-inclusive gourmet
weekends and cooking classes*

➤ **Koendidda Country House**   Pooley's Rd/RMB 2137, Barnawartha,
VIC 3688   61 2 6026 7340
*Luxury accommodations in two-story country mansion in historic
goldrush region*

Pension Grimus   149 Breathtaker Rd., Mt. Buller, VIC 3723   61 3 5777
6396
Well known boutique hotel is an ideal winter base for skiers

➤ **Yaridni**   RMB 1090, Goorambat, VIC 3725   61 3 5764 1273
*Join in farmlife on a 600-ha merino sheep property in northern Victoria.
Easily reached from Melbourne-Sydney freeway*

PHILLIP ISLAND

➤ **Narrabeen Cottage**   16 Steele St., Cowes, VIC 3922   61 3 5952 2062
Seaside guesthouse set in delightful garden on Phillip Island

➤ **Watani Waters**   9 Cleeland St, Newhaven, VIC 3925   61 3 5956 6300
Waterfront bed & breakfast with fabulous views

WILSON'S PROMONTORY

➤ **Vereker House**   10 Iluka Close, Foley Rd., Yanakie, Gippsland, VIC
3960   61 3 5687 1431
Scenic rural setting with sweeping mountain & sea views

The AnsoniA

The AnsoniA is an elegant, independently owned and operated, 4½-star boutique hotel in the heart of historic Ballarat. The classic Victorian building, built as a solicitor's office in 1860, was restored in 1996 by Gerard Ballantyne and Rosie King who preserved its heritage, while introducing contemporary style and modern amenities. Its striking interior is filled with commissioned furniture, artwork, and an abundance of flowers. A glass-roofed atrium, the focal point of this intriguing European-style hotel, extends the length of the building and is flanked by twenty guest suites, each with private facilities. Guests are encouraged to use the hotel's public spaces. In addition to the atrium, library, and garden courtyard, there is a guest lounge that provides a place for a rendezvous with friends, a pre-dinner drink, or a quiet retreat in front of the open fire with the latest best-seller. The guest rooms vary in size and configurations, and each features polished floors, hydronic heating, generous queen beds, luxurious bed linen, bathrobes, hairdryers, toiletries, and ironing facilities

Food is a significant feature of the AnsoniA, which is proud to have been included in The Age Good Food Guide each year of operation. The menu changes frequently to include seasonal delicacies, and the wine list is extensive and includes some wonderful local and other Australian wines. The AnsoniA is a multi-award winner with recent kudos including a 1999 Victorian Tourism Award for Superior Accommodations and Goldfields Tourism Certificate of Merit for Deluxe Accommodations. While not a traditional bed & breakfast, The AnsoniA offers a variety of packages that include dinner, bed, and breakfast. With children welcome and family suites available, this is a perfect choice for those traveling with kids.

Name: AnsoniA

Category: Boutique Hotel

Location: Central/Goldfields region; Ballarat (nearest city)

Address: 32 Lydiard St South, Ballarat, VIC 3350

Phone: Tel. 61 3 5332 4678 **Fax** 61 3 5332 4698

E-mail: ansonia@ansonia.ballarat.net.au

Web site: www.ballarat.com/ansonia.htm

Innkeepers: Gerard Ballantyne & Rosie King

Rates: From A$150 per double includes accommodation; B&B packages available

Rated: **** 1/2 RACV; 1999 Victorian Tourism Award

Number of rooms: 20

Baths: Private

Services & amenities: Licensed restaurant, valet parking, concierge, guest lounge, library

Restrictions: No smoking

Handicap access: no

The Avoca

V isitors to Melbourne are in for a real treat if they book a stay at The Avoca, an elegant two-story Victorian terrace house close to Albert Park. This turn of the century residence is located close to the beach, trendy shops, cafes and restaurants, yet only 3 kilometers from the heart of the city. Catch a tram from Victoria Avenue and you'll be in the central business district within 10 minutes via the Arts Centre and Southgate.

The traditional inner city B&B features gracious hospitality and three guestrooms with either king or queen-sized beds, private bathrooms, and stylish appointments. Hand-made chocolates before bed are just one of the decadent indulgences in store for you. Breakfast is another. A scrumptious meal consisting of fresh fruit juice, a homemade fruit compote, fresh fruit platter, and a gourmet "dish du jour" served with quality teas, coffee and toast, awaits you.

After venturing out to see all the local attractions, take time to curl up with magazines and newspapers in the comfortable guest parlor, and savor the log fire burning in winter. In the summer, join the walkers, joggers, and in-line skaters heading for the beach, or relax and watch the big ships coming into port. Also within walking distance of The Avoca, is Albert Park Lake and Golf Course, St. Vincent Gardens, the Aquatic Centre, the Grand Prix Circuit, the Craft Market, and numerous art galleries. One couple, who stayed at The Avoca after a month long journey around Australia, proclaimed it the best B&B they'd ever stayed in, providing a fairytale-like ending to their trip. This B&B, indeed, is like a fairytale and well worth a visit.

Name: The Avoca

Category: B&B Inn

Location: Melbourne region; Melbourne; 3 km (nearest city)

Address: 98 Victoria Ave., Albert Park, VIC 3206

Phone: Tel. 61 3 9696 9090 **Fax** 61 3 9696 9092

E-mail: avoca@netlink.com.au

Web site: www.theavoca.com.au

Innkeepers: Jane & John Murphy

Rates: From A$130 - 140 per double includes full breakfast

Rated: ****1/2 RACV

Number of rooms: 2 Queen, 1 King or Twin

Baths: 2 Ensuite, 1 Private

Services & amenities: Guest lounge with open fire, formal dining, TV, tea/coffee

Restrictions: No smoking, no pets, children by arrangement

Handicap access: no

Barkly House

T he four-star Barkly House is a stately 1920's home set in a tranquil English cottage garden. Conveniently located one minute from the heart of Mornington Village and just a short stroll from the beach and harbor, this splendid bed and breakfast provides easy access to all the area's attractions. Discerning visitors to the Mornington Peninsula can savor the local wineries, enjoy a round of golf, meander through the many renowned art galleries, craft and produce markets, fish, surf, sail, or cycle this exciting part of Victoria. With its long reputation as a popular summer destination, the Mornington Peninsula offers year-round tourist activities, and visitors find themselves satisfied on a myriad of levels. Less than an hour from Melbourne, Barkly House's park-like setting is the perfect antidote to the city.

Guests choose from one of three luxurious suites. Two are located upstairs with either an ensuite or private bathroom. Views of the lovely gardens and leafy yard embody the serene surroundings, and country-style furnishings harmoniously blend with the environment. Downstairs, the most popular of the suites features an open fireplace and bathroom with spa. But perhaps the most memorable aspect of Barkly House is the wondrous collection of pigs. Owners Denise and David share the same horoscope in the Chinese calendar, and in celebration of that fact, over 200 pigs adorn the shelves. Upstairs, there are even a couple of flying pigs on the wall!

In the mornings, guests are treated to a sumptuous country breakfast feast. A specialty of the house is free range eggs cooked a variety of ways: with bacon, mushrooms and tomatoes or scrambled eggs with smoked salmon.

Homemade muffins might be banana and pecan, blueberry and apple, or double chocolate. All meals are prepared by a gourmet chef to ensure total satisfaction, and evening meals are available by arrangement. Served in the formal dining room, these multi-course meals are a private, epicurean affair. Both Denise and David are gracious hosts who invite you to enjoy their hospitality and relax in the style of a gracious by-gone era.

Name: Barkly House

Category: Bed & Breakfast

Location: Mornington Peninsula region; Mornington (nearest city)

Address: 44 Barkly St., Mornington, VIC 3931

Phone: Tel. 61 3 5977 0957 **Fax** 61 3 5977 0957

Innkeepers: Denise & David Hassett

Rated: ****

Number of rooms: 3

Baths: Ensuite

Restrictions: No smoking

Handicap access: no

Beechworth House

B eechworth House is set in a large tranquil garden with lovely views of the surrounding hills. A spacious sitting room with TV, video and CD player, and graceful furnishings, provides the perfect place to relax after a day of exploring the historic gold mining town and all its attractions. Sip a port or sherry, or enjoy coffee or tea in front of an elegant open fire while gazing across the rose garden to the distant hills. There is also a grand piano, which can be utilized for special functions or an impromptu concert. Host Mark Stephens (alias Lazy Harry) is a singer and songwriter with a special interest in Australian Folk music. He has recorded numerous albums that take you on a musical journey into Australia's fascinating past, and with a bit of encouragement, he might be persuaded to share his love of music with guests. His repertoire of traditional Australian ballads includes such favourites as Waltzing Matilda and Botany Bay. Wendy is an award-winning artist who displays her colorful paintings throughout their lovely home, transforming it into an art gallery. It's obvious her gifted eye contributed to the stylish décor and design. Recently expanded and upgraded, Beechworth House features five delightful bedrooms (two with double spas), all with queen-sized beds and thick doonas, ensuites, heating, cooling, and stunning views. The property is only 2 kms from the center of town, and there are many walks and tourist sites, including restaurants, galleries, and historic buildings.

Fine dining is a special feature of Beechworth House. The distinctive dining room has a cedar dining table, fine dinnerware, silver cutlery, starched linen, and delicious food.

Name: Beechworth House Bed & Breakfast
Category: Bed & Breakfast
Location: North East region; Beechworth; 1.5 KM (nearest city)
Address: 5 Dingle Rd., Beechworth, VIC 3747
Phone: Tel. 61 3 5728 2817 **Fax** 61 3 5728 2737
E-mail: bworthbb@dragnet.com.au
Web site: www.lazyharry.dragnet.com.au/dragnet.com.au
Innkeepers: Wendy & Mark Stephens
Rates: A$120-A$150 includes cooked breakfast
Number of rooms: 5 Queens
Baths: 5 Ensuite (2 with spas)
Services & amenities: Quality furnishings, TV, ensuites (2 with spa baths), guest sitting room with open fire
Restrictions: No children
Handicap access: no

Bodlyn

B odlyn is a beautifully built and redecorated Federation home in the heart of Victoria's gold country. Built for a Welsh merchant family in 1910, this gracious residence was restored by hosts Jan and Geoff Kitterly who fell in love with the abode at first sight. The guest accommodations are privately contained on one side of the house with three bedrooms, three bathrooms, and two guest sitting rooms. There are open fires for ambiance, and the entire home is hydronically heated.

Two of the guest rooms have their own fire places, and the third has an aero spa in the ensuite. All rooms are large enough to accommodate romantic dinners for two. The guest sitting rooms make you want to take off your shoes, pull up a chair, and relax in front of an open fire. Television, CD player and stereo, homemade cakes or biscuits served with tea or plunger coffee, make this a very relaxing room. For those retiring late after enjoying one of Ballarat's fine restaurants, port and chocolates await. The formal dining room, where breakfast is served, is furnished with Australian Cedar furniture. Breakfast consists of freshly squeezed juice, cereal with seasonal fruits, followed by such delights as Eggs Benedict, or perhaps Scrambled Eggs and Smoked Salmon. All are topped off by freshly brewed coffee or tea as you peruse a selection of morning papers or plan your day.

Bodlyn is situated within one block of Ballarat's Main Street, and just a few short blocks from the best restaurants and galleries in town. Lake Wendouree and the Botanical Gardens are within walking distance, and Sovereign Hill is just a few minutes by car. The secluded garden at Bodlyn is beautiful year round, and the rear of the property is fully decked, providing an opportunity for guests to take breakfast in the garden throughout the summer months. The Kitterleys are only the third family to own Bodlyn, and they've restored it with the help of the former residents who shared the home's fascinating history. Much of the architectural detail was intact, and the upgrade included adding some modern conveniences and making the home guest-friendly. Their devoted efforts paid off, and Bodlyn once again reflects its former glory.

Name: Bodlyn B&B

Category: Bed & Breakfast

Location: Central/Goldfields region; Ballarat (nearest city)

Address: 9 Errard St. North, Ballarat, VIC 3350

Phone: Tel. 61 3 5332 1318 **Fax** 61 3 5332 2899

E-mail: kittelty@netconnect.com.au

Web site: www.ballarat.com.au/bodlyn.htm

Innkeepers: Jan Kittelty

Rates: From A$120 per double includes breakfast

Number of rooms: 3 Queen

Baths: 3 Ensuite

Services & amenities: Spa in one bathroom

Restrictions: No smoking

Handicap access: no

Carlyle House

L ocated in the heart of historic Rutherglen, Carlyle House is one of the area's grandest homes. Built in 1895 by a local doctor, Carlyle House has been lovingly restored by hosts Robyn and Jon Webb who worked hard to recapture the best qualities of the Victorian era. Naturally, all modern conveniences have been incorporated along with a host of luxurious appointments. Carlyle House is air-conditioned and centrally heated, but it's the crackling log fire blazing in the plush guest lounge that's the main attraction on a cool winter's day.

The house is tastefully decorated with antiques and beautiful reproduction furniture, most of which were handcrafted by Jon in his workshop out back. Guests can indulge and relax in one of four guestrooms, each with private bath and exquisitely tasteful décor. Most rooms have king-sized beds and high quality linens, along with a number of thoughtful touches. A hearty country breakfast is served in the sunroom overlooking the re-established cottage garden. The menu changes daily, but Jon's corn and bacon fritters with poached eggs and salsa is a frequent favorite. Robyn and Jon also run The Shamrock Restaurant (staggering distance from Carlyle House), an Age Good Food Guide–listed restaurant that provides fresh regional cuisine of international quality.

Rutherglen is located between Sydney and Melbourne and is an ideal stopover. The mighty Murray River is nearby, and Rutherglen is an internationally famous wine region surrounded by many historic sites and first class golf courses. Well known for its full-bodied Reds, Muscats, Tokays and superb fortified wines, Rutherglen boasts many fifth-generation winemakers, and tours of the wineries are a highlight of the region. The four and a half star Carlyle House is conveniently situated near the Town Hall and the center of town, providing easy access to the main street with its many historical attractions and eateries. Whether you take advantage of everything ... or do nothing at all, Carlyle House is the perfect base from which to spend a few days. With a well deserved reputation as one of the area's most popular B&B's, Carlyle House books up quickly with locals on the weekends, but special mid-week packages offer an attractive option and are well worth checking out.

Name: Carlyle House Rutherglen

Category: Bed & Breakfast

Location: North East region; Rutherglen (nearest city)

Address: 147 High St, Rutherglen, VIC 3685

Phone: Tel. 61 2 6032 8444 **Fax** 61 2 6032 7119

E-mail: carlylehouse@bigpond.com

Innkeepers: Jon & Robyn Webb

Rates: From A$110-160 per double includes full breakfast

Rated: ****$1/2$ RACV

Number of rooms: 3 King, 1 Queen and Single

Baths: 2 Ensuite, 2 Private

Services & amenities: Sunroom, lounge area, verandah

Restrictions: No children

Handicap access: no

Cipriani's Flinders Country Inn

Nestled in the heart of Flinders, a quiet fishing village located amidst some of Victoria's most rugged and beautiful coastline, is Cipriani's Flinders Country Inn. This unique bed and breakfast and restaurant offers superb accommodations and old-fashioned country hospitality. With views across Bass Strait and Westernport Bay to Phillip Island, Cipriani's boasts an extraordinary locale, in addition to exceptional service. The graceful verandahs, terraces, and restaurant, overlook a lake and waterfall set in 2 acres of carefully tended garden. Beautifully appointed guest lounges, with open fires, provide ample space to unwind. And the individually designed bedroom suites feature private bathrooms and sitting rooms. Delightful self-contained accommodations with spas are also available.

It's a three-minute walk to Flinders Village and beaches and a 25-minute drive from the Queenscliff-Sorrento car and passenger ferry.

If you're lucky, your stay will coincide with one of Cipriani's special 'Feature Evenings' held during the year. Especially popular, is the Summer Concerts under the stars, which include dinner and live music beside the lake. Other highlights include lazy Sunday lunches, which need to be booked in advance.

Enjoy the ambiance and cuisine of Cipriani's Restaurant (BYO) where elegant, unrushed dining is highlighted by authentic Italian cuisine. In the cooler months, join your host by the fire for a complimentary glass of red wine while you sample great winter dishes cooked in the wood-fired oven. Overnight guests at Cipriani's feast on hearty country-cooked breakfasts before heading out for the day to discover the nearby Mornington Peninsula wineries or world class golf courses.

Whatever the season, whatever the reason—Cipriani's offers great food and friendly service. After a walk along the beach on a wintry Flinders day, imagine curling up by a cozy fire with your favorite book, or in the heat of summer, lazing on a shady verandah overlooking a cool lake and sipping ice-cold champagne. Whether dining on the terraces overlooking the delightful lake and gardens, or enjoying a romantic getaway, quiet rest, or exciting weekend, Cipriani's promises you'll thoroughly enjoy every moment of your time away.

Name: Cipriani's Flinders Country Inn

Category: Bed & Breakfast

Location: Mornington Peninsula region; Flinders (nearest city)

Address: 165 Wood St., Flinders, VIC 3929

Phone: Tel. 61 3 5989 0933 **Fax** 61 3 5989 0059

Innkeepers: Susie Cipriani

Rates: from A$130–A$150 double includes breakfast

Rated: **** RACV

Services & amenities: Restaurant, guest lounge, lake, gardens

Handicap access: no

Claerwen

A top the highest hill along the Great Ocean Road overlooking the coast, and with panoramic views from all rooms, Claerwen Retreat offers four spacious suites in the guesthouse and two self-contained three bedroom holiday houses. The property serves as a relaxing base from which to explore the natural wonders of the famous surfcoast and rainforest hinterland. For those lucky enough to visit this stunning area, Claerwen provides stylish country living at its best. The elegant homestead features commanding views of the Wild Dog Valley, Otway National Park, and the rugged coastline. The 130 acres of park-like grounds, horse paddocks, and rainforest, also includes a golf course, tennis court, saltwater pool, and heated spa.

It's not just the beauty of Apollo Bay or the property's amenities that draw guests to Claerwen, however. It's the intimacy and hospitality. With a maximum of eight guests in the main house, visitors feel as if they are personal friends of the host sharing her gracious country house. Each of the four bedrooms have extensive views of the surrounding area, along with more intimate views of the courtyard garden and pool. The guest suites are all airy, luxurious, and individually decorated. The three-bedroom cottages on the property are self-contained and a perfect choice for those looking for more privacy or those traveling with children.

A spacious lounge in the guesthouse features open fireplaces, library, VCR, and CD player. For the more active, tennis racquets are provided, as well as gumboots for rainforest walks. Complimentary tea/coffee and biscuits are served on arrival, and those staying in the guesthouse are treated to a sumptuous German breakfast.

Name: Claerwen

Category: Guesthouse/Country cottages

Location: Great Ocean Road region; Apollo Bay (nearest city)

Address: Tuxion Rd., Apollo Bay, VIC 3233

Phone: Tel. 61 3 5237 7064 **Fax** 61 3 5237 7054

E-mail: cornelia.elbrecht@claerwen.com.au

Web site: www.claerwen.com.au

Innkeepers: Cornelia Elbrecht & Bill Whittakers

Rates: From A$154 per double includes full breakfast

Rated: ****1/2 RACV

Number of rooms: 4 in house, 2 cottages

Baths: Ensuite

Services & amenities: Pool, tennis court, spa, helipad

Restrictions: 2 night minimum on weekend; children by arrangement

Handicap access: no

Déjà Vu

Déjà Vu was specially designed and built in 1993 to provide guests with the best views of Lakes Entrance. The contemporary architectural tour de force is sculpted into the landscape and built on four levels, with three private studio suites attached to the main building. Perched high on a narrow strip of land above the waters of the North Arm, the property overlooks the ocean, lakes and wilderness, as well as the nearby township. Six acres of undulating land with rainforest and wetlands surround the house, and an abundance of bird and wildlife reside on or near the property—including a family of Kookaburras that wake up laughing each morning. Peace, privacy, and pampering are just some of the reasons guests return again and again to this premium bed and breakfast. Each of the suites feature a private balcony and in-room spa where guests can enjoy the panoramic views. Sunrises and sunsets are particularly memorable with the colorful sky reflecting off shimmering waters below.

Drift off to sleep watching the twinkling lights of Lakes Entrance and awaken to the soft glow of the rising sun. The list of unique and personalized features that this luxury bed and breakfast offers, is extensive. Devonshire

Tea is offered upon arrival, and hosts Beverley and Gerard Goris will be more than happy to advise on specialized activities. Although it's difficult to leave this stunning residence, especially after enjoying a gourmet breakfast served on one of the balconies, it's worth setting out to discover the region's abundant attractions.

Many well known artists call East Gippsland home, and galleries and studios are plentiful. There is also the Wyanga Park Winery Boat Cruise where you can explore the Lakes and cruise to the nearby winery for lunch or dinner. Endless natural attractions, including the coastal waterways and pristine beaches, also make the area worth visiting. Beverley and Gerard can also arrange raft trips, horse and carriage rides through the bush, 4WD tours of Snowy River Country, as well as a private seafood dinner platter, a table at the best restaurant in town, or an aromatherapy massage. To discover this delightfully different property is to experience a true sanctuary that satisfies on all levels.

Name: Déjà Vu

Category: Boutique Bed & Breakfast

Location: Gippsland region; Lakes Entrance (nearest city)

Address: Clara Street (PO Box 750), Lakes Entrance, VIC 3909

Phone: Tel. 61 3 5155 4330 **Fax** 61 3 5155 3718

E-mail: dejavu@dejavu.com.au

Web site: www.dejavu.com.au

Innkeepers: Beverley & Gerard Goris

Rates: A$135-A$210 per double includes full breakfast

Rated: ****1/2 RACV

Number of rooms: 6 Queen

Baths: 6 Ensuite, some with spas

Services & amenities: Canoe and boat hire, cruises, BBQ, massage

Restrictions: No smoking; no children

Handicap access: no

Emeu Inn

T he Emeu Inn, a restored 1857 hotel located an hour north of Melbourne in the heart of Victoria, offers visitors a tempting combination of luxury accommodations and gourmet food. When the hotel was first built, Portuguese inhabited the area and the current name "Emeu" refers to the Portuguese word for ostrich. The painstaking restoration places great emphasis on the ambience of each room. Three elegant guest suites feature queen-sized beds, private ensuites, a comfortable sitting area, and period style furnishings. Outside, a private garden provides lovely shaded areas for relaxing. There is also a guest lounge offering tea and coffee, cold drinks, biscuits, games, and current reading material. The Brady Suite, named after the first owner of the hotel, features a large spa bath; The Charlett Suite, named after the first licensee of the hotel, features a wood-burning fireplace; and the Heidi Suite, named after the owner's favorite pug, features a private entrance and large spa bath. Hosts Fred and Leslye Thies like to pamper their guests with gastronomic delights in Fred's eponymous restaurant. Fred combines the culinary traditions of Europe, Asia, and Australia with special treats from his native Germany. Hearty country breakfasts, included in the tariff, are enjoyed in the wood paneled restaurant, which was once a concert hall. There are also numerous special packages available to guests that take advantage of the culinary delights offered here. Several incorporate two or three day getaways that include dinner, bed and breakfast.

Leslye has thoughtfully prepared several itineraries for the region, with suggestions of activities including a visit to the nearby Pink Cliffs, a tour of the local boutique wineries, or a drive around Lake Eppalock. For anyone who enjoys fresh country air, delicious food, crackling log fires, and superb Shiraz, this delightful inn provides a memorable retreat in an Australian bush setting.

Name: Emeu Inn Restaurant and Bed & Breakfast

Category: Bed & Breakfast

Location: Central/Goldfields region; Heathcote (nearest city)

Address: 187 High Street, Heathcote, VIC 3523

Phone: Tel. 61 3 5433 2668 **Fax** 61 3 5433 4022

E-mail: emeuinn@netcon.net.au

Web site: www.babs.com.au/vic/emeuinn.htm

Innkeepers: Fred & Leslye Thies

Rates: A$ 140 per double includes full breakfast; Other packages available

Rated: ****½ RACV

Number of rooms: 3 Queen

Baths: 3 Ensuite

Services & amenities: Guest lounge, Licensed restaurant

Restrictions: No smoking indoors

Handicap access: yes

Glynt Manor

Built by descendents of Victoria's first permanent white settlers as a holiday retreat overlooking Port Phillip Bay, romantic Glynt Manor provides the perfect setting to enjoy old world grace and hospitality. The impressive residence is surrounded by manicured gardens, many of which were established more than 70 years ago. Exquisite floral arrangements can be found inside and out, with roses particularly plentiful. A stroll through the gardens leads to an archway and intimate area with garden bench and statuary. Continue past the circular bed of cannas to the open lawn with a wisteria covered summerhouse and tropical garden. The poplar, silver birch, and pine trees have witnessed the evolution of this grand property from a farm, to a holiday house, to a private family home, and finally to an exclusive bed and breakfast that is meticulously operated by owners Mark Callan and William Gilchrist .

The imposing stucco and granite mansion, its tower engulfed by Virginia Creeper, offers exceptional guest accommodations. Meticulously renovated during the 1980's, each of the individual king and queen suites provide bedroom, bathroom, and sitting room with all of the amenities you would expect from a grand hotel. The drawing, dining, and sitting rooms are furnished with tasteful antiques, and a fine collection of paintings by Australian and European artists are displayed throughout the house. Breakfast is enjoyed in the vast garden room with elegant arched windows that afford a view across Port Phillip Bay to the city of Melbourne.

Glynt Manor provides the ideal base to explore the outstanding attractions of the Mornington Peninsula, arguably Melbourne's best kept secret. Some of the highlights include arts and craft markets, antique stores, coastal and bushwalks, and koala and penguin reserves. The region has much of Victoria's earliest history, excellent golf courses, great restaurants, and one of Australia's finest wine producing regions. A variety of private Wildlife and Heritage Tours are designed to introduce visitors to the unique attractions around Melbourne's islands, bays, and peninsula. With pick-up available from Melbourne and accommodations at Glynt Manor, this is an ideal way to experience the beauty, style, and historic sites of the Mornington Peninsula while enjoying some of the finest restaurants and vineyards in the country.

Name: Glynt Manor

Category: Country Manor

Location: Mornington Peninsula region; Mornington (nearest city)

Address: 16 Bay Rd., Mt. Martha, VIC 3934

Phone: Tel. 61 3 5974 1216 **Fax** 61 3 5974 2546

E-mail: glynt@smart.net.au

Web site: www.glynt.com.au

Innkeepers: Mark Callan & William Gilchrist

Rates: From A$275 per double includes breakfast

Rated: **** 1/2 RACV

Number of rooms: Garden & Bay view suites

Baths: Ensuite

Services & amenities: Licensed, tennis court, formal gardens, specialized tours

Handicap access: no

Holcombe Country Retreat

H olcombe Country Retreat is situated in a secluded country setting in Victoria's Central Highlands. It is just seven minutes from the Mineral Spa resort towns of Daylesford and Hepburn Springs, and only one hour from Melbourne. Built in 1891 by Irish immigrants, Holcombe House is a beautifully preserved brick Victorian homestead that has remained in the Marshall family for over a century. The rooms of the homestead are furnished with family antiques and heirlooms handed down for generations, and each of the main rooms is decorated in the period style with warm pastel colors. Original features, like the iron lacework of the verandah, slate-tiled roof, ornate plasterwork, open fireplaces, and marble and polished walnut mantelpieces, have been carefully retained. With three spacious bedrooms, each looking out onto the verandah and the fields beyond, the house can comfortably sleep six to eight people.

The two-story Holcombe Lodge, overlooking a gentle pastoral landscape, is an exclusive, self-contained, modern dwelling that provides fine country living of the highest standard. Spacious indoor and outdoor areas, a full country kitchen, dual spa, and barbeque area, are just some of the features of this special place. The Lodge boasts two luxuriously-appointed bedrooms with granite bathrooms. The upstairs ensuite even has panoramic views from both the spa bath and double shower. Downstairs, the living room is dominated by a marvelous stone fireplace and mantel. Both the Homestead and Lodge sit alone in tranquil and surreal natural beauty, offering guests complete privacy and total luxury. Provisions for a generous country breakfast are included in the tariff, and for guests wishing to be truly indulged, Annette will provide a picnic hamper—or can arrange an intimate dinner in the Lodge or the Homestead's formal Regency-style dining room.

Set on 800 acres of rolling hills with commanding views of the surrounding countryside, the sheep and cattle grazing property is one of the largest in the area. With both old world charm and luxurious amenities, Holcombe Country Retreat evokes fantasies of life in a bygone era. There's a 124 foot waterfall on the property, plenty of opportunities for bushwalking, and an abundance of wild kangaroo. There's also a floodlit tennis court, mountain bikes, trout fishing, lazy evening barbeques (perhaps with fresh fish caught on the property), champagne on the verandahs at sunset, romantic candlelit dinners, or evenings curled up in front of a crackling log fire.

Name: Holcombe Country Retreat

Category: Self-contained Homestead & Lodge

Location: Central/Highlands region; Daylesford (nearest city)

Address: Holcombe Rd/RMB 3683, Glenlyon, VIC 3461

Phone: Tel. 61 3 5348 7514 **Fax** 61 3 5348 7742

E-mail: holcombe@netconnect.com.au

Web site: www.babs.com.au/vic/holcombe.htm

Innkeepers: John & Annette Marshall

Rates: From A$200 per double mid-week

Number of rooms: 3 in home, 2 in lodge

Baths: Ensuite, Private

Services & amenities: Tennis, trout fishing, mountain bikes, meals provided by prior arrangement

Handicap access: no

Howqua Dale

T ucked away in exquisitely landscaped grounds on the banks of the Howqua River, is a secluded resort that has established itself as one of the leading country house hotels in the world. A combination gourmet cooking school and sophisticated country inn, Howqua Dale Gourmet Retreat was established in 1977 by two old school friends as a haven for those wishing to enjoy gourmet food and excellent wines in a relaxed rural environment.

Host Sarah Stegley, a wine expert who once worked as an agricultural scientist for the United Nations, and gourmet chef Marieke Brugman, a noted Australian food connoisseur, provide complementary creative talents, which are the force behind this exclusive gourmet getaway. Originally the Stegley summer home, Howqua Dale is a rustically elegant country homestead with six first class guestrooms accommodating up to 12 guests. Each of the comfortable ensuite rooms has private access to the garden and an individual decorative theme. The Balinese Room has batik bedspreads and Asian wallhangings, while the storybook Victorian Room features dainty broderie Anglais and nineteenth-century prints. The innkeepers' passion for natural light is evidenced in the skylights and the wide windows providing panoramic views of the neighboring valleys.

A contemporary annex of cedar and glass sits next to the original homestead, housing the inspirational kitchen, cooking school, and magnificent dining room with floor-to-ceiling windows. Here, creatively presented meals emphasizing local produce and imaginative flavor combinations, are accompanied by selections from the well-stocked vintage wine cellar. Vegetable Terrine Provencal with basil and pine nut mayonnaise, mussel and leek tarts with saffron champagne sauce, and roast duck sausage with ginger Sauterne sauce, are just a sample of the entrees that might be found on the ever-changing menu. Although dress is casual at Howqua Dale, guests sometimes choose to dress up on Saturday nights.

During the day, there is no lack of recreational activities. A sparkling freshwater pool, tennis court, walking and bridle trails, and trout fishing, are all available on the 40 acre property. Wild parrots and kookaburras make the only noise, and a nearby nature preserve provides guests with the opportunity to see other Australian wildlife in their natural environment. In addition to the extraordinary Howqua Dale country weekends, Marieke and Sarah offer gastronomic cycling tours of Australian wine regions that incorporate charming accommodations, VIP wine tastings and gourmet meals.

Name: Howqua Dale Gourmet Retreat

Category: Country House Hotel

Location: North East region; Mansfield (nearest city)

Address: Howqua River Rd./ P.O. 379, Mansfield, VIC 3724

Phone: Tel. 61 3 5777 3503 **Fax** 61 3 5777 3896

E-mail: howqua@mansfield.net.au

Innkeepers: Sarah Stegley & Marieke Brugman

Rates: From A$650 per person all inclusive Friday night - Sunday night

Number of rooms: 6 Queen

Baths: 6 Ensuite

Services & amenities: Swimming pool, tennis, horse-riding, fly-fishing, bushwalking, birdwatching, gastronomic tours

Restrictions: No children

Handicap access: no

Keebles of Clunes

A s Victoria's first gold mining town, Clunes once boasted a population of 30,000. Today the tiny township is home to only about 1,000 people, but the legacy of the affluent gold mining days remains. Nestled in a small hamlet beside the Creswick Creek, Clunes' streets are still lined with numerous buildings of historical interest including the former Telegraph Hotel (1863). This grand Georgian building was transformed into an elegant English-style guesthouse in 1989, and over the years, has developed a reputation as one of Victoria's more prestigious B&B's.

Owners Tim Hayes and Michael Waugh, previously from Melbourne, have furnished the three lounge areas, the formal dining room, and the breakfast room with antiques and original works of art. Log fires are located in the dining room, the main lounge, and the library/billiard room with its impressive array of books. Upstairs, the former ballroom has been divided into six large, comfortable, private guestrooms, each with full ensuite facilities and one with a spa bath. The rooms are delightfully decorated with Australian period furniture.

The breakfast room has a glass atrium that overlooks three acres of English style gardens, a pleasant location for guests wishing afternoon tea or a glass of wine. Evening meals are served in the elegant ambiance of the dining room with its interesting collection of royal British and Russian memorabilia. Over the years, Keebles has established a well-earned reputation for food and is consistently included in Victoria's respected The Age Good Food Guide. During the week, a set three-course menu is available, and on Saturdays, a more varied four-course meal is served. A main entrée may consist of a tender fillet of rack of lamb in a rich wine sauce, or for those wishing something more traditional, a steak and Guinness pie. The hosts take advantage of local products, when possible, and can cater to dietary requests with notice. While stressing high quality service, they also know how to respect the privacy of their guests and are judicious with their personal attention.

Clunes, which has remained much as it was in the nineteenth century, has a lot to offer. It is close to the regional centers of Ballarat and Bendigo, the spa and mineral district of Daylesford, and over 15 boutique wineries. It has also recently established a "sister city" association with Coloma, California, so don't be surprised to see the 'Stars and Stripes' flying over the Town Square.

Name: Keebles of Clunes

Category: Bed & Breakfast

Location: Central/Goldfields region; Clunes (nearest city)

Address: 114 Bailey St., Clunes, VIC 3370

Phone: Tel. 61 3 5345 3220 **Fax** 61 3 5345 3200

E-mail: keeblesofclunes@bigpond.com

Web site: www.ballarat.com/keebles.htm

Innkeepers: Tim Hayes & Michael Waugh

Rates: From A$120-190 per double includes full breakfast; dinner by arrangement

Rated: ****½ RACV

Number of rooms: 8 Queen

Baths: 8 Ensuite

Services & amenities: 3 guest lounges, games room, licensed restaurant

Restrictions: Children by arrangment

Handicap access: no

Koendidda Country House

E xperience the sublime. Koendidda is a gracious, Georgian estate built in the 1850's with a goldrush fortune. It has been tenderly restored and now operates as one of Victoria's most evocative country retreats. At first glance, the imposing manor house conjures up images of a time when elegance and serenity were an art. Warm and inviting, Koendidda lives up to its expectations with generous attributes at every turn. Open fires, comfortable verandahs, and beautifully furnished sitting and dining rooms, all reflect exquisite taste. Five luxurious upstairs bedrooms, each with an ensuite, look out over the gardens below.

Nestled on 4 hectares of delightful grounds, Koendidda guests can picnic down by the lake, read a book under an ancient River Red Gum, or wait quietly by the Indigo Creek for a platypus to appear. Each time of year offers different delights, from golden autumn leaves to the perfumes of spring, and the property seems to absorb the best from each season.

Hosts Ann & Geoff are accomplished hosts who take great pride in their ability to make their guests feel at ease. Their love of life is reflected in every detail of Koendidda, and a warm reception immediately makes guests feel comfortable. Step into their world and leave everything else behind as you soak up the elegant country ambiance. The Crawfords' leisurely country breakfasts are worth relishing, and in the evening, Rutherglen, Beechworth and the quaint hamlet of Chiltern are close enough to drive to for dinner. Even better is a fine meal cooked by Ann (by prior arrangement) served in the formal dining room. Ann has a creative instinct in the kitchen, and her talents range from gourmet vegetarian cuisine to classic Australian fare. The meal is perfect with a bottle or two of local wine collected during the day. A hiatus at Koeniddida is memorable on a myriad of levels, from the incomparable accommodations, to the superb, friendly service and attention to detail. It's no wonder they're included in the prestigious The Age Good Food Guide and have been voted two times in a row as one of Victoria's Top Ten Hospitality Establishments. The kudos are well deserved.

Name: Koendidda Country House

Category: Guesthouse

Location: Northeast region; Albury/Wodonga; 25 km (nearest city)

Address: Pooley's Rd/RMB 2137, Barnawartha, VIC 3688

Phone: Tel. 61 2 6026 7340 **Fax** 61 2 6026 7300

Innkeepers: Ann & Geoff Crawford

Rates: Call for tariff/includes full breakfast

Rated: ****1/2 RACV

Number of rooms: 4 Queen, 1 King or Twin

Baths: 5 Ensuite

Services & amenities: Two sitting rooms; two dining rooms; log fires; many nearby natural attractions

Restrictions: No smoking inside, no children, no pets

Handicap access: no

Narrabeen Cottage

P hillip Island, just 130 kilometers south of Melbourne, has long been known for its beautiful coastline—from quiet and often empty sandy coves, to long, open surf beaches. The island is also home to thousands of fairy penguins, whose nightly struggles out of the water to feed their young nestled in the sand dunes, is a ritual that is increasingly popular with camera-bearing tourists.

Another reason to visit Phillip Island is Narrabeen Cottage. Located on the northern shore of Phillip Island at the southern edge of Westernport Bay, this seaside guesthouse is set in delightful gardens on a quiet, tree-lined street only a minute walk from the beach. Built in the 1920's for the retired captain of the Narrabeen, the ferry that ran across to nearby Stoney Point, the former family home now provides cottage-style accommodations for a limited number of discerning guests. In winter, the log fire in the comfortable guest lounge offers warmth to relax and read by, while in the summer, a wide, shady verandah filled with plants invites guests to sit back with a cool drink.

Narrabeen Cottage's real strength is in its superb kitchen. Hosts Marlene Forrester and Peter Berry, former guests who fell in love with the place, take great pride in the range and quality of the homemade food they provide—including breads, patés, jams, marmalades, sweet and savory sauces, biscuits, ice creams, preserved fruit, and fresh scones. Once the hosts have established the individual food preferences of their guests, a new menu is designed daily around the best fresh, local produce available. The result is a fixed menu with three or more courses that allows the hosts to serve delicious and inventive meals, often with French accents, at individual candlelit tables in the intimate dining room.

The island abounds with wildlife—penguins, a large colony of seals, and a substantial koala population. Tennis courts and a golf course are both within easy walking distance, and the European-style gardens boast over 150 rosebushes. Narrabeen Cottage has earned a devoted clientele, so it's wise to book in advance. Gourmet weekend getaways are especially popular and include dinner, bed and breakfast on Friday and Saturday, Devonshire tea on Saturday afternoon, and a delectable brunch on Sunday. Mid-week bed & breakfast only tariffs are also available, and midweek guests receive the same wonderful gourmet cuisine, comfort, and hospitality.

Name: Narrabeen Cottage

Category: Guesthouse

Location: Phillip Island region; Cowes; 1/2 km (nearest city)

Address: 16 Steele St., Cowes, VIC 3922

Phone: Tel. 61 3 5952 2062 **Fax** 61 3 5952 3670

Innkeepers: Peter Berry & Marlene Forrester

Rates: From A$240 per double Saturday/A$210 midweek includes dinner, bed & breakfast (midweek B&B available)

Rated: **** RACV

Number of rooms: 5

Baths: 4 Ensuite

Services & amenities: Restaurant, cottage garden, nearby tennis, golf & beach

Restrictions: No smoking indoors; No children

Handicap access: no

Peppers Delgany

P eppers Delgany, located on Victoria's Mornington Peninsula, is an
oasis of calm luxury and sophistication just one and a half hours from
Melbourne. The property was originally the private estate of a
wealthy Melburnian, Harold Armytage, who named it Delgany after a small
village in County Wicklow, Ireland. The impressive sandstone building, built
in the style of a European castle with Roman arches and crenellated tower,
was built in 1923 atop a hill overlooking the quiet seaside town of Portsea. It is
surrounded by five hectares of secluded manicured gardens—with its own
tennis courts, croquet lawn, and heated swimming pool—and adjoins the
acclaimed Portsea Golf Course.

With only 32 spacious suites and guestrooms, Peppers Delgany is a small
retreat with an air of intimacy, rest, and relaxation. Inside, the atmosphere is
elegant and peaceful with an accent on country house comfort and unobtru-
sive service. The public lounge area boasts a huge open fire, concert grand

piano, relaxing lounges, and beautiful artwork. Guests can unwind with a work out, spa, sauna, aromatherapy massage, or beauty treatment at the on-site Portsea Spa. Afterwards, indulge at the renowned Castle restaurant, where executive chef, Craig Gorton, offers an innovative modern Australian menu that marries Eastern and European influences. Away from the tranquility of Peppers Delgany, guests can enjoy all the Mornington Peninsula has to offer, including great beaches, dolphin watch cruises, fishing excursions, and wine tasting at award-winning local vineyards.

Name: Peppers Delgany

Category: Country House Hotel

Location: Mornington Peninsula region; Portsea (nearest city)

Address: Point Nepean Rd, Portsea, VIC 3944

Phone: Tel. 61 3 5984 4000 **Fax** 61 3 5984 4022

E-mail: delgany@peppers.com.au

Web site: www.peppers.com.au

Innkeepers: Wes Mann

Rates: From A$265 per double/B&B package

Number of rooms: 32 Suites

Baths: Private

Services & amenities: Portsea Spa offering health & beauty treatments including aromatherapy, massage, yoga; tennis courts, pool, golf nearby

Restrictions: 2 night minimum on weekends

Handicap access: no

Pines Ridge

P ines Ridge Country Retreat Bed & Breakfast is a true sanctuary where guests can soak up the stillness and serenity of the Mornington Peninsula. Nestled in two acres of garden planted with native and exotic trees, shrubs and flowers, Pines Ridge offers proximity to all of the area's major attractions while providing peace and privacy. The house is on a ten acre property, half of which is now a vineyard, and hosts Mary and Paul O'Connor plan to begin cellar door sales in 2000. Just an hour from Melbourne, this relaxing bed & breakfast is a perfect refuge from the stress of the city.

The private guests' wing at Pines Ridge consists of original timber cottages, built in the late 1800's, connected by a well-designed modern extension, which contains two additional bedrooms and guests' lounge. All rooms have views of the verdant garden in which native birds and butterflies abound. After a restful night sleep, enjoy a satisfying breakfast while engulfed by the lush greenery. The guests' breakfast room is fully equipped for guests to make snacks and small meals with tea, coffee, and other provisions complimentary to guests.

The bucolic setting is so calming, you may find it difficult to leave this lovely country retreat, but if you do, the Mornington Peninsula offers a multitude of attractions and activities. Nearby are vineyards, horse riding, bushwalking, fine restaurants, gardens, and beautiful rural and coastal landscapes. Pine Ridge is also only five minutes drive from the famous Red Hill Market (first Saturday of each month from September to May), ten minutes from bay and ocean beaches, and thirty minutes from the picturesque and historic resorts of Sorrento and Portsea.

Name: Pines Ridge Country Retreat

Category: Bed & Breakfast

Location: Mornington Peninsula region; Mornington (nearest city)

Address: 255 Main Creek Rd., Main Ridge, VIC 3928

Phone: Tel. 61 3 5989 6170 **Fax** 61 3 5989 6459

Web site: www.bol.com.au/pines.html

Innkeepers: Mary & Paul O'Connor

Rates: From A$150 per double includes breakfast

Number of rooms: 3 Queen, 1 Twin

Baths: 2 Private, 1 Share

Services & amenities: Guest lounge, games room

Restrictions: No pets

Handicap access: no

PINES RIDGE
COUNTRY RETREAT

Red Hill Retreat

R ed Hill Retreat is a boutique country house situated in the heart of the spectacular Mornington Peninsula, an area known for exceptional quality, "cool climate" wines, regional cuisine, and a vibrant art community. This enchanting forest haven is only minutes away from the sheltered beaches of Port Phillip and Western Port Bays or the rugged coast of Bass Strait. At every turn, there are incredible discoveries. A secluded forest valley where native birds provide perfect wake-up calls, sweet mountain air, drinking rainwater straight from heaven, and pathways that meander along the creek through lush tree-ferns. Just over an hour south east of Melbourne, the rural mountain retreat is a working farm with native gardens that provides an exquisite environmental experience.

Two self-contained guest suites at opposite ends of a rambling mudbrick homestead, showcase hosts Trevor and Jan's extraordinary attention to detail. The passive solar mudbrick hideaways feature expansive glass doors opening to private, sunny courtyards and the forest. Each guest suite has a private entrance through the garden and into a lounge-dining area with log fire, cozy chairs, books, and refreshing country treats. The Forest Suite has two queen-size bedrooms, each with private access to the bathroom. The Orchard Suite has one king-size (or twin-share) bedroom with ensuite bathroom. The elegant Chloe Room, with its iron bed, tasteful decor, and floor to ceiling views, is indicative of the high quality accommodations.

In the morning , let Jan pamper you with a delicious breakfast. Menus vary with the seasons and take advantage of the organic produce grown in the rich, volcanic soil of the property. However, you can always count on home-baked breads and farm-fresh eggs. The cooked breakfast is served in the privacy of your suite—by the crackling log-fire in winter, or in a shady garden room in summer. There are a number of relaxing walks on the property and depending on the season, you can pick your own fruit in the organic orchard. You'll also find abundant birdlife along with possums, echidnas, and an occasional wallaby or koala. For those who want to take advantage of the area, there are bay and ocean beaches, wineries, restaurants, galleries, scenic views (Arthurs Seat Lookout), as well as golf, tennis, fishing, horseback riding, surfing, and shops—all within a short distance of the perfectly delightful Red Hill Retreat.

Name: Red Hill Retreat

Category: Self-contained suites

Location: Mornington Peninsula region; Mornington (nearest city)

Address: RMB 6262, William Rd., Red Hill, VIC 3937

Phone: Tel. 61 3 5989 2035 **Fax** 61 3 5989 2427

E-mail: rhr@alphalink.com.au

Web site: www.redhillretreat.com.au

Innkeepers: Jan & Trevor Brandon

Rates: From A$120-150 per double includes full breakfast

Rated: Australian Tourism Operators

Number of rooms: 2 self-contained suites

Baths: Private

Services & amenities: Library, piano, games, log fires, microwaves in suites

Restrictions: No smoking; children by arrangement

Handicap access: no

Rotherwood

S ituated 'on the hill' in Richmond, Rotherwood is at the heart of Melbourne's attractions. Guests enjoy elegant, self-contained accommodations within walking distance of the Melbourne Cricket Ground, the Royal Botanic Gardens, the National Tennis Centre, and the bustle of Bridge Road's shops and restaurants.

Rotherwood is a five-minute tram ride from the City and has easy access to the National Gallery, the Concert Hall, Crown Casino, and Southbank promenade. After a busy day, have a bite to eat at the Richmond Hill Cafe & Larder or the world famous Vlado's. If you want to soak up the neighborhood atmosphere, drink with the locals at the famous Barrassi's Hotel just up the corner, or retreat and relax in peace in this home-away-from-home.

This beautifully appointed Victorian-era apartment has a private entrance and large sitting room with French doors that lead to a terrace overlooking the garden. The comfortable bedroom has a queen-size bed and a private bathroom with a claw footed tub. A separate dining room with cooking facilities offers convenience, whether it's preparing a picnic lunch or enjoying a private dinner. In the morning, a lovely French breakfast is provided. This graceful residence will suit a single or couple with the option of a foldout bed for families. Transport to and from Melbourne Airport is available, and many local activities can be arranged including golf excursions.

Name: Rotherwood

Category: B&B Apartment

Location: Melbourne region; Melbourne (nearest city)

Address: 13 Rotherwood St., Richmond, VIC 3121

Phone: Tel. 61 3 9428 6758 **Fax** 61 3 9428 6758

E-mail: rotherwood@a1.com.au

Web site: www.babs.com.au/vic/rotherwood.htm

Innkeepers: Flossie Sturzaker

Rates: A$150 per double includes French breakfast

Number of rooms: 1 Queen

Baths: Private

Services & amenities: Sitting room, terrace, garden, dining room with cooking facilities

Handicap access: yes

Sundowner Lodge

S undowner Lodge Guesthouse offers the ultimate in boutique accommodations. Built in 1996 by hosts Fay & Di, Sundowner Lodge is situated in Venus Bay, South Gippsland, which borders the Cape Liptrap Coastal Park. The tranquil atmosphere of this guesthouse envelopes you the moment you cross the threshold. Once inside, you'll catch a glimpse of the elegant restaurant and cocktail bar where an intimate dinner can be enjoyed. In the late afternoon, discover what the term "sundowner" means as you sit on the front pergola surrounded by beautiful fernery and watch the sun setting over the sand dunes. Upstairs, Sundowner Lodge offers four-star accommodations in a choice of four queen-sized guestrooms. Each is tastefully decorated to take advantage of the unique coastal location, and each features full ensuites and all amenities including TV, clock radio, heat, and ceiling fans.

Romance is the key word at Sundowner. Guests can relax in the spa and unwind after a busy day while sipping champagne. Once the sun dips behind the horizon, amble downstairs to the licensed, a la carte restaurant where an extensive menu features fresh, local fish and produce. The best part of staying at Sundowner Lodge is that after a candlelit dinner, guests need not drive. Instead, they can sink into a Chesterfield couch in the comfortable 'conservatory' area with a coffee and liquor before retiring for the night.

Breakfast at Sundowner is enjoyed in the dining room, which takes on a different ambiance during the day. Look out over the tranquil gardens and feast on a selection of fruit juices, cereals, eggs from Sundowner's hens, bacon, sausages, fresh fruit platters, and toast. Afterwards, take advantage of the area by visiting the coastal village of Inverloch, or the nearby Wonthaggi Coal Mine where coal was mined up until 1968. Venus Bay is situated on the coast halfway between Phillips Island and Wilsons Promontory, and guests can take advantage of the natural delights of both locations. Those who have had the opportunity to stay at Sundowner are enthusiastic in their praise and quick to comment that this "great little haven is excellent in every respect."

Name: Sundowner Lodge Guesthouse & Restaurant

Category: B&B/Guesthouse

Location: Gippsland region; Inverloch; 35 km (nearest city)

Address: 128 Inlet View Rd/PO Box 789, Venus Bay, VIC 3956

Phone: Tel. 61 3 5663 7099 **Fax** 61 3 5663 7674

E-mail: sundown@tpg.com.au

Web site: www.interbed.com.au/sundowner.htm

Innkeepers: Fay Brown & Diane Thomas

Rates: From A$110 per double includes full breakfast

Rated: ****RACV

Number of rooms: 4 Queen

Baths: 4 Ensuite

Services & amenities: Spa, TV, tea/coffee, Air-con, Licensed restaurant, conservatory

Restrictions: No smoking inside; no pets

Handicap access: no

The Tilba

O ne of Melbourne's most gracious small hotels, The Tilba has a well-deserved reputation for pampering its guests. Built as a private home in 1907, the building has been meticulously restored to the Victorian elegance of its heyday. Would-be guests should book well in advance, as this is a favorite among knowledgeable travelers.

Lofty ceilings, garnished with intricate roses and cornices, original leaded glass windows, and delightful Victorian furnishings, help to create the timeless environment of The Tilba. The 15 guestrooms are individually furnished and decorated with appealing simplicity, using period antiques and colors appropriate to the era. Ensuite bathrooms are specious, with such personal touches as wildflower soaps, Victorian shaving mirrors, and thick fluffy towels.

Continental breakfast is the only meal served at The Tilba, but it's a generous offering, with freshly squeezed orange juice, freshly brewed tea or coffee, and croissants, brioches, or bagels with a choice of conserves. Guests may have breakfast in their room, in the airy glass-roofed atrium amidst a profusion of palms and greenery, or in the enchanting Norman Lindsay dining room. The atrium and dining room are also open throughout the day, serving tea or coffee and delicious homemade pastries.

Situated in the trendy suburb of South Yarra, The Tilba overlooks a 100 acre park that is perfect for a leisurely stroll amid the sounds of kookaburras and cockatoos. It is also conveniently close to the activity of Melbourne's City Centre. Guests can enjoy a short walk to the Victorian Arts Centre, wander down St. Kilda Road, or browse in South Yarra's exclusive shopping area where boutiques intermingle with a rich variety of restaurants and coffee shops

Name: The Tilba

Category: Town House Hotel

Location: Melbourne region; Melbourne (nearest city)

Address: Toorak Rd. West & Domain St., South Yarra, VIC 3141

Phone: Tel. 61 3 9867 8844 **Fax** 61 3 9867 6567

Innkeepers: General Manager

Rates: A$140–195 per double includes continental breakfast

Number of rooms: 15 Doubles

Baths: Ensuite

Services & amenities: Room heaters, celing fans, telephones in all rooms

Restrictions: No children under 12

Handicap access: no

Tuki Retreat

T he one of a kind Tuki Retreat is just an hour and a half's drive from
Melbourne in the heart of Victoria's Gold and Spa country. Billed as
an establishment that incorporates trout fishing, a licensed restaurant,
natural springs, sheep farming, and accommodations, it's truly an extraordinary place to unwind, eat wonderful food, and sleep wonderful sleep.

To find Tuki, you have to drive through "Stoney Rises," a large historic
1850's sheep grazing property. Two kilometers down a private road, you'll
find a series of exquisite, uninterrupted views. In the center of the grazing
property are Tuki's stone cottages, which look out over the Loddon-Cam-
paspe valley. The distant horizon is cut by an outline of the Great Dividing
Range. The cottages are surrounded by dry stone walls, landscaped gardens,
and established trees. Each cozy, Colonial-style cottage has an open stone
fireplace, cathedral ceiling, and a private verandah. The master bedrooms
have a queen-size bed with large, fluffy pillows and electric blankets. There is
a double sofa bed in the sitting area to accommodate additional guests if
necessary, and one of the stone cottages features a spa. The Miner's Cottage
is a restored heritage cottage with three bedrooms, a master bedroom, and
two other bedrooms with four single beds. It has a cast woodbox in the living
area and is ideal for families or groups. All the cottages are self-contained and
include provisions for a self serve breakfast. After a delightful night's sleep,
pad into the rustic kitchen and whip up a real Tuki brekkie of eggs and
homemade lamb sausages

At Tuki, there is also a licensed restaurant featuring fresh regional food and local wine. The restaurant is open daily from 11 am until 6 pm, and evening meals can be served later in your cottage. Tuki is the home of serious trout, and hosts Robert and Jan have been perfecting this succulent fish for well over a decade. Be forewarned: one nibble of the freshest trout pate you've ever tasted, and you will be hooked.

The Tuki farm provides a quiet time away, with private walks and breathtaking views. Magnificent sunsets and unique bird life abound, and guests often feel they've been transported to another time and place. Feel like a little exertion? Step outside, cast a line, and snare your lunch or dinner; fresh trout is at your fingertips. Cottage guests have complimentary use of fishing gear and access to eight ponds abundant with rainbow trout. Afterwards, while Robert cleans and cooks your prize catch, you can contemplate the serene sunset from your deck chair by the lake.

Name: Tuki Retreat

Category: Self-contained cottages

Location: Central region; Smeaton (nearest city)

Address: Stoney Rises, Smeaton, VIC 3364

Phone: Tel. 61 3 5345 6233 **Fax** 61 3 5345 6377

E-mail: info@tuki.com.au

Web site: www.tuki.tmx.com.au

Innkeepers: Robert & Jan Jones

Rates: From A$120 per double includes breakfast; weekend dinner, bed & breakfast packages available

Number of rooms: 3 cottages

Baths: Private

Services & amenities: Licensed restaurant, fishing gear & 8 trout-filled ponds, TV & fireplace in cottage

Handicap access: no

Vereker House

V ereker House is a charming traditional guesthouse with a rustic atmosphere, ambience, charm, and a reputation for quality home cooked
food. The house affords panoramic views across Corner Inlet Marine
Park, the dairy farms of the Yanakie Isthmus, the rugged north face of the
Vereker Mountain Range, and other peaks of Wilsons Promontory. The combination of mountain, land, sea, sky, and southern light provides fabulous
opportunities for photographers, artists, and tourists alike. Vereker House is
located just 3 km from the boundary of Wilsons Promontory National Park
where you can select one of the many coves for a quiet picnic or refreshing
swim.

Back at the comfortable bed and breakfast, guests can relax by the log fire
in the lounge hall on cool evenings. Wide eaves and massive adobe construction keep night temperatures even throughout summer. Enjoy a four- course
dinner prepared from fresh, local produce (request when booking, please)
along with local wines. There is also a well stocked reading and tape/CD
library, and for a real treat, you can also set up the telescope for observation
of the night sky. South Gippsland's almost pollution-free atmosphere provides spectacular views of the Southern Cross and Milky Way.

Name: Vereker House

Category: Bed & Breakfast/Guest House

Location: Wilson's Promontory region; Foster; 30 KM (nearest city)

Address: 10 Iluka Close, Foley Rd., Yanakie, Gippsland, VIC 3960

Phone: Tel. 61 3 5687 1431 **Fax** 61 3 5687 1480

E-mail: vereker@tpg.com.au

Innkeepers: Mary & John O'Shea

Rates: A$50–65 per person Double/Twin share

Rated: ****RACV

Number of rooms: 4

Baths: 4

Services & amenities: Lounge, Dining Room, Log Fire, Stereo, Library

Restrictions: No smoking indoors

Handicap access: no

Warrawee Homestead

Built in the 1860's as an inn for the Cobb & Cove Stage Coach route, award-winning Warrawee Homestead has a long and colorful history. The property became a working farm until the turn of the century when it became an inebriates' colony. It was abandoned until 1983, when it was purchased by a couple of urban escapees who initiated the extensive renovation necessary to recreate Warrawee's original Victorian character. The improvements, made with painstaking attention to detail, have apparently met with the approval of Warawee's longest standing guest, Joe the Blacksmith, a friendly ghost who is still known to pay occasional visits.

Owners Jane and Kieran Scott live in private quarters above the area of the homestead reserved for guests. With more than a decade of experience owning and operating a bed and breakfast, the couple are knowledgeable hosts who know how to treat their guests. Warrawee boasts four spacious bedrooms with ensuites (two with spa) and a fully self-contained cottage in the garden. All the rooms have beautiful brass beds, and each has been individually and comfortably furnished in the style of the period. Spare doonas are thoughtfully provided under each bed for those unexpectedly chilly evenings, and open fires warm the lounge and dining room. A guest lounge, lovely gardens, and library complete the picture.

The public restaurant in the homestead has established itself as one of the best in the area, with Jane's mother, Shirley, as the imaginative chef. Diners select from an a la carte menu that changes daily and which features fresh, homegrown produce, local meats, and seafood. Houseguests order breakfast the night before and are served in the sunny, private breakfast room. A choice of fruit from the local orchards, toast, cereals, crumpets, jams, juices, and tea or coffee are offered.

Jane is an accomplished painter who specializes in abstract acrylics. The walls of the homestead have been turned into an art gallery where Jane displays her large canvases as well as the work of other talented local artists. Just an hour's drive from Melbourne, Warrawee Homestead is a world away in terms of atmosphere and pace. The beach is only a 20 minute walk, and there's plenty to do in the area including several historic properties, popular Arthur's Seat (a scenic lookout with chairlift), wineries, and two national parks that feature scenic walks and breathtaking views of Port Phillip Bay.

Name: Warrawee Homestead

Category: Bed & Breakfast

Location: Mornington Peninsula region; Balnarring (nearest city)

Address: 87 Warrawee Rd., Balnarring, VIC 3926

Phone: Tel. 61 3 5983 1729 **Fax** 61 3 5983 5199

E-mail: kieran@waraww.com.au

Innkeepers: Jane & Kieran Scott

Rates: From A$150-165 per double includes full breakfast

Rated: 1998 National Trust Heritage Award

Number of rooms: 4 Double and cottage

Baths: 4 Ensuite (2 with spa)

Services & amenities: Gardens, a la carte restaurant, guest lounge and library

Restrictions: No smoking

Handicap access: yes

Watani Waters

Watani Waters is a unique four and a half star bed and breakfast overlooking the bay on Phillip Island. With its magnificent waterfront views, Watani Waters offers a choice of superbly appointed queen or twin share suites, complete with ensuite bathrooms, comfortable beds, fully equipped kitchens with dining setting, relaxing armchairs, and a glorious sun-drenched north facing balcony. For those who feel like socializing, there is a cozy living room with comfortable seating and a wood fire that's perfect on cold wintery nights. A delightful gourmet breakfast is served each morning by hosts Wendy and Ian who are extremely helpful and enthusiastic about the many delights of their special corner of the world. After your lavish breakfast, breathe in the fresh sea air and enjoy the views of Westernport Bay and the Marina, which are stunning by day and absolutely magical by night. Once you set out, it doesn't take long to discover the many attributes of Phillip Island. The scenic beauty and contrast between coast and country is breathtaking. For those captivated by wildlife, there's the famous Penguin Parade, which takes place on the beach at dusk each day. There's also seals frolicking off Seal Rocks, koalas in easy viewing distance at the Koala Conservation Centre, pelicans fed daily at San Remo pier, and numerous sea birds that constantly delight and entertain.

For those looking for a bit of activity, Phillip Island offers beautiful seaside walks, horseriding on the beach, boating, fishing off the pier, and motor bike or car racing at the world famous Phillip Island Race Track. Of course, there's also shopping with many craft, gift, and antique shops offering hard to find treasures. At the end of the day, unwind on the balcony where you can watch the boats sail in and out of the harbor and view the star-filled night sky, which seems to blanket this charming island.

Name: Watani Waters

Category: Bed & Breakfast

Location: Phillip Island region; Cowes/15 km (nearest city)

Address: 9 Cleeland St, Newhaven, VIC 3925

Phone: Tel. 61 3 5956 6300 **Fax** 61 3 5956 6301

E-mail: watani_waters@bigpond.com

Web site: www.netstar.com.au/watani

Innkeepers: Ian & Wendy Lusted

Rates: A$125-160 includes full breakfast

Rated: ****1/2 RACV

Number of rooms: 4 Queen suites

Baths: 4 Private

Services & amenities: Off-street parking, balconies, views, TV, fully equipped kitchens

Restrictions: No smoking indoors; not suitable for children

Handicap access: no

Yaridni

Yaridni—aboriginal for wallaby—is a scenic 2,000 acre merino and wheat property only 10 minutes (13 kms) from Hume Freeway, making it an ideal stopover between Sydney and Melbourne. For those traveling by train, the Siggers will gladly arrange for your pick-up. Yaridni is a great place to experience country life in a rural yet convenient setting. Guests can see kangaroos, native birds, shearing, working sheep dogs, wonderful night skies as well as enjoy gliding, tennis, golf and skiing in season. Only 2½ hours from Melbourne, this ranch-style homestead will immediately feel like home.

Accommodations are in two twin or double rooms with a private bathroom (with spa bath) or one double room with ensuite. Evening meals are served in a formal dining room while breakfast is taken in the large farm kitchen or in the sunny front patio where there are wonderful views of the property. Rhyllis was a cooking demonstrator and teacher who enjoys cooking for guests.

Two-course dinners can be arranged, if requested, when booking and dinner is served with excellent local wines. After dinner, there is a games room with billiard table, table tennis, TV, video player, piano and library.

Seasonal activities can be enjoyed with family members on this host farm. Experience sheep shearing and feeding, or watch sheep dog demonstrations with the beautiful Border Collies—Spotty, Kelly and Jud. There is usually a lamb to bottle-feed and small animals to play with. Scenic drives, wineries, Kelly Country, Winton Raceway and the Murray River are all within a half-hour's drive.

Several options are available at this inviting property including bed & breakfast; dinner, bed & breakfast; or full board. Whatever level of accommodation you choose, you will be made most welcome by the gracious Siggers family.

Name: Yaridni

Category: Farmstay

Location: North East region; Benalla (nearest city)

Address: RMB 1090, Goorambat, VIC 3725

Phone: Tel. 61 3 5764 1273 **Fax** 61 3 5764 1352

E-mail: yaridni@iname.com

Web site: http://business.hde.com.au.yaridni

Innkeepers: Rhyllis Siggers & family

Rates: From A$120 per double includes full breakfast

Rated: **** RACV

Number of rooms: 2 King or Twin, 1 Double

Baths: 1 Ensuite, 1 Share

Services & amenities: Farm activities, games room

Restrictions: No smoking

Handicap access: yes

South Australia

Authentic australia

Discover the Bed & Breakfasts of South Australia;

- *Adelaide* — delightful capital surrounded by parklands.
- *Kangaroo Island* — best place to see Australian animals in their natural environment, including koalas, kangaroos, sea lions and more.
- *Wine Country* — 6 major wine regions including the world famous Barossa Valley.
- *Outback* — unique places like Coober Pedy and the Flinders Ranges.
- *Festivals and Events* — Home to the Adelaide Arts Festival; March 2000.

FOR FREE INFORMATION PLEASE CALL US ON
TOLL FREE *1-888-768-8428*

SouthAustralia
Relax. Indulge. Discover. Enjoy.

VISIT OUR WEB-SITE AT:
www.visit-southaustralia.com.au
OR E-MAIL US AT:
info@southoz.com

A lthough it shares boundaries with each of the mainland states, South Australia has a character distinctly its own with gently rolling countryside, century-old stone mansions, and award-winning wines. Magnificent beaches along with the Mighty Murray River, the colorful Flinders Ranges, and the vast Outback typify Australia's driest state.

Adelaide, the state capital, is one of Australia's best planned cities. Laid out in a straight-forward grid pattern, Adelaide is flat and compact and easy to get around. Beautifully manicured parks and squares are interspersed throughout the city, catering to the many pedestrians who explore Adelaide on foot. The relaxed pace of this gracious city, however, comes alive several times a year for special events. The International Horse Trials, held each October or November, are a prestigious three-day event, and the highly acclaimed Adelaide Arts Festival (and accompanying Fringe Festival), hosted at the Festival Centre every other year, epitomizes the city's cultural spirit.

The Adelaide Hills, with their stately homes and giant gum trees, flank the city and are just a 20 minute drive away. The country atmosphere and natural beauty of the hills attracts visitors to the many tiny towns tucked into the valleys or perched on hillsides with splendid views of the city. The hills offer an abundance of home hosted and cottage accommodations where visitors can take advantage of the close proximity to the city, as well as easy access to the wineries and other points of interest.

Just an hour's drive northeast of Adelaide is the most famous of Australia's wine districts. The Barossa Valley is responsible for producing 25% of Australia's wine. Settled in 1842 by immigrants of Prussia and Silesia, the area's rich Germanic heritage is particularly evident in its vineyards, churches, restaurants and bakeries. Wander the streets of Tanunda, the heart of the Barossa and discover some of the region's traditional architecture. Or go hot-air ballooning or bicycling to view the rolling green vineyards, small towns and country churches that dot the valley.

Just north of the Barossa Valley is the Clare Valley, one of the most picturesque areas in the state and home to a number of award-winning boutique wineries. South of the town of Clare is the Jesuit's Sevenhills Cellars, the oldest winery in South Australia. Country accommodations in the wine regions range from luxurious guest houses and blue stone mansions that provide gourmet food, wine and lodging to romantic self-contained cottages. All offer a good base from which to explore the historic villages and towns of the area. Nearby Burra is a historical treasure, steeped in the history of the early copper mines and surrounded by sheep-grazing country.

The South-East region of the state, one of South Australia's most productive pastoral areas, centers around the town of Mt. Gambier, built on the side of a volcano and known for its unusual crater lakes—most notably Blue Lake which changes colors according to season. The towns of Robe and Coonawarra in the South-East are both good halfway points on the road from Adelaide to Melbourne. Coonawarra (aboriginal for Honeysuckle), is a well-known wine producing region, and the lush wine and fruit district produces some of the best red wines in Australia. Robe, which is reminiscent of a Mediterranean fishing village, is a charming old seaport town and one of South Australia's earliest settlements.

The Fleurieu Peninsula, an hour's drive south of Adelaide, is considered South Australia's holiday playground. Sunlovers in particular appreciate the string of magnificent surf and swimming beaches along with the many popular watersports available here. Victor Harbor, once a whaling port, is a popular coastal resort and around the headland, Port Elliot offers powerful surf crashing onto rocks and fine views along the coast to the mouth of the Murray River. Close to the sea is McLaren Vale, the historical heart of the area's wine region. With more than fifty small wineries, many of them family concerns, scattered throughout the hills and vales, this is fast becoming a popular boutique wine region.

One of Australia's best kept secrets, Kangaroo Island, is also a popular retreat. Located 113 kilometers southwest of Adelaide, the island is a wonderful wildlife habitat and home to one of Australia's largest sea lion colonies. Long established as a farming community, Kangaroo Island is best visited in spring, summer or autumn when the koalas, kangaroos and wallabies can be seen in Flinders Chase National Park.

The Mighty Murray River, Australia's greatest river, was once the watery corridor of transport for an expanding pioneer colony: populated by paddle-steamers and dotted with bustling ports. Today it is the lifeblood of a thriving wine and fruit industry, flourishing under year-round sunshine. But the Mighty Murray is also an aquatic playground offering a plethora of watersports. Vacationers can glide regally on the gleaming river, listen to the lapping of water against the hull of a houseboat or cut a swathe through its center while on waterskis.

During the summer months, the state's nearly 25 hundred miles of coastline attracts water enthusiasts from around the country. From the Yorke Peninsula, where golden plains of barley crops give way to secluded coves and rocky headlands, to the surf beaches and striking coastal scenery of the Eyre Peninsula, both regions are popular resort areas with magnificent beaches that offer excellent swimming, surfing, fishing and sailing.

One of Australia's most remarkable mountain ranges is the rugged Flinders Range, with its colorful cliffs, granite peaks, sharp ridges and deep ochre gorges. Beyond the Flinders Ranges is South Australia's arid, and sometimes desolate, Outback. A large part of the world's opal is found in this region, particularly at Coober Pedy, a frontier-like town famous for it's fine opals and underground houses and churches. Perhaps the legendary Birdsville Track best epitomizes the state's Outback. The 500 kilometre track runs between Marree and Birdsville and is characterized as the driest, most desolate road in all of Australia. But it's exactly the freedom that comes from traveling the open road that captures the imagination. It's seeing nothing but the natural world on the horizon hour after hour and following the footsteps of explorers and cattlemen from bygone years that opens the heart towards South Australia's many surprises.

For more information write or telephone:
South Australia Tourism Commission
17880 Skypark Circle, Suite 250
Irvine, CA 92614 USA
Tel: (949) 476-4081
Toll Free (888) 768 8428
Fax: (949) 476 4088
E-Mail: info@southoz.com

South Australian Tourism Commission
Terrace Towers
178 North Terrace, Level 7/8
Adelaide, South Australia
AUSTRALIA 5000
E- Mail :info.visit-southaustralia@saugov.sa.gov.au
Website :
www.visit-southaustralia.com.au

REGIONAL DIRECTORY

➤ denotes review

ADELAIDE

➤ **Kirkendale**   16 Inverness Ave., St. Georges, SA 5064 61 8 8338 2768
Appealing country-style 3 room suite in peaceful, leafy garden

➤ **Leabrook Lodge B&B**   314 Kensington Rd., Leabrook-Adelaide, SA
5068 61 8 8331 7619
Stone bungalow in Australian native garden

➤ **Myoora Heritage Accommodation**   4 Carter St./PO Box 1124,
Thorngate/N. Adelaide, SA 5082/5006 61 8 8344 2599
Exceptional five-star Victorian residence close to all attractions

ADELAIDE HILLS

➤ **Marengo Hame**   Mannum Road, Tungkillo Postal Code: 5236
Tel: 61 8 8568 2011
1930's villa on the edge of the Barossa Valley

Mount Lofty   74 Summit Rd, Crafers, SA 5152 61 8 8339 6777
*Magnificent and gracous country house (1850s) with beautifully
appointed guest rooms*

➤ **Thorngrove Manor Hotel**   2 Glenside Lane, Stirling, Adelaide, SA
5152 (08) 8339 6748
Enchanting fairy tale like setting in a chateau-style manor house.

➤ **Villa Monte Bello** "Top of" Harris Rd., Lenswood, SA 5240 61 8 8389 8504
Superb Tuscan villa overlooking a vineyard estate

BAROSSA VALLEY

➤ **Lawley Farm**   PO Box 103, Tanunda, SA 5352 61 8 8563 2141
Six suites in converted cottage and barn on lovely Barossa Valley property

➤ **Oxley Farm**   Fairlie Rd/PO Box 1530, Kangaroo Flat/Gawler, SA 5118
61 8 8522 3703
*Luxury accommodations set in tranquil surroundings on working goat
dairy farm.*

➤ **Stonewell Cottages**   Stonewell Rd/PO Box 96, Tanunda, SA 5352
61 8 8563 2019
Delightful stone cottages on picturesque vineyard property

➤ **Strathlyn Coach House**   Nuriootpa Rd./PO Box 205, Angaston, SA
5353 61 8 8564 2430
Cottage style haven for two in tranquil, secluded setting

➤ **Strathlyn House Garden Room**   Nuriootpa Rd./PO Box 205,
Angaston, SA 5353 61 8 8564 2430
*Superior accommodations exclusively for two in stately marble residence
with private entrance.*

CLARE VALLEY

➤ **Thorn Park Country House**   College Road, Sevenhill, SA 5453
61 8 8843 4304
Beautifully restored 1850's homestead on 60 acres of pastoral land.

FLEURIEU PENINSULA

➤ **Bartrells**   47 Rapid Dr./PO Box 678, Victor Habor, SA 5211
61 8 8552 7758
A haven for body and soul in an Australian contemporary style home on golfing estate

P.S. Federal   Fleurieu Peninsula region

➤ **Willunga House**   1 St. Peter's Terrace, Willunga, SA 5172 61 8 8556 2467
Lovely Heritage accommodations in the McLaren Vale wine region

KANGAROO ISLAND

➤ **Correa Corner Bed & Breakfast**   Second Street/PO Box 232, Brownlow/Kingscote, SA 5223 61 8 8553 2498
Elegant five-star hosted accommodations in delightful garden setting beside the sea

MURRAY RIVER/COORONG

➤ **Poltalloch Station**   Poltalloch Rd./PMB 3 via Tailem Bend 5260, Narrung, SA 5259 (08) 8574 0088
Lakeside cottages on one of Australia's grand historic farming properties

SOUTH EAST

➤ **Padthaway Homestead**   Padthaway Homestead/Riddoch Highway, Padthaway, SA 5271 61 8 8765 5039
Victorian mansion set on 124 acres of vineyards and gardens in Padthaway wine region

➤ **Tintagel B&B**   Riddoch Highway/RSD 1088, Naracoorte, SA 5271
61 8 8764 7491
Private 3-bedroom suite, with lounge and own bathroom.

Bartrells

O n a golfing estate overlooking the Hindmarsh Valley and Encounter
Bay, Bartrells is a contemporary style home that provides a haven for
body and soul. Friendly hosts Barbara and Trevor Ellis make certain
that their home is their guests' home as well. The family room and outdoor
spa are available for guest use and almost anything you need can be provided. It's not uncommon for visitors to be driven to Granite Island to have
dinner and watch the penguins come up at night. The couple works with
other attractions and restaurants in the area, providing personalized service
that is rare and difficult to find. On request, custom designed packages can be
designed including anything from special diets, to relaxation massage, or a
motorized buggy.

Victor Harbor has been a South Australia beach resort town for many
years and Bartrells is perfectly located close enough to all the activities yet
far enough away not to be disturbed by the noise. A two minute walk to the
golf clubhouse and a six minute walk to the beach, this bed and breakfast is
great for golfers and guests wanting to unwind, relax and take advantage of
the beautiful coastal location.

Bartrells is part of the Fleurieu Unique Accommodation Group, an association of tour operators that offers walking or cycling tours around the Fleurieu. Guests are set on their way with maps, backpack, and all necessities while their luggage is transported to the next B&B where they're met by a hot shower, dinner, and the friendly faces of wonderful hosts. The guest book at this specially built home with views of the Bluff and Granite Island is filled with praise for the comfort and hospitality and it's easy to understand why the accolades are so frequent.

Name: Bartrells

Category: Bed & Breakfast

Location: Fleurieu Peninsula region; Victor Harbor; 3 km (nearest city)

Address: 47 Rapid Dr./PO Box 678, Victor Habor, SA 5211

Phone: Tel. 61 8 8552 7758 **Fax** 61 8 8552 7768

E-mail: bartrell@granite.net.au

Web site: www.ozemail.com.au/˜fuag/

Innkeepers: Barbara & Trevor Ellis

Rates: From A$105–125 per double includes full breakfast

Rated: ****1/2 RAA

Number of rooms: 2 Queen/Twin

Baths: 2 Ensuite

Services & amenities: Family room with TV, video, music; relaxation/ therapy massage, outdoor spa

Restrictions: No smoking; children by arrangement

Handicap access: yes

Correa Corner

Kangaroo Island's only five star accommodation, Correa Corner is a traditional style Bed & Breakfast where elegant luxury meets friendly, relaxing hospitality. Situated on the shores of beautiful Nepean Bay, just 3 km from Kingscote, the island's main township, Correa Corner enjoys the perfect location from which to explore the many wonders of this unique area. The sprawling residence features three romantic guest suites, a living room with cozy wood fire, intimate dining room, and beautiful, garden surroundings.

Each spacious guest suite features a comfortable king-sized bed, graceful furnishings complimented by ornate ceilings, romantic stained glass and lace décor, writing table and chairs, fresh flowers and an assortment of treats. The Rose Suite, with its large walk-in closet, reading nook, private bathroom with two person corner bath and separate large shower alcove, has a private patio overlooking a bush garden retreat. The Willow Suite, offering double, twin or triple accommodation, features a bay window reading nook with pleasant views of the garden in the main bedroom and a private patio. The adjoining dressing alcove is accessed through an ornate archway and includes a luggage area and large single bed. Willow Suite's private bathroom has a full size bath and separate double shower. Lastly, the Lavender Room has an entrance foyer complete with luggage rack and ornate archways that lead to the bedroom and private ensuite. A bay window reading nook offers pleasant garden views.

Helen and Terry Dennis are accomplished hosts who've been awarded the 1998 & 1999 Kangaroo Island Tourism Award for Best Hosted and Deluxe Accommodation. Among the many services they can provide are chauffeured transfers in a luxury 4WD vehicle and exclusive tours with your host, a biologist who can personally introduce you to the nearby penguin colony. In the mornings, an elaborate breakfast is served featuring home-baked bread, fresh fruits, cheeses and a selection of cooked fare. Evening meals, available by arrangement, feature fresh local produce, premium wines, candlelight, and gourmet country cuisine at its best. Delightful gardens surround the residence with a secluded relaxation area in the garden pavilion or rose court. There is also prolific birdlife and a bush garden retreat that is home to a family of resident wallabies.

Name: Correa Corner Bed & Breakfast

Region: Kangaroo Island; Kingscote; 2 km (nearest town)

Category: Traditional B&B

Innkeepers: Helen & Terry Dennis

Address: Second Street, Brownlow Postal Code: 5223; (Mailing) PO Box 232 Kingscote 5223

Phone: Tel: 61 8 8553 2498 **Fax** 61 8 8553 2355

E-mail: correac@kin.on.net

Web site: www.correacorner.com.au

Rooms: 3 King

Baths: 3 Ensuite

Rates: From A$155–175 per double includes full breakfast

Services and amenities: Licensed bar, in-house dining by arrangement, airport transfers available, exclusive touring, air-conditioning

Rating: ***** RAA; 1998 & 1999 Winner Kangaroo Island Hosted & Deluxe Accommodation

Restrictions: No smoking; not suitable for children

Handicapped facilities: No

Kirkendale

L ovely Kirkendale offers a hint of Provence just minutes from the heart
of Adelaide. With all the comforts and service of the city combined
with gracious country living, this delightful B&B provides the best of
both worlds. Situated in St. Georges, a leafy suburb near the Adelaide foot-
hills, Kirkendale is a secluded retreat perfect for one couple or family. The
open plan, self-contained suite includes two bedrooms, a bathroom, kitchenette and lounge. Guests enjoy exclusive use of the appealing, fresh and airy
accommodation nestled in a peaceful, verdant garden. The double bedroom
overlooks a rose garden while the French doors in the lounge room open
onto a sun-dappled, paved patio where alfresco breakfasts can be enjoyed.
Provisions for a generous continental breakfast are included with the tariff.

The suite is surrounded by a canopy of trees, home to many birds and a
possum family. The peaceful setting attracts numerous repeat guests. Fruit
basket, fresh flowers, an assortment of books and magazines, and the aroma
of fresh-baked bread are just a few of the treats in store for you. The country
style furnishings and terracotta floors add to the idyllic setting.

Guests are always assured of a warm welcome by gracious hosts, Jenny
and Steve, a well-traveled couple who know how to make travelers feel at
home. In addition to a hospitable welcome, they can also help with a myriad
of tour and travel arrangements. Day and half-day tours of the Adelaide Hills,
Barossa and McLaren Vale wine regions, and the Fleurieu Peninsula can all
be arranged and recommendations on nearby wildlife parks, historical and
scenic sites are readily available. Numerous restaurants, parks, shopping and
bus to the city are also nearby. Kirkendale is a great home away from home

for visitors to Adelaide; a private sanctuary that is always welcoming and inviting.

Name: Kirkendale

Category: Bed & Breakfast/Homestay

Location: Adelaide region; Adelaide; 5 km (nearest city)

Address: 16 Inverness Ave., St. Georges, SA 5064

Phone: Tel. 61 8 8338 2768 **Fax** 61 8 8338 2760

E-mail: kirken@merlin.net.au

Web site: www.wheretostay.com.au/pages/50300010.htm

Innkeepers: Jenny & Steve Studer

Rates: From A$90-105 per double includes continental breakfast

Rated: ****

Number of rooms: 2 Bedroom Suite

Baths: Private

Services & amenities: Tea/coffee, kitchenette, lounge, TV, video

Restrictions: No smoking inside

Handicap access: no

Lawley Farm

The influence of the Barossa Valley's original English and German settlers can be felt throughout the region—in the old farm cottages, soaring church spires, and especially, in the wines, cuisine, and traditional breads and pastries of the area. Lawley Farm, located near Tanunda (considered the most Germanic of the Barossa towns), offers delightful accommodations combining privacy, old world charm, and tranquility, with a touch of luxury. Hosts Sancha and Bruce Withers bought the farm in 1987 and each year have improved on the style of hospitality for which the charming bed and breakfast is so well known.

Accommodations are provided in a restored cottage and converted barn (circa 1850), and two new units built in the same style as the cottage. All are situated a short distance from the farmhouse in a three-acre garden of fruit trees, shrubs, and flowers. Each building has two self-contained suites complete with ensuite bathroom and bedroom with sitting area. The Lyndoch Suite, in the new cottage, is larger than the others and offers a separate sitting room. The suites are comfortably furnished in cottage style and include such amenities as a mini refrigerator and color TV. All suites are air-conditioned and two other suites have spa bathrooms.

Guests have a choice between a cooked breakfast in the farmhouse or preparing their own. Tea, coffee, jams, and muesli can be found in the cupboard along with crockery, silverware, toaster, and an egg cooker—virtually everything needed to prepare a light breakfast at your convenience. A gas barbeque is available for guests use, and with a little notice, Sancha can provide barbecue meat trays with salad or picnic lunches to be eaten on the rustic table under the almond trees. There is also a brick vaulted wine cellar, which can be used for small private parties; guests often prepare a barbecue and dine in the quaint underground room before having a soak in the hot tub beneath the night sky. Lawley Farm offers a charming alternative in bed and breakfast accommodation, with private, self-contained cottages in an attractive environment, and delightful hosts who help with winery tours, restaurant reservations, daily outings, and personal introductions to local winemakers. Guests are welcome to relax and enjoy farm life or wander further afield to explore the property and the 10 acres of champagne grapes the Withers have planted.

Name: Lawley Farm

Category: Self-contained cottages

Location: Barossa Valley region; Tanunda (nearest city)

Address: PO Box 103, Tanunda, SA 5352

Phone: Tel. 61 8 8563 2141 **Fax** 61 8 8563 2141

E-mail: withers@dove.net.au

Innkeepers: Sancha & Bruce Withers

Rates: From A$130-160 per double includes breakfast

Rated: ****/****½

Number of rooms: 6 Suites

Baths: Ensuite

Services & amenities: Air-conditioning; TV, refrigerator; some suites with spa & log fires

Restrictions: Limited facilities for children

Handicap access: no

Leabrook Lodge

Surrounded by majestic gum trees, Leabrook Lodge is a traditional stone bungalow set in one of Adelaide's most prestigious suburbs. The convenient location makes Leabrook Lodge a great choice for visitors who want easy access to all the city's attractions in addition to a home spun environment. The quiet and comfortable accommodations overlook a picturesque walled garden where breakfast can be enjoyed most mornings. Start the day off reading the paper in the courtyard and planning your day. For first-time visitors to Adelaide, host Barbara Carter will help personalize your trip and make sure you see all the things that interest you. For repeat guests, Leabrook Lodge is like coming home. A typical guest comment reflects Barbara's gracious generosity. "Thank you for a lovely room, delicious breakfasts, and your wonderful suggestions on Adelaide sightseeing—your hospitality was great!"

Barbara is an experienced world traveler quick to help tourists who wish to explore the quintessential character of the area thoroughly and efficiently. She suggests leaving your car behind and using public transport which is inexpensive and efficient (a lock-up garage is available). Or, she recommends using a bicycle. Her family cycles into the city and suburbs on a regular basis.

Adelaide, with its pleasant Mediterranean style climate, enjoys a reputation as a clean, civilized city featuring a wealth of attractions. Visitors should check out the Adelaide Oval (cricket etc), Botanic Gardens, Art Galleries, Museum, Festival Theatre, National Parks, Walking Trails, Adelaide Hills (great bushwalking), and the Opal Centre. Adelaide is also the gateway to the Outback and Flinders Ranges, Alice Springs, Coober Pedy, Kangaroo Island, the Barossa Valley and Southern Vale Wineries and serves as a great base for short or extended side trips. After taking advantage of all that Adelaide has to offer, unwind at Leabrook Lodge with a book from the extensive "who-dun-it" library or join Barbara for an impromptu Wednesday night dinner included in the tariff.

Name: Leabrook Lodge B&B

Category: Bed & Breakfast

Location: Adelaide region; Adelaide; 5 km (nearest city)

Address: 314 Kensington Rd., Leabrook-Adelaide, SA 5068

Phone: Tel. 61 8 8331 7619 **Fax** 61 8 8364 4955

E-mail: barbara.carter@bigpond.com

Web site: www.users.bigpond.com/barbara.carter

Innkeepers: Barbara Carter

Rates: From A$85–90 per double includes full breakfast

Rated: ***1/2

Number of rooms: 2 Queen, 2 Single

Baths: 2 Ensuite, 1 Share

Services & amenities: Log fires, guest lounge, TV, tea/coffee

Restrictions: No smoking inside

Handicap access: no

The Lodge

O ne of the most elegant places to stay in the Barossa Valley is The
Lodge at Seppeltsfield. The former Seppelt family homestead, extensively renovated in 1987, has been transformed into a luxurious country house. The early Edwardian home, built solidly of South Australian bluestone, is set in the middle of a vineyard on three acres of beautiful gardens. In
addition to the house itself, the property boasts lovely picnic spots by the
creek, an English rose garden, vegetable garden, and vine-covered summer
house with views across the lawn tennis court and swimming pool.

The Lodge accommodates a maximum of eight guests in four charming
guestrooms. A comfortable sitting room separates the formal area of the
house from the guest wing. Complete with open fireplace, sofa and assortment of books, games, and magazines, the sitting room is an inviting lounge
with an informal eating area and a guest refrigerator stocked with beer, wine
and soda. Each of the guestrooms is only a step away from the sitting area. All
have large bay windows with upholstered box windowseats and ensuites
with thoughtful extras like big fluffy towels and towel warmers.

At the front of the spacious and tastefully decorated house is a formal
living room, perfect for listening to music or reading. Pre-dinner champagne
is often served here before dining by candlelight at the enormous Irish-
Georgian table in the dining room. Dinner can be a formal affair with fine
crystal, silver, and Wedgwood china showcasing the excellent country-style
cuisine and Barossa Valley wines. Hosts Craig Harris and Graeme Mustow
like to create different moods for different meals, so breakfast might be
served in the sitting room and lunch (weather permitting) either in the
summer house or by the creek. The hosts have also been known to invite

local winemakers to join guests for dinner and an evening of talk about the vintner's art. Although fine wine is definitely the reason for the Barossa's fame, The Lodge is a welcome addition to a valley, well known for excellent cuisine and fine hospitality.

Name: The Lodge

Category: Country House

Location: Barossa Valley region; Tanunda/6 km (nearest city)

Address: RS 120, Seppelstfield, SA 5355

Phone: Tel. (08) 8562 8277 **Fax** (08) 8262 8344

E-mail: thelodge@dove.net.au

Innkeepers: Craig Harris and Graeme Mustow

Rates: From A$265 per double includes breakfast; From A$365 for dinner, bed & breakfast

Rated: *****RAA

Number of rooms: 4

Baths: 4 Ensuite

Services & amenities: Licensed, air-conditioning, pool, tennis court

Restrictions: No smoking; no children

Handicap access: no

Marengo Hame

Marengo Hame B&B offers two private suites in a 1930's villa plus a self-contained cottage on a 25 acre property nestled in the rolling hills on the edge of the Barossa Valley. Fully licensed, Marengo Hame provides luxury and convenience in a fully hosted traditional B&B run efficiently by Lesley and Gary Johns. The luxuriously appointed suites include a choice of the Tartan Room, with the warmth of timber walls, comfortable queen-size bed, separate dining area and a wonderful two person spa bath. Or, the Blue Room, with a romantic queen size 4 poster canopy bed, intimate candlelit dining area and a period bathroom with clawfoot bath plus a separate spa room for exclusive use. Both rooms have their own private entrances and come complete with full, personalized service or, if you prefer, complete privacy. Allow yourself to be pampered in the beautiful suites, situated close to many of South Australia's major tourist attractions, including the Barossa Valley, Hahndorf (25 mins), National Motor Museum at Birdwood (10 mins), the beautiful Murray River (15 mins), and yet only 50 minutes from the heart of Adelaide.

The cottage is nestled amongst native gum trees overlooking a rural setting. It is fully self contained for a couple, with private spa, kitchen and lounge/bed room. It is far enough from the main homestead to ensure total privacy yet close enough to enjoy a chef prepared candlelit dinner in the main dining room.

All guests enjoy delicious afternoon tea on arrival, perhaps taken in the garden, and strawberries and cream with your bath. Each room has a CD player with a selection of CDs, a remote controlled TV, video, and complimentary tea, coffee and port, plus other little luxuries like fluffy dressing robes, electric blankets, reverse cycle air conditioning, sweets, biscuits etc to make your stay a wonderful experience. Laundry service is also available at no extra charge. Marengo Hame is an intimate and delightful property that allows couples to be as comfortable and self-sufficient as they want.

Name: Marengo Hame Bed & Breakfast

Location: Adelaide Hills Adelaide; 57 km

Address: Mannum Road, Tungkillo Postal Code: 5236

Phone: Tel: 61 8 8568 2011 **Fax**: 61 8 8568 1739

E-mail: marengo@camtech.net.au

Innkeeper: Lesley Johns

Bedrooms: 2 Suites + Cottage

Baths: Private

Rates: From A$125-145 per double includes full breakfast

Services & amenities: Spa, Kitchen, CD Player, TV/video, tea/coffee, electric blankets, air-conditioning

Rated: **** 1/2

Restrictions: No smoking; Children by arrangement

Handicap access: No

Myoora Heritage Accommodation

T he only five-star heritage accommodation in the Adelaide Metropolitan region, Myroora is a superbly restored historic mansion only three kilometers from the city's central business district. Built in 1892, this aristocratic Victorian guesthouse combines the warmth of a private home with all the amenities of a fine hotel. Tucked away behind a wide ornate verandah, Myoora has been decorated in a gracious period style that recalls the opulence and hushed decorum of the Victorian era. The den houses glowing jarrah floors covered with Oriental rugs and a handsome leather Chesterfield. The sitting room boasts a marble-topped walnut cabinet. From the impeccable physical attributes to the superlative service, South Australia serves up a special treat with this unique bed and breakfast.

Along with its staunch devotion to tradition, Myoora makes a few important concessions to the modern world: reverse cycle air-conditioning in the bedrooms, linens by Ralph Lauren, plush bathrobes and either ensuite or private bathrooms for each of the four guestrooms—including two with large spa baths. Guests even have a private entrance. The third bedroom is a handsome apartment with its own sitting room. Behind the house there's a sparkling heated swimming pool and at the side, a grass tennis court where many a spirited match has been played. Myoora is set amongst half a hectare of lovely gardens .

Breakfast is a silver service affair in the elegant dining room with all the pomp and circumstance that the surroundings suggest; or you may choose to partake of breakfast in your guestroom. Beverley Pfeiffer is an exceptional host who has welcomed guests from around the world. All depart with the sense they have discovered something special; a secret too good to keep, yet too precious to share. Located in the patrician leafy suburb of Thorngate on the fringe of North Adelaide, Myoora is within strolling distance of O'Connell Street—where fashionable Adelaide comes to wine and dine. For both easy access to Adelaide with all its special attractions, and comfortable accommodation with all the bells and whistles, Myoora is an exceptional find in an exceptional city.

Name: Myoora Heritage Accommodation

Category: Bed & Breakfast

Location: Adelaide region; Adelaide; 3 km (nearest city)

Address: 4 Carter St./PO Box 1124, Thorngate/N. Adelaide, SA 5082/5006

Phone: Tel. 61 8 8344 2599 **Fax** 61 8 8344 9575

E-mail: myoora@chariot.net.au

Web site: www.cyberium.com.au/Myoora/

Innkeepers: Beverley Pfeiffer

Rates: From A$180-240 per double includes full breakfast

Rated: ***** RAA

Number of rooms: 3 Queen, 1 Double

Baths: 3 Ensuite, 1 Private

Services & amenities: Tennis court, swimming pool, spa, open fires, 3 private sitting rooms

Restrictions: None

Handicap access: no

Oxley Farm

O xley Farm, set in acres of native gum trees in the heart of some of the best farming country in the South Australia, offers four star accommodations on a working dairy goat farm. Perfect for those who want to experience something unique, hosts Andrew & Rhonda Brooke offer a nice blend of rural charm and modern comfort. Each of the four suites, furnished with solid Colonial timber furniture, accommodates up to two adults and three children. Families are welcome and there's a lot to keep everyone busy. Guests can feed the baby farm animals, collect eggs, help with the daily milking of the goats, or just enjoy a pleasant walk around the farm. There are even donkey rides, organized by the Brooke's enterprising daughter. For the energetic, a game of half court tennis, or table tennis is always fun. There is also a pool table, darts and quoits in the large game room. Bring along a bottle of champagne and end the day relaxing in the heated spa under the stars.

A traditional cooked farm-style breakfast is included in the tariff and an evening meal is available on request. BBQ facilities are also available, for those who wish to cook their own meals. Breakfast is served inside the suite or in the palm studded garden.

Historic Gawler, just five minute away, offers numerous activities including greyhound, trotting (free entry for guests) and horse racing tracks. The world renowned Gawler Gliding Club and Roseworthy College, with its' Agricultural Interpretation Centre are nearby. The Mallala Motor Sport Park and world-class indoor Equestrian Centre are less than 20 minutes drive. And, of course, the famous Barossa Valley Wineries are only a half hour drive away. Book at Oxley Farm for a week and enjoy a 10% discount.

Name: Oxley Farm

Category: Farmstay/B&B

Location: Barossa Valley region; Gawler; 7 km (nearest city)

Address: Fairlie Rd/PO Box 1530, Kangaroo Flat/Gawler, SA 5118

Phone: Tel. 61 8 8522 3703 **Fax** 61 8 8522 3703

E-mail: oxleyfarm@dove.net.au

Web site: www.dove.net.au/~oxleyfarm

Innkeepers: Andrew & Rhonda Brooke

Rates: From A$120 per double includes full breakfast; other meals available by arrangement

Rated: ****RAA; Barossa wine and tourism

Number of rooms: 4 Queen with trundle bed

Baths: Ensuite

Services & amenities: Spa, games room, half court tennis, BBQ, farm activites

Restrictions: No smoking inside or near animals

Handicap access: no

Padthaway Estate

S teeped in history, the Padthaway Estate was once an 80,000-acre pastoral holding established by Scottish immigrants in the middle of the nineteenth century. Located near the Victoria border in South Australia, the main homestead was built by the Lawson family in 1882.

Padthaway Homestead is a gracious and elegant two-story Victorian mansion set on 124 acres north of Naracoorte. One hundred acres of the estate are planted with Pinot Noir and Chardonnay vines, the classic grape varieties for champagne. The proprietors, Ian Gray and Dale Baker, bought the property from founder Robert Lawson's heirs. Padthaway is now efficiently run by Rosemarie Hayes and Dianne Brown who take obvious pride in the management of this historic homestead.

A long sweeping driveway, winds through the vineyards to the main house, surrounded by broad verandahs and well-manicured lawns. The house, which has been completely restored to its original style and glory, is filled with beautiful antiques, old pictures, and tasteful furnishings. Accommodations are provided in six individually decorated guestrooms with queen-sized beds. There are hand basins in every room and more than adequate share bathrooms for guests (bathrobes are provided). A study and an upstairs den are also available for guest use.

Padthaway Homestead takes great pride in the quality of its food and wine. Dinners are served in a small formal dining room overlooking the floodlit garden. Silver service, candelabra, and Royal Doulton china complement the simple menu; the food is not only delicious but beautifully presented. The wine list emphasizes the best wines of the region as well as the estate's own vintages. There is also a wine-tasting area on the grounds for aficionados, and a tennis court for athletic guests. Padthaway Estate is a very special retreat for discerning guests who appreciate quality accommodations and the best in food and wine. Staying at Padthaway Homestead is like living in a private residence on a grand country estate, with all the amenities of an elegant guesthouse.

Name: Padthaway Homestead

Category: Country House

Location: South East/Padthaway Wine Region region; Padthaway (nearest city)

Address: Padthaway Homestead/Riddoch Highway, Padthaway, SA 5271

Phone: Tel. 61 8 8765 5039 **Fax** 61 8 8765 5097

E-mail: padthawayhmstd@rbm.com.au

Web site: www.weblogic.com.au/bed_n_breakfast/padthaway.html

Innkeepers: Rosemarie Hayes & Diane Brown

Rates: From A$200 per double includes breakfast; A$300-320 dinner, bed & breakfast

Number of rooms: 2 King or Twin, 4 Queen

Baths: 4 Share

Services & amenities: Licensed, tennis court, TV, nearby golf

Restrictions: Closed Tues.- Thu./ no children

Handicap access: no

Poltalloch Station

A long Lake Alexandrina's southern shores, near the mouth of the Murray River and just 90 minutes southeast of Adelaide, lies the historic grazing property of Poltalloch. Comprised of a stately 13-room homestead and nine residences, the property has been likened to an English village, its many limestone and iron cottages evoking the charm of a bygone era. In its pre-machinery heyday, all of these residences were needed to house the many workers necessary to run the nearly 25,000 acre property. In order to be self-sufficient, the property needed a meathouse, a blacksmith, carpentry shop, stables, gardens, a store, a shearing shed and quarters, and a jetty. There is even its own lighthouse—the only inland lighthouse in the southern hemisphere.

Classified by the National Trust and on the Register of the National Heritage, the two-story homestead was built in 1876 from local sandstone, with intricate iron lacework running along the eaves and upper balcony. Poltalloch's "village" has been transformed into self-contained cottages available for guest use, fully renovated to maintain historic authenticity but complete with modern facilities. There are two bed and breakfast cottages that accommodate four guests, with a continental breakfast included. In addition, there are two, larger, fully self-contained cottages with living room and kitchen.

Guests can boat or fish on the lake, swim near a private beach, play tennis, go bushwalking in the pine forest, or observe the pelicans, ibis, egrets, and other local wildlife. Rubber boots come in handy for muddy lakeside walks. The breathtaking Coorang National Park, an area of worldwide ecological significance, with 150 kilometres of unbroken beach and 135 kilometres of sand dunes and peaceful lagoons, is also nearby. June through August is particularly nice, but this beautiful property is an ideal place, at any time of year, for relaxing in the warmth of the north-facing verandahs and watching the spectacular sunsets on the lake.

Name: Poltalloch Station

Category: Self-contained cottages

Location: Murray River/Coorong region; Narrung/ 8 km (nearest city)

Address: Poltalloch Rd./PMB 3 via Tailem Bend 5260, Narrung, SA 5259

Phone: Tel. (08) 8574 0088 **Fax** (08) 8574 0065

E-mail: poltalloch@lm.net.au

Innkeepers: Beth & Chris Cowan

Rates: From A$95 per double includes continental breakfast

Number of rooms: 2 Cottages

Baths: Private

Services & amenities: Tennis court, swimming, fishing

Handicap access: no

Stonewell Cottages

B etween the rolling hills of the Barossa Ranges and the blue-green hue of the valley below lie the many vineyards that have brought the Barossa Valley international fame. Situated on Stonewell Road between Tanunda and Seppeltsfield in the heart of this popular region, Stonewell Cottages provide a wonderfully unique and picturesque stay on an 80 acre vineyard property. Nestled among the vines on the edge of a private lake, three self-contained stone cottages, each surrounded by its own picket fenced cottage garden, provide a peaceful respite.

Enjoy the luxury of perfectly appointed cottages stocked with tea, coffee, milk, sugar, homemade biscuits, and chocolates for afternoon tea. Sip on a local port as you watch the sun go down, and enjoy the homemade bread and jams that are included in the specially prepared breakfast baskets delivered fresh each morning. Eat breakfast under the verandah and delight in the ever-changing beauty of the vines. Enjoy a barbeque in the summerhouse, or row to the island for a picnic with your favourite wine. Feed the friendly ducks, or drop in a line to catch redfin perch or yabbies. Stonewell Cottages is more than just a place to stay; it's a wonderful Barossa experience.

While staying on this property, choose from the following accommodations: Cupid's Cottage, tucked away amongst the native trees on the edge of the vineyard, is a private cottage featuring a luxury sunken spa and beautiful leadlight window. It offers an exclusive accommodation for one couple in a peaceful setting overlooking the water; The Hideaway Cottage, built on the water's edge, is a two bedroom cottage for one or two couples and features queen-sized beds, a two person spa, lounge, and a kitchen that opens onto a private patio; and The Haven Cottage Suites is one cottage with two delightful suites, each with its own kitchen and lounge, a cozy wood fire, queen size bedroom, ensuite bathroom, and sunroom featuring a private luxury two person spa. This quiet rural retreat offers peace and privacy in an idyllic vineyard setting and Stonewell hosts Yvonne and John Pfieffer have a decade old reputation for pleasing guests from around the world.

Name: Stonewell Cottages

Category: Self-contained cottages

Location: Barossa Valley region; Tanunda (nearest city)

Address: Stonewell Rd/PO Box 96, Tanunda, SA 5352

Phone: Tel. 61 8 8563 2019 **Fax** 61 8 8563 3624

E-mail: stonewel@dove.net.au

Web site: www.dove.net.au/~stonewel

Innkeepers: Yvonne & John Pfeiffer

Rates: From A$135 per double includes breakfast

Rated: Barossa Wine & Tourism Ass'n; SA B&B Town & Country Ass'n

Number of rooms: 2 self-contained Cottage Suites / 2 Cottages

Baths: Private

Services & amenities: Air-conditioning, TV, CD player, private spas, kitchen facilities, rowing, fishing

Restrictions: No smoking inside; 2 night minimum on weekend

Handicap access: no

Strathlyn Coach House

S trathlyn Coach House, meticulously restored and refurbished in 1995 as a luxury accommodation by Heather Anderson, is a self-contained retreat set in the beautiful Barossa ranges. The secluded blue stone coach house, dating from 1906, stands in an almond orchard on a gentle slope in the north-west corner of the historic Strathlyn Estate. Once used to store the family coach and stable the horses, the structure maintains all of its unique character while affording one lucky couple tranquility and seclusion. The private accommodation features a tastefully decorated mezzanine level double bedroom reached by a red cedar staircase. The kitchenette is well stocked with provisions for a country-style breakfast. There is a beautifully decorated bathroom with full bath and separate shower and a large balcony with panoramic views across the Valley all the way to the Greenock ranges. Guests can sit outside and sip a glass of wine while watching the setting sun or enjoy an intimate breakfast for two on a warm, sunny morning. Rise whenever you want and enjoy country breads, fresh fruit, eggs, bacon and tomato, jams and cereal.

The Coach House is situated next to the Saltram Wine Estate and Bistro and is close to the award-winning Vintners Bar and Grill with its array of fine food and wine. Regardless of the season, visitors to this premier wine-growing region of Australia can enjoy a diverse range of activities. The small township of Angaston, with its blend of early English and German heritage, features a main street of small shops, fine public buildings, galleries, restaurants and cafes. Ask about special Stress Relief packages featuring deluxe skin and body therapies.

Name: Strathlyn Coach House

Category: Self-contained

Location: Barossa Valley region; Angaston; 1 km (nearest city)

Address: Nuriootpa Rd./PO Box 205, Angaston, SA 5353

Phone: Tel. 61 8 8564 2430 Fax

E-mail: strathlyn@telstra.easymail.com.au

Web site: www.cyberium.com.au

Innkeepers: Heather Anderson

Rates: From A$150-165 per double includes full breakfast provisions

Number of rooms: 1 Double

Baths: Private

Services & amenities: kitchenette, living area, balcony, TV, complimentary wine, toiletries, robes, games

Restrictions: No smoking inside, no children, no pets

Handicap access: no

Strathlyn House Garden Room

B uilt from local bluestone and marble, Strathlyn House is a stately gentleman's residence that was once home to Fulton Salter, son of William Salter, the founder of Saltram Winery and one of the leading figures in South Australian winemaking history. Accommodation within the historic residence is offered in the Garden Room, renovated and opened in October 1999. The double bedroom, featuring an ensuite with luxury spa and large shower, overlooks serene garden surroundings and a pleasant patio. Privacy and comfort are ensured in the elegantly furnished room with its large double vanities and assortment of complimentary amenities including fruit, wine and biscuits. The accommodation is close to restaurants, wineries, galleries, antique shops, historic churches and scenic country walks. Host Heather Anderson, a former teacher, is a qualified Beauty Therapist and Masseuse who offers specialized beauty treatments and Aromatheraphy at Strathlyn Skin & Body Therapies in nearby Nuriotpa. She has resided at Strathlyn Estate for 20 years and has extensive knowledge of the history and features of the district. She can offer expert advice on where to go and what to see. Having operated the adjacent Strathlyn Coach House since 1995, Heather's experience as a host has prompted recent guests of the Garden

Room to comment "wonderful hospitality," "just perfect," and "we'll be back."

Name: Strathlyn House Garden Room

Category: Bed & Breakfast

Location: Barossa Valley region; Angaston; 1 km (nearest city)

Address: Nuriootpa Rd./PO Box 205, Angaston, SA 5353

Phone: Tel. 61 8 8564 2430 Fax

E-mail: strathlyn@telstra.easymail.com.au

Web site: www.cyberium.com.au

Innkeepers: Heather Anderson

Rates: From A$130-165 per double includes gourmet breakfast

Number of rooms: 1 Double

Baths: Ensuite with luxury spa

Services & amenities: TV, tea/coffee, complimentary wine, biscuits, fruit basket, robes, toiletries, private entrance

Restrictions: No smoking inside, no children, no pets

Handicap access: no

Thorn Park Country House

T horn Park Country House is located in the heart of the township of Sevenhill, just opposite the Church of St. Aloysius and the historic Sevenhill Cellars, the oldest winery in South Australia. Set on 60 acres of pastoral splendor, the homestead overlooks farmland studded with towering gum trees, grazing cattle, and a dam which is home to ducks and other native birdlife. The homestead, built in the 1850's from stone quarried on the property and Mintaro slate, was rescued from decay in 1986 and beautifully renovated over a two-year period by owners David Hay and Michael Speers. The 120 year old hawthorn hedge from which the property takes its name has been retained, complemented by new plantings of roses, perennials, and deciduous trees.

Guests relax in gracious accommodations amid the peaceful countryside. Beautifully appointed bedrooms, each with private facilities, include cozy sitting areas and panoramic views of the property. A converted stone barn and a coach house provide additional accommodations, perfect for those who want a little privacy. The spacious drawing room, intimate library, large country kitchen, and splendid dining room in the homestead are all enhanced by collections of antique furniture, books, and art. Guests can set their own schedule or just relax on the wide verandah, in one of the many comfortable rooms, or stroll around the beautiful grounds.

Dining is a memorable event at Thorn Park with food prepared with the greatest of care, in modern Australian style. Dinner might include curried parsnip soup, quail with sweet soy, lime juice, and fresh grapes, and fillet of beef with pickled walnuts, served with baby potatoes, fresh asparagus and a watercress salad. The hosts are happy to discuss any special dietary requirements prior to arrival. With its tranquil setting, small scale, and emphasis on luxury and quality, Thorn Park appeals to a discerning clientele who appreciate country living. One guest summed it up well in the guestbook: "Thorn Park is like home away from home, except home was never this good!"

Name: Thorn Park Country House

Category: Country House

Location: Clare Valley region; Sevenhill (nearest city)

Address: College Road, Sevenhill, SA 5453

Phone: Tel. 61 8 8843 4304 **Fax** 61 8 8843 4296

E-mail: thornpk@capri.net.au

Innkeepers: David Hay & Michael Speers

Rates: From A$135 per person B&B; A$180 D,B & B

Rated: ****

Number of rooms: 7 Doubles

Baths: Ensuite / private

Services & amenities: Licensed, air-conditioning, heated towel warmers, tea/coffee, TV in main house rooms

Restrictions: No smoking inside; 2 day minimum on weekends

Handicap access: no

Thorngrove Manor Hotel

Thorngrove Manor is a boutique property that has won countless regional and international accolades and awards including: "Best Romantic Hideaway in Australia," and "Super Star Hotel." The stately French-style castle is straight out of a fairy tale; an enchanting experience for anyone with a sense of romance. Set in picturesque grounds, this grand residence, with spires, arches, and turrets, offers privacy, luxury, and unprecedented excellence in guest accommodations. The dream and creation of owners Nydia and Kenneth Lehmann, the five storied, 22 room manor house features an array of private suites ranging from the three roomed King's Chambers, with it's baronial fireplace, restored German antique piano, and rare stained-glass windows, to the Tower Room, which is accessed by a spiral staircase and contains an exotic original handcarved bed. Described as one of the truly outstanding properties in the world, Thorngrove blends medieval history with superlative service. For a truly memorable night, candlelight and silver service dinners are served privately and individually in the privacy of your suite. Plan to indulge since the daily changing menu has been praised by gourmets from all corners of the world. The creative approach to accommodation and the unprecedented attention to detail at Thorngrove, can be appreciated by the most discerning of connoisseurs. So pamper yourself with this once in a lifetime experience. From North America, bookings can be made toll-free through Small Luxury Hotels—(011) 800 525 4800.

Name: Thorngrove Manor Hotel

Category: Luxury Inn

Location: Adelaide Hills region; Adelaide; 16 KM/20 mins (nearest city)

Address: 2 Glenside Lane, Stirling, Adelaide, SA 5152

Phone: Tel. (08) 8339 6748 **Fax** (08) 8370 9950

E-mail: thorngro@cobweb.com.au

Web site: www.slh.com/thorngro/ also: babs.com.au/thorngrov

Innkeepers: Kenneth & Nydia Lehmann

Rates: A$280–A$920 (double)

Rated: *****RAA, Small Luxury Hotels of the World, International Super Star Hotel 1997,98,99,2000

Number of rooms: 4 Themed Private Suites, 3 B&B areas

Baths: Ensuite, some with spas

Services & amenities: Spa, nearby golf, riding, botanic gardens, award-winning cuisine, wineries

Restrictions: No Smoking in bedrooms

Handicap access: no

Tintagel

L ocated near South Australia's Coonawarra wine region, Tintagel is a rural property surrounded by beautiful bush and vineyards. There are many popular attractions in the South Eastern area, including Mount Gambier with its Blue Lake, and Port MacDonnell, both about an hour away. World Heritage listed Naracoorte Caves, with guided tours running every day except Christmas and the Wonambi Fossil Centre, with its impressive animal fossil collection, are also nearby. During warm weather, the local lake provides great swimming and scenic walks, and in winter, Tintagel has a wood fire that is lovely to curl up beside after a full day of sightseeing. Summer or winter, look out towards the open plains and watch a beautiful sunset.

At Tintagel, the accommodations is in a private self-contained suite that consists of three bedrooms, a guest lounge, bathroom, and barbecue area. Six people can be accommodated making it ideal for a group traveling together or a family. Since Tintagel only takes one booking at a time, guests have exclusive use of the suite. Furnished with a nice blend of antique and modern furniture combined with collectables and treasures, the accommodation is both comfortable and relaxing. Bathrobes are supplied in each room, and all beds have comfy wool doonas and electric blankets. The sitting room provides a central lounge area with stereo system, colour TV, VCR, and cozy wood heater. On arrival, unwind with your hosts, Val and Malcolm, over a delicious afternoon tea. In the morning, enjoy a generous continental or full cooked breakfast using homemade preserves and farm eggs. By arrangement, Val will prepare an evening meal or there are numerous restaurants within a short drive. Picnic hampers can also be arranged and there is a BBQ for preparing your own meal.

A large fenced backyard allows kids to roam, and 18 acres of lightly wooded natural bush provide plenty of good trails to explore. For the more adventurous, there are 100 acres of Heritage bushland for walking, bird watching, and searching for native orchids or other flora. At night, hand feed the possums or watch the kangaroos feed on the front lawns. Tintagel is the winner of the SE Tourism Award for Traditional Hosted B&B, and it's easy to see why this four star property wins accolades.

Name: Tintagel B&B

Category: Bed & Breakfast

Location: South East region; Naracoorte/Coonawarra; 25 km (nearest city)

Address: Riddoch Highway/RSD 1088, Naracoorte, SA 5271

Phone: Tel. 61 8 8764 7491 **Fax** 61 8 8764 7491

E-mail: tintagel@rbm.com.au

Innkeepers: Val & Malcolm McGlashan

Rates: From A$100 per double includes full breakfast

Rated: ****RAA; Winner SE Tourism Award for Traditional Hosted B&B

Number of rooms: 1 Queen, 1 King or Twin, 1 Twin

Baths: Ensuite

Services & amenities: Guest lounge, great bushwalks, parking

Restrictions: One group, couple or family at a time

Handicap access: no

Villa Monte Bello

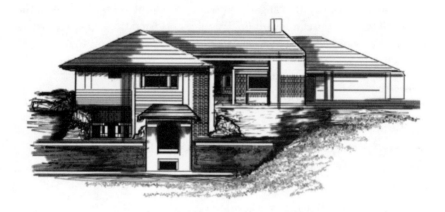

V illa Monte Bello is a beautiful luxurious country home overlooking the magical Onkaparinga Valley with views that make the universe seem to stand still. Seclusion, relaxation, deluxe accommodation, and wholesome country cooking can all be found in this superb mud-brick Tuscan villa in the Adelaide Hills. The unique bed and breakfast is a picturesque half hour drive from Adelaide and close to all the famous wine regions of South Australia. Set high on a ridge, Villa Monte Bello evokes an enchanting Northern Italian atmosphere, while offering discerning guests supreme comfort and friendly dining matched by a fine Lenswood wine cellar.

Dinner at Villa Monte Bello is a special experience; whether feasting with old or new friends, you're sure to feel like you've been invited to an exclusive dinner party. On winter nights, logs burn in the huge fireplace providing a warm focus for the evening. The terrace is a sublime spot to sip a glass of fine local wine or take in the view that could easily be mistaken for the gentle rolling hills of Tuscany. On a summer's day, gentle zephyrs soothe as you watch workers in the vineyard below. A visit to Villa Monte Bello is a journey not soon forgotten.

The accommodations are in three king-sized rooms, each with ensuite and double spa baths. The rooms overlook the valley and vineyards, and all feature modern fixtures and handmade wrought iron furniture. Villa Monte Bello is a great base from which to explore the Barossa, Clare, McClaren, or Vale wine valleys. It is also close to golf, fishing, and bushwalking. A favorite acitivity is a scenic walk along the winemakers ridge. Back at Monte Bello, a games room with snooker table contributes to the recreation. Just as good, is sitting with a glass of fine Lenswood wine in a comfy leather chair with your feet up and an enjoyable book in your lap.

Name: Villa Monte Bello

Category: Guesthouse

Location: Adelaide Hills region; Adelaide; 29 km (nearest city)

Address: ""Top of"" Harris Rd., Lenswood, SA 5240

Phone: Tel. 61 8 8389 8504 **Fax** 61 8 8389 8114

Web site: bello.mtx.net

Innkeepers: Gaetano Ceravolo

Rates: From A$220 per double includes full breakfast

Rated: Aust Tourism Council/ '99 Award of Distinction

Number of rooms: 3 King or Twin

Baths: 3 Ensuite

Services & amenities: Double spa, games room, country walks, open fire

Restrictions: Unsuitable for children

Handicap access: yes

Willunga House

Willunga House, in the picturesque McLaren Vale wine area less than 50 minutes from Adelaide, is a State Heritage listed Georgian stone residence built in 1850. Originally the first general store and post office for the village of Willunga, the structure has been meticulously restored by Rosie and Kingsley Knott. Retaining all of the old character they transformed it into a first-class bed and breakfast. The guest wing offers five queen and double bedrooms furnished with antiques and genuine old brass and iron beds. Each color-themed room features a private or ensuite bathroom, crisp cotton sheets, and handsome furnishings. The downstairs Green Room is a popular choice with its open fire and bay window to the front garden. Upstairs the Ruby Room, with its queen size bed, French doors on to the balcony and an ensuite bathroom is also popular. Electric blankets and extra bedding are provided in all rooms, along with hairdryers and toiletries in the bathrooms.

The guest sitting room, which has an open wood fire, offers a wide range of reading material, puzzles and games, and a selection of music. To help you settle in, afternoon tea and homemade cake is offered upon your arrival. A selection of teas and coffees is available at all times, as well as fresh fruit and other nibbles. The extensive breakfast menu features a wide variety of local and home-grown produce from the hosts' organic garden, including fresh eggs from their hens and a range of homemade jams, marmalades and chutneys. According the visitors' book, guests find breakfast at Willunga House special, both for the cuisine and conversation. Many guests take the opportunity to experience the luxury and relaxation provided by one of Kingsley's massages; while for others, the garden and solar heated pool provide a refreshing diversion during the summer months. If you prefer the ocean, you'll find some of South Australia's best beaches just ten minutes' drive away. Also nearby are several excellent restaurants (the Salopian Inn, The Barn, D'Arry's Verandah, Magnums, the Limeburners, The Star of Greece) and over forty wonderful wineries.

Name: Willunga House

Category: Guesthouse

Location: Fleurieu Peninsula region; McLaren Vale; 5 km (nearest city)

Address: 1 St. Peter's Terrace, Willunga, SA 5172

Phone: Tel. 61 8 8556 2467 **Fax** 61 8 8556 2465

E-mail: knotts@intertech.net.au

Web site: www.willungahouse.com.au

Innkeepers: Rosie & Kingsley Knott

Rates: From A$130-160 per double includes full breakfast

Number of rooms: 3 Queen, 2 Double

Baths: 3 Ensuite, 2 Private

Services & amenities: Solar heated pool, massage available in-house

Restrictions: No smoking; not suitable for children

Handicap access: no

Northern Territory

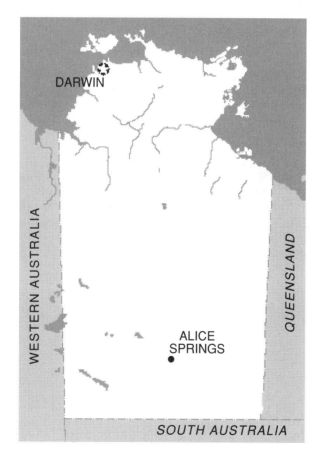

I n the Northern Territory, the vast wilderness and blanketing stillness are largely still intact after more than a century of permanent European settlement. Here is the real Outback, one of the most exciting, unspoiled, and undiscovered destinations left on Earth. It's the land of wonder, untamed and surreal landscapes, of the Aboriginal Dreamtime, mystical legends, and sacred sites that date back thousands of years. The least populated and most barren area of the continent, the Northern Territory is Australia's last frontier. It covers one-sixth of the continent but has less than 1 percent of the population.

Darwin, the Northern Territory's capital city, is perched at the "Top End" of the country—Australia's northernmost border. It's a pretty, bougainvillea-clad city with a reputation as a hard-drinking frontier town. Once a sleepy tropical outpost, Darwin has emerged as a modern commercial center situated on a magnificent harbor. As the northern gateway to the country, this colorful, cosmopolitan city is a harmonious melting pot of nationalities that hosts a constant flow of international and domestic travelers. The Top End's attractions are many, and Darwin is a good base for tours into Kakadu National Park. Kakadu (made famous by Paul Hogan's Crocodile Dundee films) is on the World Heritage List. Spanning 12,000 square miles of lush greenery, roaring falls, and surreal rock formations, the park is the product of two million years of continuous erosion. In the caves and rock shelters, are Aboriginal rock paintings which were done before the ice age. Rich in bird and wildlife, Kakadu is blessed with soaring sandstone escarpments, lush green forests, and mighty waterfalls tumbling from brightly colored cliffs to the enormous waterholes below.

The immensity of the Top End seems to swallow up the residents and swelling numbers of tourists. Along the Stuart Highway, the 1500 kilometer "track" that connects Darwin and Alice Springs, there are only a couple communities of any note. Katherine is a bustling town and an important stopping off point. The largest attraction here is the Katherine Gorge, a miniature Grand Canyon where a river runs between towering multi-colored walls. Boat trips through the sheer-walled gorge are popular and a highlight of a visit to the area. The desert oasis of Mataranka, 103 kilometers south of Katherine, offers soothing thermal springs, which provide a chance to bath away the dust and cares of the day. Huge grazing properties and cattle stations along the track to Alice Springs, are measured in square miles rather than acres, and Tennant Creek, located 511 kilometers north of Alice Springs, is the only other town of any size.

Alice Springs—"The Alice" as it is known—is in the geographic center of Australia. This Outback town, built on red soil where millions of colorful wildflowers grow, is surrounded by mountains and desert. Originally a telegraph station built near a waterhole in the bed of the dry Todd River, today Alice Springs is a modern town with a number of good shops and restaurants. It's a melting pot of cultures as well as part trading post and part artistic center.

Around Alice Springs are a number of awesome natural diversions. The spectacular folds and colors of the MacDonnell Ranges are in view from most of the town. It is an easy drive to explore the many gorges that cut through the rocky cliffs and swim in cool watering holes. Just moments out of town, the enormity of the sun-baked Red Centre sinks in as the blue sky and endless wilderness stretches to the horizon. There is little traffic on the roads, and many hours may pass without seeing another vehicle. To the southwest is Ayers Rock towering high above the desert floor. The Rock, known by its aboriginal name, Uluru, is the world's largest monolith and as a sacred site is one of Australia's most significant landmarks. Noted for its spectacular color changes as the sun moves across the sky, the rock turns pink, mauve, brown, orange and finally blood red at sunset. Equally as impressive, are the nearby Olgas, a collection of huge rock domes. More than 600 million years old, the Olgas are peaks of a buried mountain range that provide fascinating opportunities for exploration.

In many ways, Australia's legendary Outback echoes the American Wild West. The Northern Territory can be inhospitable during certain times of year and is best visited in the dry season, between May and October. However, the beauty of the mysterious Northern Territory is well worth a visit, for this area is unlike any other place on Earth.

For more information write or telephone:

Northern Territory Tourist Commission
3601 Aviation Boulevard, Ste 2100
Manhattan Beach, CA 90266
(310) 643 2636   (310) 643 2627

Or check out their websites:
www.nttc.com.au
www.insidetheoutback.com

REGIONAL DIRECTORY
➤ denotes review

CENTRAL
➤ **Bond Springs Station**   Alice Springs, NT 0871 61 8 8952 9888
Elegant and charming retreat in the majestic MacDonnell Ranges
➤ **Nthaba Cottage Bed & Breakfast**   83 Cromwell Drive, Alice Springs, NT 0870 61 8 8952 9003
Beautiful B&B cottage on a lovely hillside in Alice Springs

➤ **Orangewood**   9 McMinn St./PO Box 8871, Alice Springs, NT 0871
61 8 8952 4114

MACDONNELL RANGES

➤ **Glen Helen Resort**   Namatjira Dr., Glen Helen, NT 0870   61 8 8956 7489
*Wilderness lodge in the MacDonnell Ranges with comfortable motel style
guestrooms*

TOP END

Acacia Homestead Bed & Breakfast   5 Forest Drive, Humpty Doo,
NT 0836   61 8 8988 4000
Five acres of natural tropical bushland near major tourist attractions

Bonrook Lodge   Stuart Highway, Pine Creek, NT 0847   61 8 8976 1232
Attractive accommodations on the only wild horse sanctuary in Australia

Cape Don Experience   Gurig National Park, Cobourg Peninsula, NT
0820   61 8 8979 0263
*Head lighthouse keeper's homestead provides lodging for serious
fisherman*

➤ **La Escondida Homestead**   Lot 75 Brewerton Rd/, McMinns Lagoon,
NT 0835   61 8 8988 1598
Homestyle accommodations near Darwin's popular tourist attractions

Lake Bennett Wilderness Resort   152 Chinner Rd, Lake Bennett, NT
0845   61 8 8976 0960
Award-winning resort on a beautiful lake near Litchfield National Park

➤ **Maud Creek Country Lodge**   Lot 4179, Gorge Rd., Katherine, NT
0851   61 8 8971 1814
Quiet rural property in unique setting, minutes from Katherine Gorge

➤ **Melaleuca Homestead**   163 Melaleuca Rd., Howard Springs, NT
0820   61 8 8983 2736
Six acre rural property at Howard Springs

Mount Bundy Station   Haynes Rd., Adelaide River, NT 0846
61 8 8976 7009
Lovely homestead midway between Katherine and Darwin

➤ **The Summer House**   3 Quarry Crescent, Stuart Park, NT 0820
61 8 8981 9992
Variety of personalized accommodations on the outskirts of Darwin

➤ **Tropical Gardens Bed & Breakfast**   15 Bathurst St., Woodleigh
Gardens, NT 0812   61 8 8945 3215
Quality accommodations in lush tropical gardens in suburb of Darwin

➤ **Wildman River Wilderness Lodge**   Pt Stuart Rd. Wildman,
Winnellie, NT 0821   61 8 8978 8912
Nature-based tourism in the Mary River wetlands

Bond Springs Station

B ond Springs Station is a historic homestead situated on the banks of a tree-lined creek, a tributary of the normally dry Todd River within the majestic MacDonnell ranges. A working cattle station spread over 1500 square kilometers of arid zone land, Bond Springs is owned by the Heaslip family, a family with long traditions in the outback South Australian and Northern Territory pastoral industry. At Bond Springs, Poll Hereford cattle are bred for local and international beef markets. Since 1996, Jan Heaslip has opened the homestead to guests wanting to experience a little of life on an Australian Outback station and the natural beauty of this unique place. She has renovated and restored the homestead's guest accommodations furnishing these rooms in the style of "early Australiana," appropriate to the historic significance of the house.

In the main house, the guestroom has a large bedroom with a king-size bed and a small lounge area opening into the garden. Attached to the homestead proper is a separate wing originally built as the guest quarters. This wing is now offered to visitors a suite of two double bedrooms sharing a large bathroom. This room opens onto a shady enclosed verandah that in turn opens into the garden. The enclosed verandah is comfortably furnished as a place to relax with a drink or a book (or both!). For guests seeking even more private luxury, there is the beautifully restored "Corkwood Cottage." Originally built for the Station's head stockman and his family, Corkwood Cottage is a fully self-contained residence with three bedrooms, lounge, dining area, kitchen and bathroom. A wide shady verandah surrounds the cottage in the true tradition of a Australian bush dwelling. It is an ideal spot for morning coffee or to relax in the early evening to catch the ever changing colours on the distant hills as daylight fades. Don't be surprised if a kangaroo hops through the garden, or a dingo howls in the distance. At night you'll get to fully appreciate the wonder of the Southern night sky, a truly remarkable spectacle.

Guests are invited to 'dine in' at Bond Springs Homestead. In the tradition of station life, meals are served in the homestead kitchen where everyone— guests, family and station hands—are seated around the long table. Jan's homestead cooking is renowned and sometimes even Grant, the Boss, gets into the action to carve the roast! Fine selected Australian table wines and soft drinks are served with the meal. Alternatively, the evening meal may be served around the swimming pool as the traditional bush barbecue cooked by the Boss. No one barbecues Bond Beef with more expertise than Grant! All guests are invited to use the gardens, tennis court, swimming pool, and to generally make themselves at home around the Station Homestead. Ecological safaris on Bond Springs Station and beyond can also be organized for guests. Bond Springs, with its own unique attractions, is ideally situated as a home base for visitors wanting to explore the sights of Central Australia, including Ayers Rock.

Name: Bond Springs Station
Category: Outback Retreat
Location: Central region; Alice Springs; 24 kim (nearest city)
Address: Alice Springs, NT 0871
Phone: Tel. 61 8 8952 9888 **Fax** 61 8 8953 0963
E-mail: bondhmst@alice.aust.com
Innkeepers: Jan Heaslip
Rates: Call for tariff
Rated: ****½ AANT
Number of rooms: 2 Suites, 2 Cottages
Baths: Ensuite, Private
Services & amenities: Air-conditioning; heating
Restrictions: No smoking indoors
Handicap access: no

Glen Helen Resort

J ust an hour and a half drive from Alice Springs, the geographic "red center" of Australia, Glen Helen Homestead Lodge is situated on the banks of the Finke River in the heart of the breathtaking Western Mac-Donnell Ranges. Originally built in the 1890's, the Lodge was rebuilt in 1986 after a fire swept through the historic homestead. Today, the Lodge stands on 17 acres of freehold land surrounded by National Parks and the vast Glen Helen cattle station. Lovingly restored and remodeled with a 1930's décor to give guests absolute comfort, the Lodge appears to be a mirage in the middle of a timeless desert.

Accommodations are provided in 25 motel-style, air-conditioned gues-trooms with views of the bordering river and Mt. Sonder. Built in the style of the early 1900's with leaded glass windows and patchwork bed covers, each ensuite guestroom is individually decorated with genuine antique furnishings and fittings. A lounge area, adjacent to the popular bar, provides tea and coffee making facilities and is open to guests all day. Budget accommoda-tions, consisting of serviced rooms with share bathroom facilities and hostel accommodations are also available.

The licensed bar, with beautiful views of the brilliant red face of sheer rock towering above the Finke River, is a welcome sight after the hot dusty ride from Alice Springs. But perhaps the most outstanding feature of Glen Helen Lodge is its superb gourmet restaurant. Winner of numerous Northern Territory Awards for Excellence, Cloudie's (named after pioneer post mis-tress Cloudy Beale) has beat out more established chefs from the Four Seasons and the Sheraton in Alice Springs with an eclectic and creative à la carte menu featuring international haute cuisine (with subtle Indian and Asian influences). Lace table cloths, Grosvenor silver service, fine china and an intimate candlelit ambience, combine with excellent food presentation and a good wine list, to create a magnificent dining experience, that is made all the more memorable by the fact that it is enjoyed in the middle of the Outback.

While at Glen Helen, visitors have the opportunity to enjoy miles of walking track through spectacular gorges and red desert. They can experience the unique flora and fauna and view aboriginal rock paintings while exploring some of the oldest country on earth. The famous Ormiston Gorge (the jewel of the center), Serpentine Gorge, Palm Valley and the magnificent Gosse's Bluff and Simpson's Gap are all nearby and well worth a visit.

Name: Glen Helen Resort

Category: Homestead/Motel

Location: MacDonnell Ranges region; Alice Springs; 133 km (nearest city)

Address: Namatjira Dr., Glen Helen, NT 0870

Phone: Tel. 61 8 8956 7489 **Fax** 61 8 8956 7495

E-mail: glenhelen@melanka.com.au

Web site: www.melanka.com.au

Innkeepers: Trevor & Michelle Cox

Rates: From A$120 per double/breakfast extra

Number of rooms: 25 Double/Twin

Baths: Ensuite

Services & amenities: Licensed bar and restaurant; BBQ

Handicap access: no

La Escondida Homestead

LA ESCONDIDA
◆ H O M E S T E A D ◆

L
a Escondida Homestead offers rural home-style accommodations on six acres near the outskirts of Darwin. The property is surrounded by the tropical gardens of the Territory and en-route to Kakadu and Litchfield National Parks. The lush paradise has more than 1000 fully-grown exotic tropical palms and many different varieties of tropical fruits. Guests can help themselves to mangoes, rambutans, tamarind and custard apples in season.

Guests have their choice of three bedrooms with TV and spacious shared facilities. Two bedrooms feature queen-sized beds and the third has twin beds. A lounge with TV and video as well as a games room are also available for guest use. The bedrooms have a traditional, rustic ambience and access to the long wide verandah, landscaped gardens and large inground salt water pool. Full breakfasts are served in the enormous but comfortable dining room. Other meals can be provided on request.

There is no shortage of things to do at La Escondida. It's easy to arrange a tour to Kakadu, Litchfield Park and most tourist destinations. Days can also be spent relaxing by the pool or underneath a palm tree. Guests can take a stroll among the palms and feed the goldfish, barramundi and yabbies from the bridges over the tropical ponds. La Escondida also features a paddock of magnificent ant hills—which have been years in the growing. In outer Darwin there are river cruises, a crocodile farm, a wetlands visitor center and a host of other attractions so guests should plan on staying at least a few days.

Name: La Escondida Homestead

Category: Homestay

Location: Top End region; Darwin (nearest city)

Address: Lot 75 Brewerton Rd., McMinns Lagoon, NT 0835

Phone: Tel. 61 8 8988 1598 **Fax** 61 8 8988 4510

E-mail: terej@ozemail.com.au
   URL:

Innkeepers: Bob & Tere Jaensch

Rates: From A$100-150 per double includes breakfast

Rated: **** 1/2 AANT

Number of rooms: 4 Doubles

Baths: 2 Ensuite, 1 Share

Services & amenities: Air-conditioning; overhead fans

Restrictions: No smoking indoors

Handicap access: no

Maud Creek Country Lodge

Wile in Katherine, the lovely Maud Creek Country Lodge offers a friendly, relaxing style of bed and breakfast. This rural retreat, just five minutes from the gorges and 15 minutes from town, is set on approximately 250 acres of river frontage. The guesthouse is a recently renovated and fully refurbished stationhand's quarters set apart from the main homestead. The three ensuite bedrooms are air-conditioned and have ceiling fans as well as access to a large full length verandah where outdoor table settings can be found.

A continental breakfast is served each morning in the dining room. Modern cooking facilities are provided should guests want to prepare their own evening meal or use the outdoor barbeque. A guest lounge with television is also available. Maud Creek is a perfect choice for families with two interconnecting rooms that can accommodate two adults and two children. The lodge is only 100 metres from the Katherine River so for guests feeling energetic, they can take a wander down to the jetty. If really quiet, guests may spot a small fresh water crocodile or, if a fisherman, cast about for that elusive Barramundi. For those not so energetic, sit back and relax on the verandah, spot the birdlife, and at dusk listen to the sounds of the bush.

Hosts Julie and Kevin will share their knowledge of local attractions and will help set up local tours. Katherine Gorge, with its steep-sided ravines, flowing waterways and Aboriginal art is a highlight of the area. In the dry season, it is a peaceful haven where you can watch crocs glide silently through pools shaded by flowering trees alive with parrots. In the wet season, the quiet gorge becomes a steep mountain track of rapids diving into ravines masked by fog. Anytime of year, Maud Creek Guesthouse is a good choice.

Name: Maud Creek Country Lodge

Category: Farmstay

Location: Top End region; Katherine (nearest city)

Address: Lot 4179, Gorge Rd., Katherine, NT 0851

Phone: Tel. 61 8 8971 1814 **Fax** 61 8 8972 2763

E-mail: julies@nt-tech.com.au

Innkeepers: Kevin & Julie Sneddon

Rates: From A$85-99 per double includes continental breakfast

Rated: NTBBC

Number of rooms: 2 Queen, 1 Twin

Baths: 3 Ensuite

Services & amenities: Pool, BBQ, kitchen, air-conditioning

Restrictions: No pets

Handicap access: no

Melaleuca Homestead

S ituated 30 kilometers from both Darwin's central business district and the international airport, Melaleuca Homestead is a luxury rural home retreat, set in six acres of natural tropical bushlands that abounds with native birds and wild life. Hosts Colette & Eddie O'Connor offer their guests all modern conveniences and services, and a hideaway from the hustle and bustle of today's fast pace. Guests are greeted with a complimentary drink upon arrival and shown to their room. There are two guestrooms in the homestead and two additional cottages available. Both The Melaleuca Room and The Orchid Room have their own ensuite or private bathroom, queen-size bed, and writing desks along with period furniture from the early 1920 and 1930's. All guestrooms have large bath towels, hairdryer, a selection of natural shampoos and conditioners along with natural soaps. The Frangapani Cottage and The Hibiscus Cottage are settler-type cottages overlooking the lake and separate from the homestead. The cottages feature king-size beds, air-conditioning, a mini country kitchen as well as a spacious verandah for alfresco dining. Heritage style décor sets the tone for the comfortable cottages.

A full four-course breakfast is included in the room tariff and guests in the cottages are provided with breakfast provisions. Evening meals can be arranged under tropical skies and a full in-house liquor license offers an array of Australian wines. After dinner, relax and enjoy a glass of port with your hosts. A guest sitting room is equipped with TV/VCR, a full surround stereo system with the best of classical and relaxation music, along with a large selection of reference and other books. A variety of tours can be arranged with pick-up and drop-off at Maleleuca. Car hire can also be arranged at special discounts, and limousine airport transfers can be arranged to meet your requirements. After a day of discovery, enjoy the outdoor facilities at the Homestead including large rolling lawns, lake area, swimming pool with waterfall, outdoor spa, tropical gardens, bushland walks, and, of course, secluded hideaways where you can sit and absorb the native bush.

Name: Melaleuca Homestead

Category: Homestay

Location: Top End region; Darwin (nearest city)

Address: 163 Melaleuca Rd., Howard Springs, NT 0820

Phone: Tel. 61 8 8983 2736 **Fax** 61 8 8983 2736

E-mail: melaleucahomestead@bigpond.com

Innkeepers: Colette & Eddie O'Connor

Rates: From A$100-135 per double includes full breakfast

Rated: **** AANT

Number of rooms: 2 Queen, 2 King cottages

Baths: Ensuite / Private

Services & amenities: Licensed, swimming pool, spa, gardens

Restrictions: No smoking indoors

Handicap access: no

Nthaba Cottage

N thaba Bed and Breakfast is your home away from home in Alice Springs. Enjoy the comfort of your own separate cottage with private access and off-street parking. Set in the heart of the Golf Course Estate, Nthaba is a short walk from the Alice Springs Golf Club greens and clubhouse, and within walking distance of Lasseters Casino, and the town centre. The garden provides a tranquil oasis after visiting magnificent out-back chasms, gorges and valleys. Views of the spectacular MacDonnell Ranges can be enjoyed from Nbatha as well as from most parts of town.

The Colonial style brick Nbatha B&B cottage features a separate sitting room, double or twin share bedroom and private bathroom. An additional bedroom is also available if necessary. Enjoy breakfast in the garden or the comforts of the private sitting room. Hosts Anne and Will Cormack, who reside in the adjacent main house, are quite knowledgeable about the area and helpful when it comes to making suggestions of what to see and do.

Bird watchers will delight at the rich bird life found in the garden and surrounds. Will is a keen birdwatcher and happy to share his knowledge. There are 36 species of birds that visit the garden regularly and guests at Nthaba Cottage B&B can visit the acclaimed Alice Springs Desert Park where bird, plant and animal life are beautifully presented. Alice Springs is also a major tourist center and a variety of seasonal events and attractions can be enjoyed. Nbatha offers special rates at certain times of year so inquire about the seasonal rates.

Name: Nthaba Cottage Bed & Breakfast

Category: Self-contained

Location: Central region; Alice Springs (nearest city)

Address: 83 Cromwell Drive, Alice Springs, NT 0870

Phone: Tel. 61 8 8952 9003 **Fax** 61 8 8953 3295

E-mail: nthaba@ozemail.com.au

Web site: www.ozemail.com.au/~nthaba/

Innkeepers: Will & Anne Cormack

Rates: From A$125 includes breakfast

Number of rooms: 1 King/Twin

Baths: Private

Services & amenities: Air-conditioning; tea/coffee making facilities, refrigerator, toaster

Restrictions: No smoking indoors

Handicap access: no

Orangewood

T he "Old Eastside" is one of the earliest settled suburbs of Alice Springs. Nestled into Telegraph Station National Park, the area features historic buildings and easy access to the town center. A morning walk along the usually waterless Todd River to the restored Station is highly recommended.

On a quiet street, in this lovely neighborhood sits Orangewood, a comfortable family home maintained exclusively for the comfort and enjoyment of guests. Named for the grove of citrus trees in the back garden and extensively renovated in 1995, Orangewood features three luxurious bedrooms and a comfortable garden cottage suite. All the rooms are attractively furnished with antiques, special family pieces and original artworks. A luxuriously appointed sitting room features an open fireplace, piano and stereo system with an extensive collection of jazz and classical music. There are shelves of first edition books and an adjacent reading room where a paperback "exchange" library provides plenty of reading material. Relax with a cup of tea or coffee and homemade biscuits that are provided along with seasonal fruit throughout the day.

Breakfast is served in the "Barbara Butler" room, so named for a central Australian artist and family friend who exhibits her work in the room. The bright breakfast area overlooks the garden and swimming pool, and warmed on frosty mornings by a cottage stove. Naturally, breakfast includes a glass of freshly squeezed juice from the oranges that grow out back.

Hosts Lynne and Ross Peterkin have lived in Alice Springs for more than three decades and are active in local tourism organizations. Their beautiful home was transformed into a bed & breakfast after their youngest son moved out and they've won numerous accolades for their accommodations. Both are well traveled and they pride themselves in translating their personal experiences into a quality experience for guests. Both Lynne and Ross can offer suggestions on local attractions as Alice Springs is the gateway to Australia's vast Outback and a center for Aboriginal art and culture.

Name: Orangewood

Category: Bed & Breakfast

Location: Central region; Alice Springs (nearest city)

Address: 9 McMinn St./PO Box 8871, Alice Springs, NT 0871

Phone: Tel. 61 8 8952 4114 **Fax** 61 8 8952 4664

E-mail: oranges@orangewood-bnb.au.com

Web site: www.orangewood-bnb.au.com

Innkeepers: Lynne & Ross Peterkin

Rates: From A$160 includes full breakfast

Rated: ****1/2 AANT; 1998 Brolga Award for Excellence

Number of rooms: 2 King or Twin, 1 Queen, 1 Double

Baths: 4 Ensuite

Services & amenities: Air-conditioning/heat, guest lounge/library; open fire; piano; stereo; TV, coffee/tea, pool

Handicap access: no

The Summer House

W hether you're looking for an alternative to a hotel, or something different, The Summer House has a variety of accommodation styles. Centrally located in the balmy residential suburb of Stuart Park, three minutes from Darwin, this delightful establishment offers private and personalized accommodations. As a bed and breakfast, The Summer House offers a sense of a traditional B&B in a tropical setting. Guests in two double bedrooms share a fully equipped kitchen, bathroom and living area. For families or groups, four self-catering units with two bedrooms each are available. "The Studio" is a contemporary suite with polished cement floors and a hint of the orient. "The Suite" has a blended style which features a giant Balinese cane lounge, wrought iron and glass queen-sized bed. And "The Apartment" is a simple and fun unit with just a hint of 1956, ideal for a family.

All bedrooms have fans and/or air-conditioning while the living areas are fan cooled for those balmy evenings. A tropical breakfast is included for B&B guests, and for those late mornings, B&B often turns into Bed & Brunch. Breakfasts can also be arranged for those staying in the self-catering units. Televisions are located in the lounge area of the cottages and B&B guests have access to a shared lounge area.

Host Jill Farrand has artistic inclinations and her interest in mosaics can be seen all around The Summer House. She can also help identify area attractions in and around Darwin. The local shopping center is within walking distance and the Mindil Beach Markets are a casual stroll on a tropical night.

Name: The Summer House

Category: Self-contained

Location: Top End region; Darwin (nearest city)

Address: 3 Quarry Crescent, Stuart Park, NT 0820

Phone: Tel. 61 8 8981 9992 **Fax** 61 8 8981 0009

E-mail: summerhouseb&b@octa4.net.au

Web site: www.octa4.net.au/summerhouseb&b

Innkeepers: Jill Farrand

Rates: From A$100 per double includes breakfast

Number of rooms: 4 Doubles

Baths: Private

Services & amenities: Air-conditioning

Restrictions: No smoking indoors

Handicap access: no

Tropical Gardens

A t Tropical Gardens Bed & Breakfast Homestay, guests enjoy the re-laxed atmosphere that bi-lingual hosts, Peter & Maria Prukner have created. The tastefully decorated guestroom features a queen-size bed along with ensuite facilities, air-conditioning and an overhead fan. Centrally located in Darwin's northern suburbs, Tropical Gardens is close to golf and other sporting venues and a few minutes drive to the beach. At the end of the short street is a bus stop for those who don't want to drive to the many attractions that Darwin has to offer. The city center, Casino, Mindil Beach Markets and the Wharf Precinct are all just 15 minutes away.

Guests are welcome to use the large in-ground spa or relax in the tropical leisure area to read a book, write postcards, or watch TV. Tropical plants abound allowing for plenty of privacy and shade. A gas barbeque is available for those fishermen who want to cook the catch of the day or you can pick up food at the market and enjoy it on the enclosed patio area.

Peter and Maria offer complimentary pick-up and drop-off service along with a complimentary drink upon arrival. They'll also point out all the things to see and do in Darwin's northern suburbs including the nearby coastal dunes, monsoon vine forest and Jungle Nature Park. There are also numer-ous recreation areas for picnics and sunset viewing as well as a myriad of sports and social activities.

Name: Tropical Gardens Bed & Breakfast

Category: Homestay

Location: Top End region; Darwin (nearest city)

Address: 15 Bathurst St., Woodleigh Gardens, NT 0812

Phone: Tel. 61 8 8945 3215 **Fax** 61 8 8945 3215

E-mail: tropical.bb@octa4.net.au

Web site: www.interbed.com.au/tropicalgardens.htm

Innkeepers: Peter & Maria Prukner

Rates: From A$110 per double includes continental breakfast

Rated: ****½ AANT

Number of rooms: 1 Queen/Twin

Baths: Ensuite

Services & amenities: Air-conditioning; overhead fans

Restrictions: No smoking indoors

Handicap access: no

Wildman River Wilderness Lodge

L ocated on a private reserve, Wildman River Wilderness Lodge provides unique accommodations and specialized wildlife tours. The reserve was developed in 1994 to protect and present the beauty and natural wonders of this exquisite part of the country. The Top End, well known for its great wildlife concentration and unique eco-system, attracts visitors from around the world. Situated within two hours drive of Darwin on the edge of Kakadu National Park, The Wildman Wilderness Lodge offers an ideal base from which to take advantage of the area's attractions. One of the most unique features of this operation is that the lodge is within 500 metres of the wetland, which puts the wildlife virtually at your doorstep. The Lodge offers daily tours and wetland cruises to view the wildlife and operates the only airboat in the area providing unparalleled access during the wet season (Nov.–April). There are over 250 species of birds to see, 2 species of crocodile and numerous wallabies and other marsupials.

Accommodations at Wildman River Wilderness Lodge are provided in individual cabins and, during the dry season, luxury fabric safari-style cabins are available. The cabins are sparse but comfortable with all the necessary furnishings. For families, there are connecting rooms and cots available.

Given the isolated location of the lodge, the tariff includes dinner, bed & breakfast. A typical dinner menu might consist of Cauliflower Soup, Chicken Hollandaise, Fresh Baked Rolls and Lemon Meringue Pie. Hearty breakfasts include cereal, fruit, bacon, eggs, tomato, toast, juice and, of course, tea or coffee. Meals are eaten in a communal dining room and the kitchen can cater for special diets and vegetarians. Wildman River Wilderness Lodge caters to many overseas visitors who come for a wilderness experience.

Name: Wildman River Wilderness Lodge

Category: Wilderness Lodge

Location: Top End region; Darwin; 186 km (nearest city)

Address: Pt Stuart Rd. Wildman, Winnellie, NT 0821

Phone: Tel. 61 8 8978 8912 **Fax** 61 8 8978 8907

E-mail: wildman-lodge@octa4.net.au

Web site: www.wildmanlodge.com.au

Innkeepers: David & Susan Churchett

Rates: From A$110 per person included dinner, bed & breakfast

Rated: Brolga Award

Number of rooms: 25 Double/Twin

Baths: 7 Share

Services & amenities: Dining room, pool, spa, wildlife tours

Handicap access: no

Western Australia

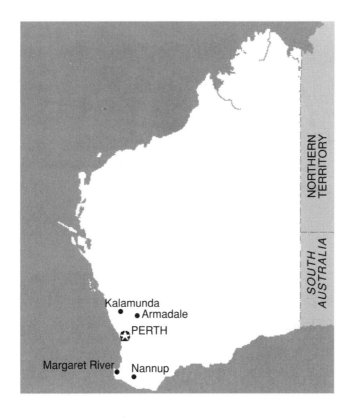

Occupying one third of the Australian continent, Western Australia stretches from the spectacular Kimberley region in the north, to the lovely beaches of the South West coast and is bordered by the vast desert to the east. Spanning over 1 million square miles, Western Australia is so large, it extends into different climatic zones simultaneously. Adored for its brilliant blue skies, warm sunny climate and white sandy beaches, Western Australia is blessed with some of the world's most precious natural phenomena including the dolphins of Monkey Mia, the 350-million-year-old Bungle Bungle Range and the towering karri forests of the South West. Great weather is also one of Western Australia's most appealing attractions. The temperate climate throughout much of the state provides year-round sunshine and even during the winter months, it's possible to enjoy warm, summer-like weather.

Perth, the State's capital and gateway city, enjoys more hours of sunshine than any other capital city in Australia. First settled in 1829, it wasn't until the gold rushes of the 1890's that real growth began. Today, with a population of nearly 1.5 million, the city is renowned for vigorous growth and characterized by the casual pace of its warm, friendly people. The comparative newness of the city accounts for the modern, clean-cut look. Situated on the banks of the scenic Swan River, the pleasant river location and close proximity to clean ocean beaches make the city ideal for aquatic sports and boats of all sizes and descriptions. Windsurfers, dinghies and water skiers can all be seen enjoying the relaxed lifestyle of this dynamic cosmopolitan city.

The nearby historic port city of Fremantle, is a maze of picturesque streets lined with grand Victorian buildings (many built in the 1800's by convict labor). Recognized as the best preserved example of a 19th century port streetscape in the world, Fremantle has Western Australia's largest collection of heritage-listed buildings. Many of which are house attractions, museums, offices, art galleries, restaurants, and shops. The first group of convicts were brought to Fremantle in 1850, and many were set to work constructing roads and buildings in the colony. Existing evidence of these public works include the Fremantle Prison, the road between Perth and Albany, Government House and the Perth Town Hall.

An easy three hour drive from Perth, is Western Australia's South West, a region of lush vegetation, rich farmland, dense forests and rugged coastline. Old timber towns like Bridgetown and Pemberton, offer idyllic environments for escaping the pressures of modern life. A bushwalker's haven, the area is also a favourite for birdwatchers and freshwater fishermen.

The charming town of Margaret River, well-known as a surfer's paradise, boasts some of the best waves for the sport to be found anywhere in the world. Situated only 10 kilometers from some of the most magnificent beaches along the South West coast, the town lies in the center of the region's wine industry. Quiet roads for exploring the area's many attractions, including ancient caves and giant karri forests as well as quaint craft shops, boutique wineries and excellent country-style restaurants, wind their way through the region.

The Great Southern region is the State's most southerly point where stunning natural scenery abounds. A well kept secret, the area boasts million year old granite ranges and some of the country's most beautiful wildflowers. Walk the tracks of the Stirling Range National Park, explore coastal and country towns rich in history, or immerse yourself in natural experiences such as whale watching or the Tree Top Walk—a 600-metre steel suspension walkway. Neighboring Esperance, where some of Australia's most spectacular coastline, islands and magnificent national parks can be found, is one of Western Australia's fastest growing tourist destinations. Graced with a temperate climate year round and sugar-white sand bordered by brilliant blue-water bays, the peace and simplicity of the region is a large part of its appeal. With its abundance of wildlife including seals, dolphins, whales, emus and sea eagles, Esperance is one of the only places in Western Australia where you might see kangaroos sunbathing on the beach.

Western Australia's Outback offers a wide array of adventure for tourists of all ages and abilities. About 500 miles north of Perth, along the state's remote coastline, the Gascoyne Region is where the deep red soil meets the brilliant blue waters of the Indian Ocean. Some of the many highlights of the area are windsurfing and the tiny settlement of Monkey Mia, where dolphins regularly swim into the shallows of the beach to take fish from the hands of fascinated visitors. The region offers some of Australia's premier soft adventure and eco-tourism experiences with The Shark Bay World Heritage area and Ningaloo Marine Park—both world-famous natural attractions. Exmouth, surrounded by the warm waters of the Indian Ocean, offers some of the best game fishing in all of Australia.

The so-called "Golden Mile" near the historic town of Kalgoorlie in the Goldfields, is said to be the richest square mile of earth anywhere in the world. Today, with rows of frontier buildings, pubs and old mines to explore, Kalgoorlie still preserves the colourful character of yesteryear and remains steeped in the rich heritage of early settlement. The surrounding towns were not all so lucky, but visitors can see what remains of these ghost towns or even try their luck by at gold panning themselves.

Broome, the Western gateway to the rugged Kimberley, recalls the romantic bygone days when pearling fleets from Japan, the Phillipines, Malayasia and the Dutch East Indies discovered the bountiful riches of gem pearls in these tropical waters. The once bustling Chinatown still reflects the early community and embraces the traditions and ways of their origins.

Covering more than a quarter of a million miles, The Kimberley covers an area three times the size of England, though only 25,000 residents live there. This translates to fewer people per square mile than almost any other place on the planet. A land of spectacular gorges and ranges, cascading waterfalls and tranquil pools, the area is the natural habitat of the crocodile, the legendary barramundi game fish and a variety of birds and reptiles. This wild, untamed region, considered by many to be Australia's last frontier, is also home of the Bungle Bungle Range, a surrealistic landscape of bizarre beehive striped domes that stretch over more than 450 square kilometers of remote wilderness.

Accommodations in Western Australia is as varied as the State's landscape; from luxury resorts, private hotels and adventure lodges, to Outback stations and guesthouses, every type of bed and breakfast can be found. Due to the remoteness of many areas, caravan parks are still a prevalent style of accommodation, but a whole new generation of lodging has evolved in the more popular tourist areas—most notably the picturesque Avon Valley, the South West and Great Southern regions, as well as delightful towns such as Margaret River, Albany and Yallingup. Small and well-run, these bed and breakfasts provide an excellent introduction to a region, good value for the money, and hosts who will go out of their way to make sure your visit is enjoyable.

For more information whilst in the U.S.:

Tel: (661) 775-2000 (brochure orders)

or

Western Australian Tourist Centre
Forrest Place (at Wellington Street)
Perth WA 6000
AUSTRALIA
(GPO Box W2081, Perty, WA 6846)
Tel: 1300 361 351 (in Australia)
Fax: (+61 8) 9481 0190 (anywhere in the world)

and

www.westernaustralia.net

REGIONAL DIRECTORY
➤ denotes review

AVON VALLEY

Egoline Reflections   PO Box 1026, Northam, WA 6401 61 8 9622 5811
National Trust listed homestead set in extensive gardens one hour from Perth

Hillside Country Retreat   PO Box 12, York, WA 6302 61 8 9641 1065
Gracious Edwardian homestead in farmland setting

The Chittering Bed & Breakfast   Lot 88 Parkside Gardens, Bindoon, WA 6502 61 8 9576 0161
Airy farmhouse-style homestead in western red cedar with slate floors and extensive patio area

FREMANTLE

Fremantle Colonial Accommodation   215 High St., Fremantle, WA 6160 61 8 9430 6568
Fremantle Colonial Accommodation is the Port City's most conveniently located private accommodations

Westerley Bed & Breakfast   74 Solomon St., Fremantle, WA 6160 61 8 9430 4458
Lovely factory-conversion townhouse in Fremantle

GASCOYNE

Dirk Hartog Island Station   Dirk Hartog Island, Shark Bay, WA 6537 61 8 9948 1211
Unique sheep station and holiday destination situated on secluded private beach

GREAT SOUTHERN

Flinders Park Lodge   3 Harbour Rd., Oyster Harbour, WA 6330 61 8 9844 7062
Unique character guesthouse set in a vast expanse of landscaped gardens

Hayrocks B&B   St Werburghs Rd., Mt. Barker, WA 6324 61 8 9851 2196
Tranquil setting on nine acres of rural land with views over the vineyards and the Hay River Valley

Karri Mia Lodge   Box 500, Denmark, WA 6333 61 8 9848 2255
Designed and built for the discerning guest who appreciates attention to detail

Peacehaven Mountain Escape   4 Millinup Road, Porongurup, WA 6326 61 8 9853 2141
Peacehaven is located on the pictuesque southern slopes of the Porongurup Range

Water's Edge Guesthouse   9 Inlet Dr., Denmark, WA 6333 61 8 9848 1043
Lovely modern guesthouse with superlative views

KIMBERLEY

El Questro Station   Gibb River Road, Kununurra, WA   61 8 9161 4318
Over one million acres, El Questro provides a true Australian Outback experience

PERTH

➤ **Anne Hathaway's Cottage**   25 Canns Rd./PO Box 398, Armadale, WA 6112/6992 61 8 9497 3942
Indulgent yet affordable B&B accommodations in charming, thatched tudor replica nestled in hills

Como Heights   4 Lockhart St., Como, WA 6152 (08) 9450 6875
Australian character home 7 minutes from Perth city centre offering beautiful river views

Hansons   60 Forest Road, Henley Brook, WA 6055 61 8 9296 3366
The best of elegant living in beautiful Swan Valley

➤ **Possum Creek Lodge**   6 Lenori Rd, Gooseberry Hill, WA 6076 61 8 9257 1927
High quality fully self-contained suites set in a large garden;

➤ **Rosebridge House**   86 Williams St., Gooseberry Hill, WA 6076 61 8 9293 1741
Charming colonial homestead in traditional Australian style convenient to both the airport and Perth

➤ **William Shakespeare Guesthouse**   25 Canns Rd, Bedfordale, WA 6112 61 8 9497 4009
Elizabethan style replica of Shakespeare's birthplace

SOUTH WEST

➤ **Blackwood Inn**   Lot 4/ South Western Hwy, Mullalyup, WA 6253 61 8 9764 1138
Five-star adults only boutique B&B retreat in beautiful Blackwood Valley region

➤ **Cairnhill Homestead**   Koorabin Dr/ PO Box 28, Yallingup, WA 6282 61 8 9755 2828
Colonial style homestead in Margaret River Wine region

Cape Lodge   Caves Road, Yallingup, WA 6282 61 8 9755 6311
Boutique hotel nestled in the heart of the Margaret River wine growing region

➤ **Gilgara Homestead**   Caves Road, Margaret River, WA 6285 61 8 9757 2705
Beautiful homestead near Margaret River offering country hospitality

Heritage Lodge   31 Bussell Highway, Margaret River, WA 6285
61 8 9757 9595
Luxury suites nestled in the forest at the entrance to Margaret River

➤ **Hi*Life Guesthouse**   28 Carey St/ PO Box 551, Bridgetown, WA
6255   61 8 9761 2104
Cedar clad guesthouse situated high on a hill with outstanding valley views

Karriview Lodge   Caves Rd., Cowaramup, WA 6284   61 8 9755 5553

Kievi Farm Lodge   RMB 853, Williams, WA 6391   61 8 9885 6026
Farm lodge on 5,000 acre sheep and cattle farm

Laughing Clown   Cnr Caves & Hemsley Roads, Yallingup, WA 6282
61 8 97552341
Five-star country retreat for adults, on ten beautiful landscaped acres

➤ **Redgum Hill**   Balingup Rd., Nannup, WA 6275   61 8 9756 2056
First-class accommodations on the banks of the Blackwood River

➤ **Wildwood Valley**   Wildwood Rd., Yallingup, WA 6282   61 8 9755 2120
Country house set in bushland in heart of Margaret River region with magnificent views to the sea

Windsor House   PO Box 403, Bridgetown, WA 6255   61 8 9761 1676
Secluded riverside setting with period furnishings near the centre of Bridgetown

Anne Hathaway's Cottage

Hosts Cheryl Gillmore and Bill Banton invite you to be pampered and indulged at Anne Hathaway's Cottage, an Elizabethan escape, set in peaceful gardens in the picturesque Bedfordale hills 2km south of Armadale. Enjoy charming bed & breakfast accommodations in a thatched replica of the 16th century farmhouse of Shakespeare's wife. Guests enjoy private facilities, an informal friendly atmosphere, and discreet, attentive service. At Anne Hathaways, it's possible to step back in time. Stay in one of two charming double ensuite bedrooms, or the family suite, where everything is provided, including a choice of silver service, deluxe continental, hearty Aussie, or gourmet breakfasts, in your own private dining room. Amenities include tea and coffee making facilities, fridge, TV, VCR, videos, linen, electric blankets, crockery, cutlery, games, books, magazines, and toiletries, etc.

The Romeo & Juliet Suite is a private suite, comprising a spacious queen-size room with adjoining bathroom, separate toilet and private breakfast room. Another large queen-size room with two additional singles is decorated with period furniture and tasteful Old World décor. The Hamlet Suite is a charming double room with ensuite bathroom, an enchanting candlelit and private breakfast room just for two. Lastly, there's a Family Suite that is just perfect for those traveling with kids.

Guests can linger over breakfast, sit in the sunshine and read, or take a walk through the tranquil hills. Anne Hathaway's provides a place to stop and breathe in the fragrance of cottage flowers—roses, lavender and Australian eucalyptus. Marvel at the changing of the seasons, the myriad of birdlife, laughing kookaburras, chattering magpies and the antics of the greedy galahs. Western Australia's renowned Heritage Country boasts many scenic and man-made attractions. Anne Hathaway's Cottage is situated at the gateway to the South West/Margaret River/Albany regions and is conveniently located, just 30kms from Perth, the capital city of Western Australia, and cosmopolitan Fremantle, a popular seaside suburb. When it's time to eat, a real Old English Pub is right next door to Anne Hathaways, providing award-winning beers, brewed on the premises. Enjoy a counter meal in the cozy bar beside a log fire or al-fresco. For those seeking something more formal, à la carte dining is available in cozy Cobwebs Restaurant.

Name: Anne Hathaway's Cottage

Category: Bed & Breakfast

Location: Perth Hills region; Armadale; 2 km (nearest city)

Address: 25 Canns Rd./PO Box 398, Armadale, WA 6112/6992

Phone: Tel. 61 8 9497 3942 **Fax** 61 8 9497 2247

E-mail: cometpl@ozemail.com.au

Web site: www.annehathaways.com.au

Innkeepers: Cheryl & Bill Banton

Rates: From A$110-165 per double includes breakfast

Rated: ****1/2;Tourism Council Australia

Number of rooms: 1 Queen, 1 Queen with 2 Singles, 1 Double

Baths: Private / Ensuite

Services & amenities: Licensed restaurant, BBQ, tea/coffee, TV/Lounge area, refrigerator, games

Restrictions: No smoking

Handicap access: no

Blackwood Inn

E stablished in the 1864 for travelers making their way South by horse and coach, the Blackwood Inn is one of Western Australia's first inns and it remains a favourite with those touring the beautiful South West region. The original handmade brick building and grounds remain largely unchanged from the 19th century and are classified by the National Trust as an important link in the early heritage of the South West. But there have been important upgrades as well and visitors to the Blackwood Inn now enjoy five-star accommodations in a beautifully maintained establishment that caters to all the creature comforts.

The suites at the Blackwood Inn resemble the guest wing of a fine country house. Spacious queen-sized suites are well appointed with open fireplaces, luxurious beds, comfortable furnishing and ensuite bathrooms. There are also deluxe spa suites that feature king-sized beds, a two-person spa and a generous lounge area. All suites are simply but elegantly furnished with individual décor and meticulous attention to detail. The Tivoli Spa Suite, opened in 1992 is a favourite as is the Innkeeper's Spa Suite with its four-poster bed, writing desk and comfortable seating area.

The Blackwood Inn features a warm and cozy licensed restaurant where a log fire crackles in the grate and the wholesome aroma of good country cooking beckons to all who cross the threshold. The restaurant is very much as guests found it when the inn first opened but the menu now features an interesting selection of regional delicacies including trout, venison and beef. A selection of quality wines from nearby wineries is also available. The Inn's garden make a lovely setting for outdoor dining and, in season, guests can pick fruit from trees that were planted in the 1860s. The Inn is also central to many of the South West's attractions and guests can take advantage of the beautiful surroundings found right at the Inn's doorstep.

Name: Blackwood Inn

Category: Bed & Breakfast

Location: South West/Blackwood River region; Mullalyup (nearest city)

Address: Lot 4/ South Western Hwy, Mullalyup, WA 6253

Phone: Tel. 61 8 9764 1138 **Fax** 61 8 9764 1335

E-mail: E-mail: blackwood.inn@bigpond.com

Innkeepers: Dion Lang & Kylie Isitt

Rates: Call for tariff

Rated: ***** RAC

Number of rooms: 8

Baths: Ensuite

Services & amenities: Spa, sauna, licensed restaurant

Restrictions: No smoking, no children

Handicap access: no

Cairnhill Homestead

E njoy the beauty, romance and tranquility of this picturesque 10-acre country property, with lake, creek, hill and forest views. The five-star Cairnhill Homestead is perfectly located to take full advantage of the nearby wineries, restaurants, golf courses, beaches, dive venues, whale watching, art galleries and many other attractions of the Margaret River region of Western Australia. Hosts Dennis and Liz have traveled widely and chose to settle in the South West Capes region in late 1992. With the help of their architect son-in-law, they designed Cairnhill as a luxury guesthouse for couples. Its' accommodations are intentionally limited to three suites, to ensure a high level of personal service and comfort. Guests enjoy air-conditioned facilities throughout but may relax on a private patio or, during the cooler months, besides the log fire in the guest lounge and dining room. Lovely gardens surround the residence without obstructing the superb views from all rooms. Each king-size suite, with its individual décor, provides all the requirements of a romantic, peaceful and memorable interlude. A two person corner spa bath allows guests to enjoy the scenic views while relaxing.

In the morning, a silver service breakfast, featuring a varied menu, is provided in the guest dining room. The region is also blessed with an excellent range of restaurants, and many of the wineries have dining rooms or cafes that have gained notable awards for the food and service. Perched on a hill, the Colonial-style homestead looks down over a picturesque valley and lake. Across the valley, rises the forested hills of Leeuwin-Naturaliste National Park. The area abounds with wildlife, and kangaroos are virtually guaranteed to put in an appearance on and around the property. Within four kilometers are beautiful beaches for swimming and surfing. A dive wreck sunk off the coast in late 1997 is attracting many visitors for snorkeling and reef diving.

The limestone cave that launched tourism in the area 100 years ago, is just a short distance away and other caves along the Leeuwin Naturaliste Ridge offer visitors a unique opportunity to experience their wondrous beauty. From June to December, whales calve in the waters around the Capes and may be seen from charter boats or the shore. A good vantage point is the Naturaliste Lighthouse, just north of Cairnhill Homestead. Although the region's attractions are plentiful, be sure to plan enough time to relax and enjoy the luxury of this special homestead—it's well worth it.

Name: Cairnhill Homestead

Category: Guesthouse

Location: South West/Capes region; Yallingup (nearest city)

Address: Koorabin Dr/ PO Box 28, Yallingup, WA 6282

Phone: Tel. 61 8 9755 2828 **Fax** 61 8 9755 2829

E-mail: mail@cairnhill.com.au

Web site: www.cairnhill.com.au/

Innkeepers: Dennis & Liz Smith

Rates: From A$160-220 per double includes full, silver service breakfast

Rated: ***** RAC

Number of rooms: 3 King

Baths: 3 Ensuite with spa

Restrictions: No children; no pets; minimum 2 nights on weekends

Handicap access: no

Gilgara Homestead

A t first glance, Gilgara appears to be an historic residence passed down from generation to generation. In fact, it's a striking reproduction of a classic Australian Colonial station homestead circa 1879. Nestled on twenty-three lush acres in the superb wine-growing region of Margaret River, Gilgara is surrounded by gardens overflowing with roses and scented perennials. Guests at this exclusive bed & breakfast enjoy walking in the beautiful gardens, frequented by native birds, or to the nearby coast, past Meekadarabee Falls and Ellensbrook Homestead—home of the first settlers Ellen and Alfred Bussell (1857).

Gilgara is elegantly appointed with luxurious features in evidence everywhere. Romantic bedrooms, all with ensuite facilities, are individually decorated and miniature roses can be found on the crisp white pillowcases before turning in for the night. Host Pam Kimmel begins to extend her hospitality the moment you cross the threshold and the gracious treatment continues throughout your stay. She's eager to share her love of the region and is a wealth of information when it comes to local history.

During the winter months, an enormous open fire blazes in the graciously furnished drawing room and an English cooked breakfast is available. At other times, a gourmet Mediterranean breakfast features an array of regional delicacies that change according to the season. The varied selection might include Margaret River cheeses, smoked salmon, fresh fruits and vegetables along with freshly made breads. Enjoy the sumptuous feast while gazing across splendid views of the beautifully landscaped property.

The region surrounding Gilgara has much to offer, with craft shops, galleries and restaurants all nearby. Long stretches of secluded beaches, jeweled caves, quiet forest walks and world-renowned wineries are also there to be discovered. The country splendor found at this exclusive retreat has attracted an international clientele, including numerous celebrities, who appreciate the high standards and the extraordinary attention to detail.

Name: Gilgara Homestead

Category: Bed & Breakfast

Location: South West region; Margaret River (nearest city)

Address: Caves Road, Margaret River, WA 6285

Phone: Tel. 61 8 9757 2705 **Fax** 61 8 9757 3259

E-mail: stay@gilgara.com.au

Web site: www.gilgara.com.au

Innkeepers: Pam Kimmel

Rates: From A$175 per double includes breakfast

Rated: ****1/2 RAC, Winner Sir David Brand Award

Number of rooms: 6 Queen

Baths: Ensuite

Handicap access: no

Hi*Life Guesthouse

T reat yourself to Bridgetown's premier guesthouse. Hosts Margaret and Frank Penn have been in the hospitality business for many years and their dream was to build a special guesthouse that incorporated many of the best features they'd seen in other establishments. After searching the South West, they discovered one of the highest land points in Bridgetown where they built Hi*Life, a lovely cedar clad structure with three tastefully appointed suites and magnificent views of the Blackwood Valley. Hi*Life is situated close to the Blackwood River and within walking distance of the town, making it an ideal home away from home.

A highlight of the Hi*Life is its unusual dining room. Guests can enjoy a memorable meal in the Pemberton Room, where Frank will treat you to fine cuisine and quality local wines. Because Hi*Life entertains many couples, the dining room specializes in creating dishes for two; try the Chateau Hi*Life featuring prime South West Sirloin or the fresh fish of the day cooked Marseilles style. With its wonderful vantage point, the Pemberton Room features vaulted ceilings, a wall of glass and wondrous views across the Blackwood Valley.

The cozy, modern Hi*Life is warm and welcoming and overnight guests have a choice between three comfortable suites. The popular Anniversary Suite includes a private spa with glassed views of the verdant landscaping outside. Private balconies are large enough to accommodate four for dinner, relax with a glass of wine, and enjoy the glorious sunsets.

The Bridgetown area is rich with activities to keep you busy. Winery tours through the Warren-Blackwood Region can be organized by your hosts as well as Eco Tours and horseback riding. The Blackwood River, a five minute walk from the Hi*Life, is an ideal venue for canoeing and rafting, and many guests take advantage of the unique opportunity. After a day exploring the attractions, relax in the newly established gardens at Hi*Life and visualize the outstanding dinner you'll be served in the elegant Pemberton Room.

Name: Hi*Life Guesthouse

Category: Guesthouse/B&B

Location: South West region; Bridgetown; 2 km (nearest city)

Address: 28 Carey St/ PO Box 551, Bridgetown, WA 6255

Phone: Tel. 61 8 9761 2104 **Fax** 61 8 9761 2104

E-mail: users.mns.net.au/~hi-life

Innkeepers: Margaret & Frank Penn

Rates: From A$90-110 per double includes full breakfast

Rated: **** RAC

Number of rooms: 3

Baths: 3 Ensuite

Services & amenities: Balconies, TV, sound system, licensed restaurant

Restrictions: No children, no smoking, no pets

Handicap access: no

Martin Fields

E njoy a break at Martin Fields, a comfortable four-star country retreat set on 10 lovely acres overlooking tranquil Geographe Bay. Named for the Martins (commonly known as swallows) that populate the area, Martin Fields is nestled against a background of native Australian flora and Norfolk Island pines. The property hosts a variety of other birdlife including mountain ducks, pelicans, ospreys, white herons, black swans and migrating Siberian stints. From the South facing windows, you can see the unique Tuart forest, which is the only natural forest of its kind in Western Australia.

Hosts Jim and Jane Cummins have owned and operated hotels, tours and restaurants in the Busselton area for over two decades and have an excellent knowledge of the South West's local attractions. They'll gladly point you towards the Vasse River estuary or nearby Wonnerup Beach where you'll find safe swimming or fishing. Visit the many stellar vineyards or just plain relax on the balcony and watch the sun go down on Geographe Bay. Also feel free to stroll among the trees and bird life that abound in the beautiful gardens landscaped by Jim.

This two-story house features guestrooms with ensuite facilities and a variety of excellent amenities. The upstairs west-wing was completed in 1998. All bedrooms in the west-wing have a double and twin bed, ensuite facilities, a refrigerator, colour television and tea/coffee making facilities. From the bedroom balcony, you can see the pond, river and ocean all at once, as native birds take flight before your eyes. The ground floor east-wing bedrooms are also well appointed. Each comfortable room has ensuite facilities, a fridge, colour television and tea/coffee making facilities. A ground floor guest lounge is complete with stereo, colour television, bar and piano available to those guests who wish to relax outside their bedrooms. The dining area is centrally located on the ground floor of the main building complex. It is here that guests enjoy a fully cooked breakfast and have a chance to meet other guests in a totally relaxed environment. Jane is a seasoned chef who will also prepare a gourmet three-course dinner by arrangement. Martin Fields Country Retreat is a delight on many levels and visitors to the South-west region can't go wrong choosing this delightful B&B.

Name: Martin Fields

Category: Country Retreat

Location: South West region; Busselton (nearest city)

Address: Lot 25 Lockville Rd., Wonnerup, Busselton, WA 6280

Phone: Tel. 61 8 9754 2001 **Fax** 61 8 9754 2034

E-mail: jcummins@iinet.net.au

Web site: www.iinet.net.au/~jcummins

Innkeepers: Jim & Jane Cummins

Rates: From A$90 per double includes full breakfast; dinner, bed & breakfast from A$220 (2 nights)

Rated: ****

Number of rooms: 9 Doubles

Baths: 7 Ensuite, 1 Share

Services & amenities: Guest lounge, refrigerators in each room, TV, tea/coffee

Restrictions: none

Handicap access: no

Possum Creek Lodge

L ocated high above Perth on Gooseberry Hill, a historic area first settled in 1861, is a tranquil neighborhood where you'll find Possum Creek Lodge. This secluded bed & breakfast establishment features spacious self-contained units set in a large garden. The convenient location allows guests to experience the unique Western Australian native flora and fauna and sample a relaxed environment with local flavor. From its elevated perch, Possum Creek Lodge offers stunning city and coastal views.

Guests enjoy the Bandicoot Suite, a new ground level suite in a detached building that includes a large bathroom and open-planned living area. Some of the memorable features include lead lighting and a beautiful "Federation Albert" queen-sized bed. There is also a private patio with outdoor furniture set in a delightful cottage garden. The Possum Suite is an upstairs loft suite in a new detached building. The suite includes a private bathroom, open floor plan with fully equipped kitchen, sleeping area and sitting area. High quality furnishing and details throughout include a queen size bed and large private balcony overlooking beautiful gardens and grass tennis court.

Bush walks in the Kalamunda and Gooseberry Hill National Parks are only minutes away and Kalamunda features numerous quality restaurants and shops. There's also a historic trail that follows a railway track once popular for hauling Swan River Mahogany (Jarrah) down to the Swan River. Golfers will quickly discover Hillview Golf Course is only minutes away and tennis players can enjoy the grass court at Possum Creek, which is lit for night play. Guests can also take in a show at the local theatre, or the Performing Arts Centre, or visit the nearby Hills vineyards, which are a must for wine tastings. Bring a local bottle back and relax in the surroundings of the property's tranquil garden—perhaps while barbecuing some dinner. Hosts Helen & Leon English have lived at The Lodge since 1973, restoring and developing the property to its present day character. Helen, a qualified visual arts teacher, has traveled and taught overseas; she is also a skilled gardener who takes great pride in her design of the Lodge garden. Leon, a graduate in Agricultural Science, has a broad knowledge of Western Australia. Ask him about the unique flora and fauna of the Darling Range—he's a wealth of information. Possum Creek Lodge is perfect for those looking for a relaxed rural experience without sacrificing any modern amenities.

Name: Possum Creek Lodge

Category: B&B Self Contained Suites

Location: Perth region; Kalamunda; 2 km (nearest city)

Address: 6 Lenori Rd, Gooseberry Hill, WA 6076

Phone: Tel. 61 8 9257 1927 **Fax** 61 8 9257 1927

E-mail: possum@git.com.au

Web site: www.holiday-wa.net/possum.htm

Innkeepers: Helen and Leon English

Rates: From A$125 per couple includes generous continental breakfast

Rated: ****½ RAC

Number of rooms: 3 Queen

Baths: 2 Ensuite, 1 Private

Services & amenities: Nearby public golf course, restaurants, vineyards & orchards

Restrictions: No smoking inside; no pets

Handicap access: no

Redgum Hill

Midway between Nannup and Balingup on the picturesque Blackwood River Valley tourist drive is Redgum Hill. The delightful country home is situated on an 11-acre property on the bank of the Blackwood River in an area well known for its scenic beauty. Redgum Hill's gardens are a delightful tapestry of color and form, running in a series of terraces replete with herbs, roses and water features down to the Blackwood. The garden has been exhibited in the respected Australian Open Garden Scheme. The Federation-style brick home blends traditional design with a contemporary ambiance. Breakfast and dinner are served in the host's living room, where a wall of windows provides panoramic views of the grounds and river behind the house. The lovely setting enhances the pleasant informal atmosphere.

Kit and Edna are generous hosts who see to it that their guests are taken care of well. They have a separate guest wing offering guests complete privacy in three impeccably furnished ensuite rooms. Each four-star room opens onto front and back verandahs, enjoying a river view, and is decorated with beautifully restored antique furniture. Over breakfast, in the large formal dining area, with log fire roaring in winter, or on the verandah in warmer months, guests plan their day with help from their hosts. Redgum Hill also has two delightful two-storied self-catering cottages (air conditioned for summer comfort and wood fires for those crisp winter nights). Gumnut Cottage is ideal for a couple while Duffy's House can sleep up to six.

Edna is more than happy to prepare dinner on request. French and Italian style and traditional Australian fare using fresh local produce are part of the dinner repertoire at Redgum Hill. Barbecue facilities are available for those who want to have their own "cook-up." Redgum Hill is licensed and has a cellar boasting a selection of local wines.

Redgum Hill is adjacent to the State Forest so there are plenty of bush tracks nearby and an abundance of native bird and wildlife. Kangaroos pay regular visits to the property and bird watchers will delight in the colorful varieties to be viewed. Bocce, croquet, bikes and a canoe are available for guest use on the property. The Blackwood River and Blackwood Valley change with the seasons and each time of the year has a special attraction for visitors. Redgum Hill is also an ideal base from which to tour the scenic South West, being about an hour's drive from most of the major tourist areas.

Name: Redgum Hill

Category: Country House & Cottages

Location: South West/Blackwood River region; Nannup (nearest city)

Address: Balingup Rd., Nannup, WA 6275

Phone: Tel. 61 8 9756 2056 **Fax** 61 8 9756 2067

E-mail: bookings@redgum-hill.com.au

Web site: www.redgum-hill.com.au

Innkeepers: Kit & Edna Handyside

Rates: From A$ 105-125 per double includes breakfast (Dinner $35p/p)

Rated: **** RAC

Number of rooms: 3 Queen + cottage

Baths: 3 Ensuite

Services & amenities: TV, tea/coffee making facilities

Restrictions: No children

Handicap access: no

Rosebridge House

K alamunda began as a timber settlement in the 1860's, but by the early 1900's it was transformed into a resort destination where the residents of Perth and Fremantle could escape. Large, beautiful guesthouses with magnificent gardens were constructed to accommodate the throngs of weekend visitors. Today, Rosebridge House continues the tradition by providing superb accommodations in a colonial homestead nestled on the edge of the Gooseberry Hill National Park just one kilometre from the heart of Kalamunda Village. Hosts Rosemary and Peter Bridgement graciously offer country hospitality, an intimate atmosphere and a warm welcome to all their guests.

The rooms are all romantically furnished and offer the ultimate in comfort and style. Air conditioning, electric blankets, and heaters are provided for your comfort and French doors lead out to the magnificent gardens. The popular Summer House includes a spa, queen-size bed, and a sofa bed for additional guests. The Rose Room includes a spa and queen-size brass bed, while the Green Room features a claw foot bathtub, and the Courtyard Room has a king size brass bed (which can be made into twins). All the rooms include such standard features as ensuite bathroom, TV, radio, refrigerator, tea and coffee making facilities.

Commence the day with a scrumptious, leisurely breakfast in the sunny dining room and observe the large variety of local birdlife as they come in for their daily feed. In warmer months you may take breakfast on the verandah and savor the gentle breezes and the tranquility of the Hills. Enjoy the comfort and relaxing atmosphere of the spacious lounge complete with open fire, ample reading material and games. Or spend glorious days or balmy evenings sitting by the pool relaxing and take pleasure in the unique perfumes of the Australian bush. Kalamunda and the surrounding districts offer an amazing variety of restaurants. Also nearby are the vineyards and orchards in the Bickley and Swan Valleys, the Zig Zag Tourist Drive, numerous walking trails including the famous Bibbulmun Track (which stretches 963 kilometres to Albany on the South Coast) National Parks, galleries, and the Perth Observatory. For the adventurous, there are also camel rides, horseback riding and the Kalumunda Water Park. The century old tradition of escaping to the Hills is better than ever and it has been greatly enhanced by the addition of establishments like Rosebridge House.

Name: Rosebridge House

Category: Luxury Bed & Breakfast

Location: Perth region; Perth; 20 km (nearest city)

Address: 86 Williams St., Gooseberry Hill, WA 6076

Phone: Tel. 61 8 9293 1741 **Fax** 61 8 9257 2778

E-mail: rbridge@abacus.com.au

Web site: www.perthguide.com.au/rosebridge

Innkeepers: Rosemary & Peter Bridgement

Rates: From A$110-160 per double includes full breakfast

Rated: **** ½ RAC

Number of rooms: 3 Queen, 1 Twin

Baths: 4 Ensuite, 2 with spa

Services & amenities: Pool, BBQ, TV, radio, refrigerator, tea/coffee; close to city & airport

Handicap access: no

Wildwood Valley

W ildwood Valley is a 120-acre farming property in the heart of the Margaret River wine region. Originally established as a dairy farm at the turn of the century, it is one of the oldest and most beautiful properties in the area. Host Anne Sargent converted the family home to a stunning guesthouse in 1995, maintaining all of the original charm and character while providing spacious and luxurious accommodations for up to 14 guests. Set in natural bush with magnificent views to the sea, this timber and stone residence provides a real taste of country living. Enjoy nature in peaceful, beautiful surroundings while only minutes from the numerous beaches, wineries, restaurants and galleries for which this area is so well-known.

The guesthouse has five bedrooms, each with private or ensuite bathrooms and queen, double or twin beds. In addition, there is a large living area with high vaulted ceilings, a wood fire and stereo system; a full-size snooker room, an upstairs lounge with tea/coffee making facilities and microwave oven, a separate television and video lounge with video library, and a large gazebo overlooking the sea with barbeque facilities. For small groups and families, there is a spacious, beautifully appointed two-bedroom self-contained apartment. Children are not generally catered to in the guesthouse but are most welcome in the self-contained unit. Lovely views can be enjoyed from most rooms as you relax in the warm, rustic surroundings.

The guesthouse tariff includes a friendly country-style breakfast around the 12 foot dining table. Anne has reared many kangaroos who at times return for breakfast along with the resident sheepdog. After breakfast, take in the surrounding bushland; a true haven to wildlife and guests who take the time to stroll around the property. For the more adventuresome, there's scuba diving (the HMAS Swan Dive Wreck is sunk 2.5 km offshore), canoeing, surfing, whale-watching (the Humpbacks calve off Cape Naturaliste in October and November), horseback riding, cave and forest walks, all nearby in this magnificent corner of Western Australia.

Name: Wildwood Valley

Category: Guesthouse & Self-contained apt.

Location: South West/Margaret River region; Margaret River; 35 km (nearest city)

Address: Wildwood Rd., Yallingup, WA 6282

Phone: Tel. 61 8 9755 2120 **Fax** 61 8 9755 2120

E-mail: wwvalley@compwest.net.au

Web site: www.westernaustralia.net

Innkeepers: Anne Sargent

Rates: From A$128 -168 per double includes full breakfast

Rated: **** ½ RAC

Number of rooms: 2 Queen, 2 Double, 1 Twin + self-contained apartment

Baths: 3 Ensuite, 2 Private

Services & amenities: Snooker room, TV/video lounge, video library, piano, gazebo & BBQ

Restrictions: No smoking, no pets, children by arrangement

Handicap access: no

William Shakespeare Guesthouse

S outh of Perth, set in the Bedfordale Hills, just half an hour from Perth International Airport is William Shakespeare House, a true replica of the 'Bard's' 400-year-old birthplace in Stratford-upon-Avon in central England. The half-timbered Tudor house is situated in the Elizabethan Village as a tribute to the famous poet/playwright. Complete with a country lane, village green, Tudor cottages and an award-winning brewery serving traditional beers, this unique village transports you to back the 16th century. Nearby is the cottage of Shakespeare's wife, Anne Hathaway. Steeped in culture and history, the authenticity and attention to detail in this township is reminiscent Olde England.

In the center of Stratford Park, the four and a half star William Shakespeare House is a true English-style country retreat. Relax and enjoy the tranquil landscaped gardens and excellent hospitality with your hosts Jill and Geoff or take a two-minute stroll to the Brewhouse Inn where friendly staff will serve you excellent bar meals in the cobblestone courtyard or a la carte meals in the Cobwebs Restaurant by the cozy log fire. Wednesday through Sunday afternoon you'll be entertained with jazz and sing-alongs. Enjoy a pint of ale brewed on the premises as you imagine what life was like in the Bard's day.

Accommodations at the William Shakespeare House are in three queen-sized guestrooms, each with ensuite, tea/coffee making facilities and comfortable furnishings. All guests enjoy warm and cozy rooms in winter and cool air-conditioning in summer. A lounge and barbeque area are also available for guest use. The tariff includes a full cooked breakfast and other meals are served at the pub or restaurant within the village. With both Perth and the beautiful South West region nearby, the list of tourist attractions is extensive. Visit the Margaret River wine region and beautiful beaches, or discover the delights of Western Australia's capital city. Whether you stay for a day or a week, you'll find the William Shakespeare House a memorable experience.

Name: William Shakespeare Guesthouse

Category: Bed & Breakfast

Location: Perth Hills region; Armadale; 2 km (nearest city)

Address: 25 Canns Rd, Bedfordale, WA 6112

Phone: Tel. 61 8 9497 4009 **Fax** 61 8 9497 4544

Web site: www.wabblist.com.au/shakespeare

Innkeepers: Jill & Geoff Brough

Rates: From A$95-120 per double includes cooked breakfast

Rated: ****1/2 RAC

Number of rooms: 3 Queen

Baths: 3 Ensuite

Services & amenities: Restaurant and pub onsite

Restrictions: No smoking

Handicap access: no

Tasmania

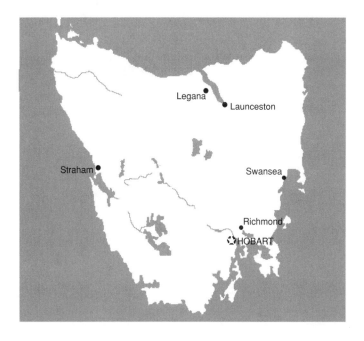

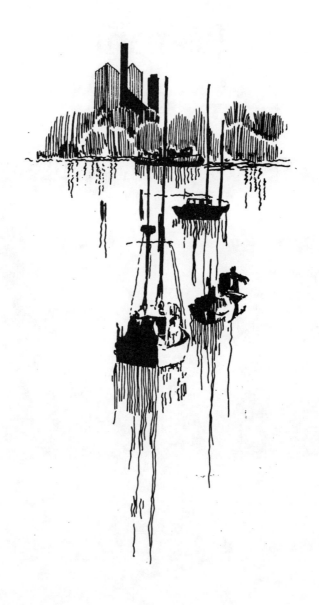

An enchanting island state located off the southeast corner of the Australian mainland, Tasmania is steeped in history and Old World charm. The pace of life here matches the surroundings—tranquil and serene, for Tasmanians live their lives in an unhurried, relaxed manner. Roughly the size of West Virginia, the population of Tasmania is small—less than half a million people—and you'll rarely find crowds anywhere. But the primary lure of this compact isle is its diversity. With four distinct seasons, each time of year offers unique events and activities. In addition to absorbing the historic charm of the island, it's possible to tramp through a rainforest, stroll through rustic fishing villages, explore old mining boom towns on the rugged West Coast or walk the endless white sand beaches. People also come from afar to fly-fish the streams and lakes, kayak the coast, or to dive the ocean's depths, peeping into seacaves and frolicking with dolphins.

Visitors to Tasmania walk in the footsteps of pioneers and convicts who have left their legacy everywhere. Fine old churches, bridges, cottages, old English-style villages, and ghostly remains of convict settlements echo `Tassie's' past. Tasmania's capital, Hobart, was founded 16 years after Sydney in 1804 and it is Australia's second oldest city. Straddling the Derwent River, the beautiful deep water port city is dominated by maritime history, and backed by mountains, many of which are snow-capped year round. A quaint mix of past and present, Hobart manages to combine the progress of a modern city with the rich heritage of its colonial past. Battery Point, the old port area, represents the historic centre of the city, and Salamanca Place, adjacent to Constitution Dock in the city centre, features beautifully preserved sandstone warehouses from the city's first settlement, as well as specialty shops, cafes and restaurants.

Roads fan out from Hobart in all directions, and the best way to get around the island is by car. South of the city, in the waterways and wilderness of the Huon Valley and D'Entrecasteaux Channel, travelers can discover an array of art and heritage; apple blossom and vineyards; farmers, foresters and fishermen. Past and present mingle on the magnificent Tasman Peninsula, almost an island apart. You'll discover fine heritage buildings, sample cool-climate wines from a vineyard overlooking the sea, and savour some of the local specialties—octopus, oysters, quail and venison. You may even see a majestic sea eagle soaring from the tall sea cliffs sculpted by centuries of waves and winds. Further south, Port Arthur, Tasmania's premier tourist attraction, has overlooked the dark waters of a quiet bay for more than 150 years. Ever since it ceased operation as a penal settlement in the late 1800's, Port Arthur has fascinated tourists interested in early convict life.

North of Hobart, the historic towns of Richmond or New Norfolk in the Derwent Valley are both easy day trips. Richmond is a delightful Georgian village with Australia's oldest bridge and New Norfolk showcases the country's oldest Anglican Church. Further inland, brown trout have been hatched for 150 years to provide some of the world's finest fly fishing, and the historic towns of Hamilton and Ouse are the centre of the surrounding farming area.

The East Coast, with its ribbon of beautiful white sand beaches, tiny fishing villages, granite outcrops and deserted coves, is edged by an un-derwater wilderness. Dive and enjoy the marine habitats of the coast with its excellent visibility and diversity of fish and plant life. Four national parks dot the East Coast – Mount William, Douglas-Apsley, Freycinet and Maria Island—providing a paradise for bushwalkers and a haven for native animals and birds. Freycinet National Park, a peninsula fringed with white beaches, crystal water and some of the most spectacular coastal head-lands in Tasmania, is one of the island's most popular destinations. Nes-tled in Great Oyster Bay on the East Coast, is the resort town of Swansea, popular for boating and fishing. Along the coast are numerous other small towns that offer a variety of special activities. Pan for sapphires near Branxholm, sample local cheese at Pyengana, climb dunes at St. Helens, or watch the penguins return to their burrows at Bicheno.

The Midlands region resembles the tranquil rolling English countryside early settlers were so familiar with. The Highland Lake Country, in the center of the island, is quite formidable in its beauty. The best-known feature of this region is the Cradle Mountain-Lake St. Clair National Park. Ten thousand years ago, glaciers carved out Lake St. Clair, Australia's deepest lake, which features an incredible array of flora and fauna and a world famous bushwalk. In addition, the magnificent glacial lakes, crystal clear streams and thundering waterfalls attract visitors to this area year round. Slow down as you travel through Tasmania's northern midlands, perhaps not to the pace of horse-drawn coaches that once rattled through the prosperous grazing land but, enough to feel the gentle pace of times gone by. The 'Heritage Highway' follows the route pioneered in 1807 when pathfinders took eight days to traverse the island. Although you can now drive from Hobart to Launceston in a couple of hours, you'd miss some of Tasmania's most beautiful country scenery.

Arriving in Launceston, on the Tamar River near the northern coast, you'll discover a gracious city nestled in a wide valley and surrounded by high, rugged mountains. Known as the "Garden City," Tasmania's second largest city features long established and beautiful public and private gardens. Launceston still reflects the wealthy days when ships loaded wool and wheat docked at the River Tamar's wharves, and it remains the hub for northern grazing and farmlands. Fine Victorian buildings and the numerous gardens make a walking tour of this city a delight. Throughout the surrounding region are the wineries, orchards and farms that produce the acclaimed fine Tasmanian wines and foods such as blueberries, strawberries, apples, pears, bush honey, and gourmet cheeses.

Blessed with a rich diversity of geographic features, Tasmania's North Coast is a picturesque mix of orchards and gently rolling hills. The port town of Stanley has a quaint village-like atmosphere and is situated in the shadow of The Nut, a landmark rock formation off the coast. The sturdy stone cottages of Stanley, established around 1826, and the graceful facade of Highfield Homestead, reflect the town's fishing and farming history.

Tasmania's wild West Coast is a region of untamed mountains, dense rainforests, deep lakes and raging rivers. Strahan, the only town on the west's forbidding coastline, is the gateway to the lower reaches of the Gordon River and the splendours of the Franklin and Lower Gordon Wild Rivers National Park, a World Heritage wilderness area. Here you'll see millions of years of evolution captured in ancient rocks. The South West region boasts a pristine natural sanctuary that's home to a wide variety of wildlife including those unique to the area, the Tasmanian Devil and the Tasmanian Tiger. Experienced bushwalkers relish the classic trails in this area, which are often difficult to negotiate but offer breathtaking scenery at every turn. The entire West Coast has a rich mining heritage spanning over 100 years. Museums, such as the West Coast Pioneers Memorial Museum, take visitors back in time while the nearby towns and villages capture the spirit of men and women who carved a boom-and-bust living from the mountains, forests and seas.

In the blue waters of eastern Bass Strait, Flinders Island and the surrounding atolls, are what remain of the land that once connected Tasmania to mainland Australia. This is an island of dramatic landscapes, from the colourful granite cliffs of the Strzelecki National Park and Killiecrankie, to the green farmland that rolls gently across the north. King Island is the guardian of the western entrance to Bass Strait. Sitting in the path of the Roaring Forties, westerly winds that endlessly circle the world's southern latitudes, it's an island of long empty beaches, offshore reefs, rocky coasts and home to Wickham Lighthouse, the tallest in the southern hemisphere.

In addition to the natural beauty, Tasmania is also renown for its many English-style bed and breakfast accommodations. Colonial and country style accommodations can be found almost everywhere—from small historic villages with carefully restored cottages and homesteads, to city back streets and rural farms off the beaten track. Many of Tassie's original cottages, coaching houses, stone villas, homesteads and grand old homes, have been transformed into gracious B&B's offering warm hospitality and fantastic home-cooked meals. The small scale of the island, combined with spectacular landscapes and delightful accommodation, should put Tassie on the top of the list for travelers looking for a special holiday.

For more information:

Tourism Tasmania   Email : intlinfo@tourism.tas.gov.au
GPO Box 399   Internet : http://www.tourism.tas.gov.au
Hobart TAS 7001, AUSTRALIA
Phone : 61 3 62 308227   Fax : 61 3 62 308307

REGIONAL DIRECTORY
➤ denotes review

DERWENT VALLEY
➤ **The Old Schoolhouse**   Lyell Highway, Hamilton, TAS 7140
61 3 6286 3292   *Gracious Victorian schoolhouse in Midlands set on three acres of English gardens*

EAST COAST
➤ **Meredith House & Mews**   15 Noyes St., Swansea, TAS 7190
61 3 6257 8119   *Colonial charm and 21st century comfort on Tasmania's Central East Coast*

FLINDERS ISLAND
Flinders Island Lodge   Franklin Parade, Flinders Island, TAS 7255
61 3 6359 3521   *Waterfront lodge on scenic Flinders Island*
Partridge Farm   Badger Corner, Whitemark, TAS 7255 61 3 6359 3554
Peaceful hobby farm on island paradise off the coast of Tasmania

MIDLANDS
Foxhunters Return   132 High St., Campbell Town, TAS 7210
61 3 6381 1602 *Luxury accommodations between Launceston and Hobart*
➤ **Racecourse Private Hotel**   114 Marlborough St., Longford, TAS
7301 61 3 6391 2352   *Traditional Georgian coaching inn offers suberb accommodations in historic setting*

NORTH EAST
➤ **Edenholme Grange**   14 St. Andrews St., Launceston, TAS 7250
61 3 6334 6666 *Glorious 1880's mansion surrounded by a parklike garden*
➤ **Freshwater Point**   56 Nobelius Drive, Legana, TAS 7277
61 3 6330 2200   *Colonial accommodations at one of Australia's oldest and most beautiful homesteads*
➤ **The Turret House**   41 West Tamar Rd., Launceston, TAS 7250
61 3 6334 7033
Charming house (circa 1902) combines the elegance of yesteryear with modern comforts

NORTH WEST

➤ **Atherfield Country Accommodation**   241 Jeffries Road, Sheffield, TAS 7306 61 3 6491 1996
Four-star country accommodations 35 km from Devonport ferry terminal

SOUTH EAST

➤ **Elms of Hobart**   452 Elizabeth St., Hobart, TAS 7000 61 3 6231 3277
Carefully restored National Trust classified mansion.

Jarem Waterfront Guesthouse 8 Clarke Avenue, Hobart, TAS 7000
61 3 6223 8216 *Waterfront guesthouse on the banks of the Derwent River*

➤ **Merre Be's**   17 & 24 Gregory St., Sandy Bay, TAS 7005 61 3 6224 2900
Spacious home (circa 1884) on quiet leafy street in Sandy Bay

➤ **Millhouse On The Bridge**   2 Wellington St., Richmond, TAS 7025
61 3 6260 2428   *Unique home situated on Australia's oldest bridge in beautifully preserved Georgian village*

➤ **Orana**   20 Lowelly Rd., Lindisfarne, TAS 7015 61 3 6243 0404
Hosted accommodations in comfortable Edwardian home across the river from Hobart.

Princes Park House   27 Castray Esplanade, Battery Point, TAS
7004 61 3 6223 2414
Restored neo Georgian home next to Princes Park in Battery Point

Prospect House   1354 Richmond Rd, Richmond, TAS 61 3 6260 2207
1830's four and a half star heritage boutique hotel with all modern conveniences

TAMAR VALLEY

Pomona Bed & Breakfast   77 Flinders St., Beauty Point, TAS 7270
61 3 6383 4073
Federation style home overlooking the river and peaceful Tamar Valley

Yorktown Manor   PO Box 138, Beaconsfield, TAS 7270 61 3 6383 4647
Peaceful bush setting on the banks of the Tamar River

TASMAN PENINSULA

➤ **Osprey Lodge Beachfront B&B**   14 Osprey Rd., Eaglehawk Neck, TAS
7179 61 3 6250 3629   *This beachfront B&B is noted for its beautiful setting and outstanding hospitality*

Wunnamurra Waterfront B&B   21 Osprey Rd, Eaglehawk Neck, TAS
7179 61 3 6250 3145   *New waterfront home with views of the coastline*

WEST COAST

➤ **Franklin Manor**   The Esplanade, Strahan, TAS 7468 61 3 6471 7311
Franklin Manor is a cozy boutique hotel offering tranquility, warm hospitality and indulgence

➤ **Ormiston House**   The Esplanade, Strahan, TAS 7468
61 3 6471 7077   *Tasmania's five star stately guesthouse and restaurant*

Atherfield Country Accommodation

A therfield Country Accommodation is a peaceful, relaxing country home with magnificent views of mountains, rural valleys and the Dashe River from every window. Situated on eight and a half acres, the property boasts lovely gardens filled with flowers, fruits and vegetables that encompass the surrounding landscape. The idyllic location is convenient yet well off the beaten track. For those interested in touring Tasmania's beautiful North West region, Cradle Mountain – Lake St. Clair National Park is 63 kilometres away and an easy drive. Limestone caves, Mt. Roland and Lake Barrington are also nearby. Visitors marvel at the huge arch of Devils Gate Dam on Lake Barrington. In Sheffield, stroll the streets and enjoy the murals and homemade ice cream. If a round of golf is more your style, there is a handy golf course and hosts Margaret & Ken keep a set of clubs on hand for guests to use.

Atherfield is a passive solar home featuring two comfortable guest rooms; one is a king/twin and the other is a double, each with ensuite. To ward off the chill on winter nights, there is a log fire in the lounge and the beds have electric blankets. In the summer, enjoy cool evenings relaxing on the verandah and taking in the panoramic vistas and vast skies. Guests have their own private dining room and lounge where they can relax with TV/video, a choice of games including billiards and darts, and an extensive library of reading material.

Afternoon tea is served on arrival and tea or coffee available at all times in the guest dining room. With so much to see and do in the area, guests who arrive for one night have been known to stay for a week!

Name: Atherfield Country Accommodation

Category: Bed & Breakfast

Location: North West region; Sheffield; 7km (nearest city)

Address: 241 Jeffries Road, Sheffield, TAS 7306

Phone: Tel. 61 3 6491 1996 **Fax** 61 3 6491 1996

E-mail: eveatherfieldpara@bigpond.com

Innkeepers: Ken & Margaret Everett

Rates: From A$110 per double includes full breakfast

Rated: ****1/2 RACT

Number of rooms: 1 King or Twin, 1 Double

Baths: 2 Ensuite

Services & amenities: Private guest lounge/dining room

Restrictions: Unsuitable for children under 5

Handicap facilities: no

Edenholme Grange

Edenholme Grange is a grand two-story Victorian house (circa 1881) set in secluded and substantial grounds in beautiful Launceston. Edenholme was the name of a three-masted Barque that plied from the Port of Launceston and unfortunately met disaster on Hebe Reef at the mouth of the Tamar River. Located close to Launceston's many fine restaurants and other attractions, including the magnificent Cataract Gorge, Edenholme Grange is classified by the National Trust and is a member of the Historic Houses of Tasmania. Hosts Paul and Rosemary meticulously maintain the residence and offer accommodations in six luxurious rooms and a self-contained cottage on the property.

The Captain's Room derives its name from Captain Edward Ditcham who was the first owner of the house and a Master Warden of the Port of Launceston. A grand Victorian half-tester bed, decorated with rich navy velvet, is a dominant feature of this room. The nautical decor includes memorabilia spanning a century. The Banker's Room is masculine and original. A carved oak bed is complemented by an antique mahogany barreltop desk complete with two early local bank ledgers dating from the commencement of the building of the house. European influence is evident in The Marchioness' Room, decorated with a French serpentine bed of brass, porcelain, crystal and cast iron. The original bathroom contains a deep claw-foot bath, a Victorian-style vanity suite and a walk-in shower. The Governess' Room is a ground floor room with an unusual barley-twist four-poster bed of French Colonial vintage. The room features a glassed-in balcony that captures the morning sun, ideal for an intimate breakfast. The popular Victoria Room is the most indulgent room in the house. With its king-size full tester four-poster bed and double spa bath, this room is a favorite with honeymooners and couples looking to rekindle their relationship. The room is connected to The Albert, a self-contained studio suite. When combined, the rooms make a luxurious two-bedroom apartment. The Albert Suite has a Victorian half-tester bed and royal portraits, including rare prints of Prince Albert. Ideal for a longer stay, there is a separate entrance, a full kitchen, a tastefully decorated dressing room and ensuite with spa bath. Lastly, The Settlers Cottage is a self-contained two bedroom, two bathroom rustic cottage located in the grounds of the property, providing serenity and private views of the ornamental garden.

Tariffs at Edenholme Grange include a full Tasmanian breakfast or equivalent provisions. Also, ask about special romantic holiday packages.

Name: Edenholme Grange

Category: Victorian Guesthouse

Location: North East region; Launceston (nearest city)

Address: 14 St. Andrews St., Launceston, TAS 7250

Phone: Tel. 61 3 6334 6666 **Fax** 61 3 6334 3106

E-mail: edenholme@microtech.com.au

Web site: www.vision.net.au/˜webspace/edenholme/

Innkeepers: Paul & Rosemary Harding

Rates: From $A140-180 per double includes full breakfast

Rated: **** 1/2 RACT

Number of rooms: 6 Queen/Double/Triple/Family 4/Self-Contained Cottage

Baths: Ensuite / Private

Services & amenities: Licensed bar, guest lounge, wood fire, BBQ. Rose gardens

Restrictions: Children only in cottage and Governess Room

Handicap facilities: no

Elms of Hobart

The Elms is one of a number of Hobart's landmark buildings that were designed by Bernard Walker, a renowned architect in Tasmania in the early 20th century. With the genuine feel of a stately old mansion that was once home to one of the city's wealthiest families, a stay at The Elms is like turning back the hands of time. The National Trust classified residence has been carefully restored to reflect the original splendor of the period and exquisite details can be found at every turn.

Guests staying at The Elms are accommodated in beautifully appointed luxury suites, each with full facilities. The rooms provide a seamless blend of Old World charm and modern day comfort. Popular rooms include the deluxe "Elms Suite" with its half-tester bed and spacious bathroom featuring a genuine clawfoot bath, and the romantic "Hawthorn Suite." In addition, there are two beautifully furnished double suites and a delightful apartment suite.

The intimate guest lounge is warm and welcoming; guests can sit by the wood fire, sample complimentary port and sherry, or enjoy a bottle of wine from the "honesty" cellar. Hospitality is a key feature at The Elms. Each morning a generous cooked breakfast is served along with a daily paper. Outside, lovely English gardens are enjoyed by guests who want to unwind after a day of sightseeing. In the evening, take advantage of The Elms central location near Hobart's gourmet restaurant strip. Over 20 establishments offer a variety of cuisines for every palate. All of the city's primary attractions are also nearby, including the waterfront area, Salamanca Place and the city center.

Name: Elms of Hobart

Category: Bed & Breakfast

Location: South East region; Hobart (nearest city)

Address: 452 Elizabeth St., Hobart, TAS 7000

Phone: Tel. 61 3 6231 3277 **Fax** 61 3 6231 3276

E-mail: elmshobt@netspace.net.au

Web site: www.ice.net.au/Elms/Elms.htm

Innkeepers: Sue & Vic Murphy

Rates: From A$100-134 per double includes full breakfast

Rated: ****1/2 RACT

Number of rooms: 3 Queen, 3 Double, 1 Single

Baths: 6 Ensuite, 2 with spa

Services & amenities: Guest lounge, wine cellar, English garden, color TV, tea/coffee making

Restrictions: No pets; no smoking indoors

Handicap facilities: no

Franklin Manor

S ituated on Tasmania's beautiful West Coast, on the outskirts of the tiny
fishing village of Strahan, Franklin Manor is a boutique hotel providing
guests with a relaxed ambience perfectly suited to the natural beauty
and solitude of the Tasmanian wilderness, with its rivers, rainforest and
shores that stretch as far as the eye can see. Built in 1896 by Strahan's first
Harbor Master, the Victorian manor house has a rich local history. An extensive restoration brought the home and gardens back to their former glory and
Franklin Manor is now synonymous with luxury and warm hospitality.

The extensive underground wine cellar is a favorite with visitors as they
descend the stairs to select their own wines for dinner. The original lounge,
with its soft lamplight and roaring log fire, and dining room remain imbued
with a feeling of Old World charm and guests can enjoy this real piece of

history from a modern day perspective. After a day exploring the area, you may wish to take a leisurely afternoon tea on the verandah or explore the garden with its century old rhododendrons, duck pond and towering trees.

Fourteen magnificently appointed queen and king-sized rooms in the main house feature ensuite facilities and some have extras like open fireplaces, spas, and showers built for two. The elegant and individually decorated rooms create the perfect haven for those who appreciate comfort and relaxation. There are also four stable apartments. Decorated in a rustic style and situated on the Manor grounds, the Stables offer the comfort and flexibility of open plan living and include a large bathroom and family room with accommodations for up to five people. Other amenities include a celebrated licensed restaurant open for breakfast and dinner, picnic baskets prepared to order, guest laundry, and off-street parking. Three acres of landscaped grounds surround Franklin Manor and just minutes away are great bush tracks leading to cascading waterfalls. Also nearby is the World Heritage Franklin-Lower Gordon River National Park. The West Coast of Tasmania offers magnificent scenery. Visitors can choose from a wide range of activities including fishing trips, seaplane tours, cruise boat tours, a jet boat ride, four wheel drive adventures, horse-riding and bushwalking. And the luxurious Franklin Manor is the ideal base for exploring the region's rugged and spectacular scenery.

Name: Franklin Manor

Category: Boutique Hotel

Location: West Coast region; Strahan (nearest city)

Address: The Esplanade, Strahan, TAS 7468

Phone: Tel. 61 3 6471 7311 **Fax** 61 3 6471 7267

E-mail: franklinmanor@bigpond.com

Web site: www.franklinmanor.com

Innkeepers: Tony Wurf

Rates: From A$110-218 per double includes breakfast

Rated: 1999 Australia's Wine List of the Year

Number of rooms: 14 in-house rooms, 4 stable apartments

Baths: Ensuite

Services & amenities: Licensed restaurant, formal gardens, duck pond on grounds

Restrictions: No smoking

Handicap facilities: no

Freshwater Point

I magine an 1820's settler's home with thick convict-built brick walls, original woodwork throughout, and verandahs that allow you to take in the perfect waterfront setting. The Heritage-listed Freshwater Point homestead, one of Australia's first waterfront properties, sits on a gentle rise above the Tamar River. Set amidst giant elm trees planted more than a hundred years ago, the beautiful homestead is a luxurious tranquil hideaway just 15 minutes from Launceston. With a maximum of 12 guests, you can look forward to privacy and pampering in park-like surroundings.

Accommodations are offered in the homestead or in one of three beautifully restored cottages on the grounds. Homestead bedrooms each have queen-size or king-size beds, antique furniture and ensuite facilities. Choose a room with a water view or one overlooking the exquisite garden. A private lane alongside the waterfront garden leads to a private jetty. Take a picnic basket or a fishing line and drink in the serpentine river views. The well-appointed cottages, all feature king-size beds, and two cottages offer additional single beds. All are fully equipped and breakfast provisions are included in the tariff. A choice of duvet or merino wool blankets, feather or hypo-allergenic pillows, hair dryers, and toiletries. Even a first aid kit is provided along with a selection of magazines, and, of course, fresh flowers from the garden.

Popular sight-seeing destinations are all within easy access of Freshwater Point. Cradle Mountain is a comfortable day trip, as are the spectacular beaches at Freycinet and Wineglass Bay. Trout fishing lakes are within 30 minutes' drive plus the majority of Tasmania's historic houses. Freshwater

Point is at the gateway to Tasmania's main vineyards, and you can sample some of Tasmania's finest wines, or lunch at excellent vineyard restaurants. Freshwater Point has also been featured in magazines like *Gourmet Traveller, Vogue Entertaining,* and *Travel & Leisure* (US). Your host has extensive knowledge of food and wine. Imaginative meals, using only the freshest produce, are served either in the homestead dining room or in the privacy of your cottage. A terrific selection of wines is offered and guests are welcome to peruse the wine cellar. The well-established garden is another highlight of this historic property, from the drifts of daffodils, azaleas and rhododendrons in spring, to the blaze of reds and gold in autumn. The garden is open to the public on certain days during spring, and has been featured in garden books and house & garden magazines.

Name: Freshwater Point

Category: Guesthouse & Cottages

Location: North East region; Launceston; 15 km (nearest city)

Address: 56 Nobelius Drive, Legana, TAS 7277

Phone: Tel. 61 3 6330 2200 **Fax** 61 3 6330 2030

E-mail: freshwtr@netspace.net.au

Web site: www.wocis.com/freshwaterpoint

Innkeepers: Jan Creed-Thomas

Rates: From $A130-155 per double includes full breakfast

Rated: ****1/2 RACT

Number of rooms: 1 King, 1 Queen in Homestead, 3 King or Twin in Cottages

Baths: Private

Services & amenities: Gardens, licensed dining, waterfront location, tea/coffee making facilities, fully equipped cottages

Restrictions: No smoking in homestead rooms

Handicap facilities: yes

Meredith House & Mews

Named after the original land owner, Charles Meredith, the National Trust classified, Meredith House was built in 1853 in the town of Swansea on the East Coast of Tasmania. Originally designed as an inn, it was never used as such. Over the years the Colonial-style building has been used as a private residence as well as a girl's grammar school, a baby hospital, and a boarding house. Perched on a hill overlooking the historical seaside village, its elevated position provides sweeping views of the magnificent Great Oyster Bay and Freycinet Peninsula.

The home has been extensively renovated and now offers every comfort for the discerning traveler including ensuite facilities, mini bars, TVs and telephones, along with a great deal of warmth and charm. Accommodations includes six rooms upstairs and a luxurious two-room suite downstairs with its own open fire and spa. There is an intimate guest lounge and elegant dining room, also with open fires. The whole house is furnished with hand-crafted red cedar furniture and family antiques. Dinner is usually a convivial affair with guests enjoying a delicious, country-style, three-course meal. Local specialties are featured with seasonal produce from the garden, complimented by a choice of local and mainland wines. A full or light breakfast is served daily in the dining room.

Four spa apartments were added to the property in 1997. These heritage-style, luxury studio apartments each feature a double and single bed and all the amenities of the guestrooms in the House. They also have kitchenettes and individual balconies overlooking the garden and barbeque area. The landscaped gardens lead down to a croquet lawn. Swansea makes a good base for touring and hosts Greer and Clive are happy to help plan a day outing. Close to the magnificence of Freycinet National Park, many Meredith House guests enjoy the area's rugged beauty, the exquisite Wine Glass Bay, and the award-winning local vineyards. Meredith House is a true Colonial classic . . . considered by many to be the pearl of Great Oyster Bay.

Name: Meredith House & Mews

Category: Colonial B&B

Location: East Coast region; Swansea (nearest city)

Address: 15 Noyes St., Swansea, TAS 7190

Phone: Tel. 61 3 6257 8119 **Fax** 61 3 6257 8123

E-mail: olbery@vision.net.au

Web site: www.focusontas.net.au

Innkeepers: Greer & Clive Olbery

Rates: From A$135-160 per double includes full breakfast

Rated: **** ½ RACT

Number of rooms: 11 King / Queen / Double

Baths: 11 Ensuite

Services & amenities: Heating, tea/coffee, TV, fridge and mini-bar in all rooms, BBQ, croquet, guest laundry, bicycles, licensed dining room

Restrictions: No smoking

Handicap facilities: no

Merre Be's

F our and a half star Merre Be's provides a warm welcome in an atmosphere of harmony and warmth, amid antique treasures and luxurious
details. Originally constructed in 1884, the grand old Victorian home is
both elegant and serene. A century after being built, in 1994, the house was
transformed into a stylish Bed & Breakfast. Merre Be's is located on a quiet
boutique street in the heart of the leafy bayside suburb of Sandy Bay close to
all of Hobart's major attractions. Guests sleep on very comfortable beds in
spacious rooms, enjoy hot strong showers in the morning and then feast on
gourmet breakfasts beautifully presented and served in the sunny dining
room. A typical morning menu may consist of potato and herb pancakes or
eggs merridew and mushrooms with fresh orange juice, homemade bread
and jams, and fresh plunger coffee or tea.

The Old World atmosphere of the family home is beautifully preserved
and complemented by a variety of modern comforts. Eight ensuite rooms,
each individually decorated with grace and charm, offer various configurations including King, Queen, Triple, Twin & Family Rooms (some with spas).
Thoughtful touches, including bowls of fresh fruit, vases of flowers and ca-
rafes of port can usually be found around the house. Additional amenities,
including off street parking, direct dial telephones, fax, electric blankets, hair
dryers, colour TV, and a guest lounge are all available to guests.

The house is within easy walking distance to historic Battery Point, Salamanca Market, Tasmanian University, Hobart Central, Royal Yacht Club,
Wrest Point Casino, and the beautiful yacht-filled harbour. Just 50 metres

from shops, banks, taxi and bus stops, this is truly an excellent location for travelers. After a busy day exploring the bustling waterfront and nearby attractions, relax in the tranquil garden at Merre Be's and contemplate the mouth-watering choice of nearby restaurants where you can enjoy a fabulous dinner. The appeal of Hobart and its surroundings is great and host Mary Bremner is a wealth of information regarding nearby walks, rainforest picnics, 4-WD Tours, wilderness air flights or sea adventures. Visitors can also visit antique shops, art galleries, attend the symphony, or enjoy world-class wines and fresh local seafood. For romance, there is a Honeymoon House and special packages that include champagne, chocolates and more.

Name: Merre Be's

Category: Bed & Breakfast

Location: South East region; Hobart (nearest city)

Address: 17 & 24 Gregory St., Sandy Bay, TAS 7005

Phone: Tel. 61 3 6224 2900 **Fax** 61 3 6224 2911

E-mail: merrebes@bigpond.com

Web site: www.merrebes.com.au

Innkeepers: Mary Bremner

Rates: From $A150 per double includes breakfast

Rated: ****1/2 RACT

Number of rooms: 8 Queen

Baths: 8 Ensuite

Services and amenities: off street parking, guest lounge, TV, electric blankets

Handicap facilities: limited

Millhouse on the Bridge

R ichmond is renowned as the best-preserved village in Australia, yet it is only 20 minutes from Hobart, Tasmania's largest city. The idyllic Coal River meanders alongside the village and beneath the Richmond Bridge. The bridge, the oldest in Australia, was built by convicts out of locally-quarried sandstone in 1823. Millhouse on the Bridge, built just 30 years later, overlooks the historic bridge. Millhouse sits in a romantic garden of majestic old trees and colorful perennials with more than 1200 feet of private riverfront shaded by huge silver poplars.

Millhouse on the Bridge, with its massive rough-hewn eucalyptus beams and convict-made bricks, was originally a steam mill—one of four flour mills in Richmond. The property is classified by the National Trust and the National Estate, and is the only mill still standing in the area. Its location, adjacent to the Australia's oldest bridge, gives it unique appeal, and the famous Australian landscape painter John Eldershaw converted the mill into his own private residence and studio in the 1920's. Millhouse on the Bridge was superbly restored in 1998 by John and Suzanne Hall, and the restoration was judged the best in Australia by the Master Builders' Association. Four exquisite guestrooms, each furnished with Australian antiques, feature queen-sized beds of brass, mahogany and Huon pine (an extremely rare and valuable Tasmanian timber) and private facilities.

In the morning, guests can look forward to a cooked breakfast, including eggs collected from the resident hens, locally harvested smoked salmon, and the freshest fruits from the property and nearby orchards. Served in the sunroom overlooking the cottage garden of perennials (including old roses), it's the perfect way to start the day. Guests can wander the gardens of the five-acre property, picnic on garden seats under the sprawling historic silver poplars, or relax in total seclusion under the weeping bough of an old willow in the shadow of Australia's oldest bridge. Richmond is the perfect base for discerning visitors to Tasmania with Hobart nearby. Numerous historic, scenic attractions, and wineries all within easy reach. But even with much to do in the vicinity, you may not want to wander too far when you stay at the lovely Millhouse on the Bridge.

Name: Millhouse On The Bridge

Category: Heritage Bed & Breakfast

Location: South East region; Hobart; 30 km (nearest city)

Address: 2 Wellington St., Richmond, TAS 7025

Phone: Tel. 61 3 6260 2428 **Fax** 61 3 6260 2148

E-mail: millhouse@millhouse.com.au

Web site: www.millhouse.com.au

Innkeepers: Suzanne & John Hall

Rates: From $A130-165 per double includes full breakfast & afternoon tea

Rated: **** ½ RACT

Number of rooms: 4 Queen

Baths: 3 Ensuite, 1 Private

Services & amenities: Open fire, central heat, air-conditioning, sunroom, tea/coffee making facilities, library, television, parking

Restrictions: No smoking, not suitable for children; stairs

Handicap facilities: no

The Old Schoolhouse

S tanding like a lovely Victorian doll house along Hamilton's main road, The Old Schoolhouse is an enchanting sandstone building with an interesting history. Built over a two-year period 1856–1858, the children of this small country town learned their lessons here for more than 75 years. In 1935, a new school was built next door and, the building lay abandoned until 1972 when it was condemned and, almost torn down. The Hamilton Council, however, raised enough money at the last minute to restore the building and offer it for private sale.

Michael Tapley and Julie Crook now own and run The Old Schoolhouse as an English-style B&B. Check to see if the old brass school bell still hangs above the front door.

There are three queen-size ensuite rooms, a cozy guest lounge with open log fire and a dining room where breakfast and dinner are served. Fresh Tasmanian produce is used in the home cooking with fruit and vegetables grown in the garden. Breakfast can be as hearty or light as you require— freshly stewed berries in season, yogurt, fruit juices, cereals, muffins to bacon, sausage, tomato, mushrooms and local farm eggs are served. The area is famous for trout that can be caught in the nearby river and brought back to be cooked. English antiques adorn the rooms and "Class Antiques," a unique shop is located on site. Nearby, a stone cottage set in the garden provides self-contained accommodation for up to 6 people.

Hamilton makes a great base to discover Mt. Field National Park with its wonderful rainforest and alpine walks. Spectacular Russell Falls features the world's tallest flowering tree. A wallaby or two may be spotted beside the walking tracks along with platypus in the nearby rivers. Further on from Mt. Field, one can discover the tremendous views of both mountain and lakes in the Southwest World Heritage area, on the way to Lake Pedder, the Gordon Dam, or golfing museum.

Name: The Old Schoolhouse

Category: Colonial Accommodation

Location: Derwent Valley region; Hamilton (nearest city)

Address: Lyell Highway, Hamilton, TAS 7140

Phone: Tel. 61 3 6286 3292 **Fax** 61 3 6286 3369

E-mail: jcrook@southcom.com.au

Web site: www.view.com.au/schoolhouse

Innkeepers: Michael Tapley & Julie Crook

Rates: From A$110-132 per double includes full breakfast; dinner by arrangement

Rated: Tourism Council of Australia

Number of rooms: 3 Queen (Twin available)

Baths: 3 Ensuite

Services & amenities: Guest lounge; wine & beer available

Restrictions: No smoking; no children under 10

Handicap facilities: no

Orana

O rana is Aborigine for "welcome" and guests find the hospitality at Orana immediately apparent. Even the "resident convict," Henry Pearce, helps provide a friendly reception. Pearce, who was sentenced to seven years for stealing lead, arrived in Hobart on an English convict ship in 1828. He went on to become a successful Hobart merchant as well as a member of the City Council and in 1909 his daughter-in-law, Ellen Pearce built Orana as a holiday house. Although there have been several owners since then, the original family history remains a large part of this gracious Edwardian home and the life-size likeness of Pearce that stands in the hall today reminds guests of the city's colourful past.

Situated across the Derwent River less than a ten-minute drive from Hobart, the lovely town of Lindisfarne was a popular summer retreat for city dwellers around the turn of the century. Ellen Pearce regularly made the journey with her maid and cook to holiday at the delightful riverside home before taking up permanent residency there after her husband's death. Extensive renovation has brought the large red brick house, with magnificent views, back to its former glory. Many of the original features like stained glass windows in the foyer and the large open fireplace in the guest lounge remain intact. Beautiful landscaped gardens surround the home and plenty of off-street parking is available for guests.

Each of the guestrooms is named for John and Ellen Pearce or one of their eight children. Many personal touches are provided, including home-cooked cake or cookies for guests to have with their tea or coffee. Some deluxe rooms have spa bathrooms and all have ensuite facilities. The tariff at Orana includes bed and breakfast, and an extensive morning menu caters to every taste and appetite. Orana stresses friendly service and individual attention.

This consideration for guests as well as the emphasis on hospitality are what make Orana such a great find.

Name: Orana

Category: Heritage Bed & Breakfast

Location: South East region; Hobart; 4 km (nearest city)

Address: 20 Lowelly Rd., Lindisfarne, TAS 7015

Phone: Tel. 61 3 6243 0404 **Fax** 61 3 6243 9017

E-mail: oranahouse@optusnet.com.au

Innkeepers: Claire Marshall

Rates: From A$90-120 per double includes full breakfast

Rated: ****1/2 RACT

Number of rooms: 10 Queen / Double

Baths: 10 Ensuite

Services & amenities: Lovely views, peaceful

Restrictions: No smoking

Handicap facilities: yes

Ormiston House

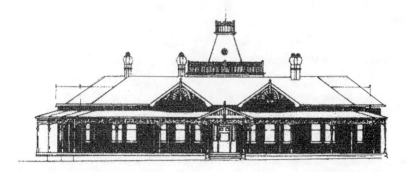

O rmiston House is a fine example of Federation architecture, built in 1899 by Frederick Ormiston Henry, the founder of Strahan. Guests enjoy the casual elegance of the Victorian era in this faithfully restored mansion, that overlooks the bay of Tasmania's charming west coast town. Owners Carolyn and Mike have done a fantastic job resurrecting both the history and the grandeur of this stately home. Each of the four guest rooms is named after a member of the Henry family and each offers its own delights.

The F.O. Henry is a grand room that was the original bedroom of Frederick Ormiston Henry. Lavishly furnished in Tartans and tassles reflecting the Scottish history of the family, the room also features the original Victorian wardrobe transported from Scotland. A four-poster bed dominates the room, along with a beautiful chaise lounge (circa 1860) in the bay window. The Mary Alice Room is named after the wife of Frederick Ormiston. This room boasts a blackwood four-poster bed along with strong but feminine decor that reflects Mary Alice's character. The fireplace supports an ornate Victorian mantle and an original gas wall lamp both that reflect on the history of the house. Light shining through the stained glass skylight brings the brass to life in the sparkling ensuite bathroom. The Amelia Room features a beautiful clawfoot bath, together with a fireplace and bowed wallpaper. These features complement the Queen Anne and Edwardian style furniture in the bedroom with drapes of roses and bows. The Jessie Room allows guests to repose on the wonderful Grandmother chair and drink in the Victorian country scene that is featured on the papered walls. In the beautiful two-bedroom suite, there is a queen-size Federation bed in one room and a double in the other. Relax in the clawfoot tub as the sun shines in through the high window in the bathroom. A private courtyard view adds to Jessie's charm. The jewel of the house is the Christina Suite overlooking the rose gardens and magnificent Macquarie Harbour. Antique Tasmanian oak furnishings with a wonderful ironlace romantic queen size bed are some of the unique features, along with a romantic spa in the ensuite bathroom.

The delights of the Ormiston House extend well beyond the accommodations. There is also an award-winning licensed restaurant for house-guests and visitors to Strahan. The menu, designed by the House's Executive Chef, features Tasmania's best seafood, beef, lamb, game and cheese. Guests also enjoy visiting the wine cellar to pick out a special bottle to accompany dinner. During the day, take advantage of Gordon River Cruises, scenic flights, the beautiful nearby beach, 4WD tours, Queenstown mine tours, the Zeehan museum, and numerous wilderness walks. Then, return to Ormiston House to wine, dine and stay in historic luxury.

Name: Ormiston House

Category: Guesthouse

Location: West Coast region; Strahan (nearest city)

Address: The Esplanade, Strahan, TAS 7468

Phone: Tel. 61 3 6471 7077 **Fax** 61 3 6471 7007

E-mail: ormiston@tassie.net.au

Web site: www.ormistonhouse.com.au

Innkeepers: Carolyn Nissen & Mike Fry

Rates: From $A150-235 per double includes deluxe continental breakfast

Rated: ***** RACT

Number of rooms: 4 Queen, 1 Double

Services & amenities: Licensed restaurant, lounge bar, drawing and morning rooms, tea/coffee, observation deck

Restrictions: No smoking

Handicap facilities: no

Osprey Lodge

The four and a half star Osprey Lodge Beachfront B&B is a tranquil retreat overlooking beautiful Pirates Bay at Eaglehawk Neck. Located on the Tasman Peninsula near historic Port Arthur, Osprey Lodge is adjacent to The Tasman Peninsula National Park (officially declared April 1999). The park takes in the entire coastal area and includes the highest sea cliffs in the southern hemisphere along with many beautiful ocean beaches.

Just one hour from Hobart, Osprey Lodge's secluded beachfront setting offers scenic beauty and complete privacy. Guests love the warmth and peacefulness of the sprawling cedar lodge along with the hospitality of hosts Diane and Bill. Built in 1997 to take full advantage of the superb views across the bay, the residence already has an established garden that is included in the National Open Garden Scheme. A path leads through the garden to a secluded ocean beach, next to the famous Tessellated Pavement. A large central lounge, library and dining area are available for guest use, and a wall of windows takes full advantage of the surrounding landscape. The guest wing features two rooms with ensuites, private balconies, televisions and other thoughtful touches including fresh flowers and quality toiletries.

Guests enjoy individual attention and spectacular views while sharing a pre-dinner snack and a glass of wine. After dinner choose a port with coffee to finish the day. The best Tasmanian produce is featured for breakfast and for the complimentary pre-dinner hors d'oeuvres. Tas smoked Salmon, the very best cheeses, local pate and mussels, abalone, anchovies and octopus are among the many delicacies served. There is a choice of restaurants in the area and, in the summer, a barbeque dinner is offered which may include Atlantic Salmon, local quail, or wallaby and venison sausages. In the morning, after a scrumptious and hearty breakfast, experience bush walks, majestic coastal scenery, and Tasmania's convict past at nearby Port Arthur. For the active-minded, go scuba diving, sea-kayaking, horseback riding, deep-sea fishing or golfing. Above all relax and enjoy the natural beauty of this special corner of Tasmania.

Name: Osprey Lodge Beachfront B&B

Category: Bed & Breakfast

Location: Tasman Peninsula region; Port Arthur; 20 km (nearest city)

Address: 14 Osprey Rd., Eaglehawk Neck, TAS 7179

Phone: Tel. 61 3 6250 3629 **Fax** 61 3 6250 3031

E-mail: osprey@southcom.com.au

Web site: www.view.com.au/osprey

Innkeepers: Diane & Bill Melville

Rates: From A$140-160 per double includes gourmet breakfast

Rated: ****1/2 RACT

Number of rooms: 2 Queen (1 with extra single)

Baths: 2 Ensuite

Services & amenities: Private balconies, tea/coffee making facilities, televisions in rooms, use of laundry

Restrictions: No smoking

Handicap facilities: no

The Turret House

The striking Turret House is one of Launceston's landmark properties, with its signature turret and fascinating widow's walk. Built in 1902 by George McKinley, the charming residence has many turn-of-the-century Edwardian features including ornate fireplaces, stained glass windows, intricate plasterwork, and elaborate fretwork on the verandahs. The house combines the elegance of yesteryear with all the modern comforts and more than a few luxuries.

Hosts Maureen and David Lindsey greet guests with a warm welcome and obvious pride for their exquisitely restored house. Purchased in 1994, the couple has put considerable time and effort into all of the details and unusual features. There is also a large garden that is lovingly tended and David is landscaping it back to its former glory. Inside the house, three luxurious ensuite guestrooms accommodate six people. An array of personal touches include freshly baked cakes, fresh flowers and handmade soaps. There is a comfortable lounge and guests are always welcome to visit with Maureen and David and join them for a glass of port before retiring. An elegant dining room with views of the garden is where a delicious breakfast is served daily.

But the highlight of this house is definitely the turret. Guests are welcome to climb the box stairs and take in the river and city views. It's a glorious sight but beware, the staircase is steep and can be difficult to navigate given the separate treads for each foot.

For those who want to experience the area, the famous Cataract Gorge is only a five-minute walk and city centre is only ten minutes away. Leave your car behind and explore the delights of this charming Victorian city. The property is also ideally situated for touring the lovely Tamar Valley. A river cruise is a popular attraction and The Turret House is at the start of the Wine Route, for those who want to take in the local wineries. Whatever your interests, you'll find this unique B&B provides the perfect respite when visiting Tasmania's North East region.

Name: The Turret House

Category: Bed & Breakfast

Location: North East region; Launceston; 1.5 km (nearest city)

Address: 41 West Tamar Rd., Launceston, TAS 7250

Phone: Tel. 61 3 6334 7033 **Fax** 61 3 6331 6091

E-mail: wivells@bigpond.com

Innkeepers: Maureen & David Lindsey

Rates: From A$100 -120 per double includes breakfast

Rated: ****1/2 RACT

Number of rooms: 2 Queen, 1 Twin

Baths: Ensuite

Services & amenities: Guest lounge, garden, heating, electric blankets, homemade cakes, fruit, homemade soaps

Restrictions: No smoking

Handicap facilities: no

Tynwald Estate

O riginally built in 1830 as a family residence, this typical square-fronted home was transformed into a glorious country mansion by a promi-nent politician around the turn of the century. Wide verandahs, deco-rated with lace-like iron fretwork were wrapped around the three-story house and large bay windows were introduced to overlook the English country garden. A graceful tower was also added and today guests can climb up the flagpole in the lofty tower for magnificent 360 degree views of the surround-ing countryside.

Set on 40 acres of grounds along the banks of the Derwent River, the old mill property still retains hints of its former days. Ruins from a granary built in the 1820's lie scattered around the front embankment and partial walls from the old Mill buildings can be found along the winding road to the house. Nearby, within easy driving distance, are several attractions that visitors to the area shouldn't miss including Salmon Ponds, Mt. Fields National Park and Russell Falls.

Faithfully restored with features of the early craftsmanship retained, Tyn-wald boasts open fires in the lounge and restaurant, 12' high ceilings and period furnishings throughout the home. There are two large comfortable guestrooms on the ground floor with private baths just across the hall and four guestrooms upstairs. All rooms are furnished with handsome brass or iron beds, Victorian furnishings and antique radios. Upstairs, beautiful stained glass windows are scattered throughout and all second floor rooms have access to the sunny verandah where glorious river views can be en-joyed.

The à la carte dining room, open to the public seven nights a week and for Sunday lunch, features international cuisine with candlelight and silver service. All of the baked goods and sweets are made on the premises and the Salzburg Nockerl is a house specialty. Breakfast is served in the small comfortable room adjoining the kitchen. While feasting on homemade muesli, yogurt, cereals, juice, cheese scones, pancakes, danish pastries, eggs, bacon, sausage, toast and tomatoes, collectors will appreciate the wonderful assortment of chamber candlesticks hanging from the fireplace and the open cupboard filled with Jubilee mugs. The daily tariff at Tynwald includes bed and breakfast and, in addition, most guests take advantage of at least one dinner in the house restaurant.

Name: Tynwald Estate

Category: Colonial Accommodation

Location: Derwent Valley, New Norfolk

Address: PO Box 51, New Norfolk, TAS 7140

Phone: (Tel.) 61 3 6261 2667 **Fax**: 61 3 6261 2040

Email: tynwald@trump.net.au

Innkeepers: Pat Kelsall & Garry Roohan

Rooms: 7 Doubles

Baths: 3 Ensuite

Rate: From A$130-150 per double includes breakfast

Services & amenities: Licensed restaurant, guest lounge, swimming pool, tennis court

Rating: TCA

Handicap access: No

THE COMPLETE GUIDE TO

Bed & Breakfasts INNS & GUESTHOUSES

in the U.S.A., Canada, & Worldwide

17th ★★ MILLENNIUM EDITION

Pamela Lanier
The best loved, best selling guide to 21,000 inns – Over 2 million copies in print!

A LANIER GUIDE

Complete Guide to Bed & Breakfasts, Inns & Guesthouses in the United States and Canada

A best-selling classic now in its twelfth fully revised edition. Over 10,000 inns listed and access to over 20,000 guesthouses. Includes specialty lists for interest ranging from bird watching to antiquing. "All necessary information about facilities, prices, pets, children amenities, credit cards and the like. Like France's Michelin ..." **New York Times.** Winner of **Yahoo's Gold Star** award on the Web.

Lanier Travel Guides
In Book Stores Everywhere!

Lanier Travel Guides have set the standard for the industry:

"All necessary information about facilities, prices, pets, children, amenities, credit cards and the like. Like France's Michelin . . ."
—New York Times.

"Provides a wealth of the kinds of information needed to make a wise choice." *—American Council on Consumer Interest.*

Golf Courses
The Complete Guide

It's about time for a definitive directory and travel guide for the nation's 30 million avid golf players, 7 million of whom make golf vacations an annual event. This comprehensive and updated guide includes over 14,000 golf courses in the United States that are open to the public. Complete details, greens fees, and information on the clubhouse facilities is augmented by a description of each of the golf courses' best features. A beautiful gift and companion to *Golf Resorts—The Complete Guide.* Introduction by Arthur Jack Snyder.

Golf Resorts International

A wish book and travel guide for the wandering golfer. This guide, written in much the same spirit as the bestselling *Elegant Small Hotels,* reviews the creme de la creme of golf resorts all over the world. Beautifully illustrated, it includes all pertinent details regarding hotel facilities and amenities. Wonderful narrative on each hotel's special charm, superb cuisine and most importantly, those fabulous golf courses. Written from a golfer's viewpoint, it looks at the challenges and pitfalls of each course. For the non-golfer, there is ample information about other activities available in the area, such as on-site health spas, nearby shopping, and more.

Introduction by John Stirling.

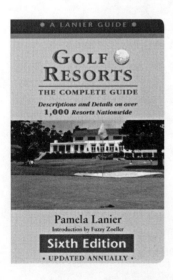

Golf Resorts
—The Complete Guide

The first ever comprehensive and recently updated guide to over 1,000 golf resorts coast to coast. Includes complete details of each resort facility and golf course particulars. "The Complete Guide to Golf Resorts is a wonderful golf destination guide."
—LPGA
Introduction by Fuzzy Zoeller.

Elegant Small Hotels
—A Connoiseur's Guide

This selective guide for discriminating travelers describes over 240 of America's finest hotels characterized by exquisite rooms, fine dining, and perfect service par excellence. Introduction by Peter Duchin. "Elegant Small Hotels makes a seductive volume for window shopping."
—*Chicago Sun Times.*

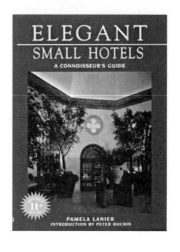

All-Suite Hotel Guide
—The Definitive Directory

The only guide to the all suite hotel industry features over 1,200 hotels nationwide and abroad. There is a special bonus list of temporary office facilities. A perfect choice for business travelers and much appreciated by families who enjoy the additional privacy provided by two rooms.

Condo Vacations
—The Complete Guide

The popularity of Condo vacations has grown exponentially. In this national guide, details are provided on over 3,000 Condo resorts in an easy to read format with valuable descriptive write-ups. The perfect vacation option for families and a great money saver!

Elegant Hotels of the Pacific Rim

Over 140 exquisite hotels and resorts located in the burgeoning Pacific Rim. Especially chosen for their inspired architecture, luxurious ambiance and personal service *par excellence*. A must for the globe trotter!

The Back Almanac
The Best New Thinking on an Age-Old Problem

by Lanier Publishing

Just in the nick of time for the 4 out of 5 Americans suffering with back pain, a practical guide to back pain prevention and care. Delightfully illustrated. Internationally acknowledged experts offer the latest thinking on causes, treatment, and pain-free life, including Danger Signals, Sex and Back Pain, and What If Nothing Works? Resource guide lists back schools, pain centers and specialty items.

Revised

"The editors have amassed a wealth of easy-to-find easy-to-read information..." —HEALTHLINE

AVAILABLE IN BOOK STORES EVERYWHERE